POLARIZING DREAMS

ALLISON ALEXY
Series Editor

Animated Encounters: Transnational Movements of Chinese Animation, 1940s–1970s
DAISY YAN DU

Pop Empires: Transnational and Diasporic Flows of India and Korea
EDITED BY S. HEIJIN LEE, MONIKA MEHTA, AND ROBERT JI-SONG KU

Puppets, Gods, and Brands: Theorizing the Age of Animation from Taiwan
TERI SILVIO

Legacies of the Drunken Master: Politics of the Body in Hong Kong Kung Fu Comedy Films
LUKE WHITE

Queer Transfigurations: Boys Love Media in Asia
EDITED BY JAMES WELKER

Alice in Japanese Wonderlands: Translation, Adaptation, Mediation
AMANDA KENNELL

Polarizing Dreams: Gangnam and Popular Culture in Globalizing Korea
PIL HO KIM

POLARIZING DREAMS

Gangnam and Popular Culture in Globalizing Korea

Pil Ho Kim

University of Hawaiʻi Press
Honolulu

© 2025 University of Hawaiʻi Press
All rights reserved
Printed in the United States of America

First printed, 2025

Library of Congress Cataloging-in-Publication Data

Names: Kim, Pil Ho, author.
Title: Polarizing dreams : Gangnam and popular culture in globalizing Korea / Pil Ho Kim.
Other titles: Asia pop!
Description: Honolulu : University of Hawaiʻi Press, [2024] | Series: Asia pop! | Includes bibliographical references and index.
Identifiers: LCCN 2024012371 (print) | LCCN 2024012372 (ebook) | ISBN 9780824899851 (hardback) | ISBN 9780824897512 (trade paperback) | ISBN 9780824899875 (epub) | ISBN 9780824899882 (kindle edition) | ISBN 9780824899868 (pdf)
Subjects: LCSH: Popular culture and globalization—Korea (South)—History—21st century. | Equality—Korea (South)—Seoul. | Popular culture—Effect of technological innovations on—Korea (South)—Seoul. | Kangnam-gu (Seoul, Korea)—In popular culture.
Classification: LCC DS925.S46 K366 2024 (print) | LCC DS925.S46 (ebook) | DDC 306.095195—dc23/eng/20240408
LC record available at https://lccn.loc.gov/2024012371
LC ebook record available at https://lccn.loc.gov/2024012372

Cover art: (top) The Han River skyline at night, including Gangnam's 123-story skyscraper Lotte World Tower; photo by mauveine.kim (Flickr); (bottom) Guryong Village Fire, November 9, 2014. Tower Palace, a luxury high-rise apartment complex in Gangnam, appears in the distance, through the smoke; photo by Chʻoe Kwangmo (Wikimedia).

This publication was supported by the 2024 Korean Studies Grant Program of the Academy of Korean Studies (AKS-2024-P-021).

University of Hawaiʻi Press books are printed on acid-free paper and meet the guidelines for permanence and durability of the Council on Library Resources.

*For my parents, who brought me to Gangnam,
and for Yoonkyung, who got me out of there.*

Contents

Series Editor's Preface	ix
Acknowledgments	xi
Note on Romanization and Translations	xv
Introduction: Gangnam, the Phantasmagoria of Korean Capitalism	1
Chapter 1 Boomtown Songs on the South of the River: The Origins of "Gangnam Style"	19
Chapter 2 Paradise across the River: Gangnam in Literature	45
Chapter 3 Two Lakes in Chamsil: Ecology, Class, Disaster	72
Chapter 4 Solidarity amid Disaster Capitalism: The Sampoong Collapse	94
Chapter 5 Place Maketh Man: Gangnam as the Locus of Social Evil	116
Chapter 6 Gentrification beyond the American Dream: The Transformation of Tree-Lined, In-Between Streets	144
Conclusion: Burning Down the House or Reaching across the River	169
Notes	179
Bibliography	199
Index	215

Color insert follows page 18.

Series Editor's Preface

When I was in Tokyo in 2012, a thoughtful student emailed me about a new craze that was sweeping the U.S.: Psy's "Gangnam Style" music video and dance seemed to be everywhere. The student, like me, doesn't speak Korean and was instinctually wary of a pop cultural item that featured an Asian man rapping to horsey dance moves. The ambiguity of it—is this guy a goofball or a self-aware genius?—enhanced the music and dancing to create a captivating pop cultural trifecta. To differing degrees, thanks to Psy, both the fantasy and the critique of Gangnam were now fixed in the global imagination.

In *Polarizing Dreams: Gangnam and Popular Culture in Globalizing Korea*, Pil Ho Kim brilliantly demonstrates that the Gangnam district deserves scholarly attention well beyond a viral music video. As a geographic place and a social space, Gangnam signifies contradictory, if not oppositional, pulls: middle-class aspirations and extreme economic inequities, possibilities and failures, infrastructural marvels and deadly collapses, layers of local histories and global pop cultural production. Contextualizing media, literature, and popular culture from sociological perspectives, this book offers vital interdisciplinary analysis that pushes any reader or fan into more complex, grounded awareness.

Tying together social meanings, media representation, and shifting geographies, *Polarizing Dreams* epitomizes both the importance of pop culture and pop cultural scholarship. By zooming in on Gangnam, Kim reveals complex realities linked with persistent fantasies echoing within and beyond South Korea.

Acknowledgments

It is all too appropriate that I am sitting here in my old roost in Togoktong, Gangnam, putting the finishing touches on the writing I have been working on since 2011, well before Psy's fateful music video. I cannot honestly say that I enjoyed the global fad the music video spawned. Unquestionably, however, it took a great deal of weight off my shoulders to explain what Gangnam is and why it matters as I was writing this book.

The decision to turn old, fragmented research on Gangnam into a book was mine, of course, but it would not have been reached without the Department of East Asian Languages and Literatures (DEALL) at the Ohio State University giving me an opportunity to prove myself as a scholar. For that, first and foremost, I would like to thank Chan E. Park, whose accomplishments as a performing artist and scholar I can only admire. Before becoming a world-renowned *p'ansori* performer, she had been a legendary modern folk singer of the 1970s' Korean counterculture I grew up with and then studied as a researcher. Not only have I appreciated her work, but I have also benefited immensely from her guidance and boundless support of my career since we first met in Ohio. My gratitude is also extended to the Korean faculty at DEALL, under the leadership of Danielle Ooyoung Pyun. Our program continues to thrive in the capable hands of Danielle, Yonsoo Kang-Parker, Hyunjin Lee-Miller, and others. The department chair, Mark Bender, was a great advisor and champion for me, from hiring me through my promotion, a period when I jokingly referred to myself as an endangered species. Mark had some senior colleagues take turns mentoring me, and from each of them I learned valuable lessons: Marjorie Chan, Kirk Denton, Naomi Fukumori, Meow Hui Goh, Mineharu Nakayama, Shelley Feno Quinn, and Patricia Sieber; there are two more who are no longer with us, Charles Quinn and Richard Torrance. Their untimely passing deeply saddened me while I was wrapping up this book's final manuscript. Charlie's warm support had been essential in my progress as a junior faculty member, and Richard gave exceptionally high praise to the manuscript as he led the departmental committee for my promotion and tenure. May their kind souls rest in peace.

A special thank-you goes to Debbie Knicely and Kelly Harless for their administrative support, without which it would have been difficult for me to carry out teaching and service duties and still find time to write. Beside my own department, the East Asian Studies Center at Ohio State is a wellspring of institutional support for my research. Etsuyo Yuasa, the previous director of EASC and a departmental colleague, as well as Mitch Lerner, the current director, both helped me in big and small ways to reach out to audiences beyond the confines of the department and the university. The wonderful administrative staff—Dani Cooke, Janet Smith, Francesco DiMarco, and others—long headed by Amy Carey and now by Chris White, more than deserve this brief thank-you. I am also indebted to Steve McEachern at the Department of Statistics, who has been a great advocate for me at Ohio State.

Although housed within the walls of a supposedly bitter rival to my own institution, the Nam Center for Korean Studies at the University of Michigan has been instrumental since the inception of this project. It was in their book manuscript workshop that the idea of writing an academic monograph on Gangnam received its first serious test. Furthermore, their administration of the Korea Foundation Big Ten Academic Alliance eSchool Program allowed me to offer my urban culture course, Making Places in Seoul, to many institutions beyond mine over the past five years. I owe gratitude to the Nam Center's former and current directors, Nojin Kwak (now with the University at Buffalo) and Youngju Ryu, and to Evan Vowell's administrative assistance. At the book manuscript workshop, I met two generous mentors, Kyung Hyun Kim and Sunyoung Park, who patiently explained how to compose an academic monograph in the humanities field and gave their ringing endorsement of my fledgling project. Se-Mi Oh also participated in the workshop voluntarily to offer her valuable insights and solidarity. After the workshop, another pivotal moment for this book came at the Korean Literature Association conference in Minneapolis, where a congregation of experts including Ellie Choi, Michelle Cho, Yoon Sun Yang, Immanuel Kim, Barbara Wall, Hye Seung Chung, Travis Workman, and others encouraged my dilettantish approach to literary and cinematic text analysis. Once the book project got on the right track, more opportunities followed to share my research and shape it. I thank Seung-kyung Kim, the director of the Institute for Korean Studies at Indiana University Bloomington, and Hyunjoon Park, the director of the James Joo-Jin Kim Center for Korean Studies at the University of Pennsylvania, for inviting me to give a public talk on their respective campuses. Not even a global pandemic stopped the momentum as I managed to visit many other places virtually to discuss my project. In particular, I thank Jae Won Edward Chung for inviting me to the University Seminar at Columbia University's Center for Korean

Research, where I received many insightful comments from Ksenia Chizhova, Jenny Wang Medina, and other participants. Jae Won was also a member of the informal Korean studies writing group that included me, Susan Hwang, and Jonathan Kief; we held regular meetings online in the spring and summer of 2022 to discuss one another's projects. Jooyeon Rhee was very kind to invite me repeatedly to the Institute of Korean Studies at Penn State University, and I took full advantage of her generosity by presenting two chapters' worth of this book in front of the virtual and live audiences there in 2022–2023.

While they may or may not have been directly engaged with this book project, numerous colleagues in the field of Korean studies have offered me professional guidance, timely advice, and personal friendship. Here are only a few of the names I can think of at the moment: Charles Kim, Hyaeweol Choi, Kyeong-Hee Choi, Bruce Fulton, Kelly Jeong, Jina Kim, Ji-Eun Lee, Dafna Zur, Juhn Ahn, Jae-Jung Suh, Henry Em, Hyun Ok Park, and Merose Hwang, among others. I alone am responsible for everything that is written in this book, but it had to go through the capable hands of editors before seeing the light of day. Most of all, I am deeply obliged to Perry Dalnim Miller for taking the indispensable role of development editor and setting my writing straight. Stephanie Chun, the acquisition editor at the University of Hawai'i Press, has been an excellent guardian for a novice like me. I also thank Nick Allaman for helping to polish parts of the manuscript.

Needless to say, a book like this could not be written without relying on academic communities in Korea. I should give credit to the Institute for East Asian Studies at Sungkonghoe University and its team of scholars for the collaborative research on which portions of chapter 1 and the entirety of chapter 6 are based: Hyunjoon Shin, Keewoong Lee, Jaeyoung Yang, Ji Youn Kim, and Taeyoun Kim. In fact, a Korean-language version of chapter 6 was previously published in the volume edited by Shin and Lee, *Seoul Speaks of Gentrification* (P'aju: P'urŭnsup, 2016). President Eun Mee Kim of Ewha Womans University hired me as a postdoctoral scholar when she served as dean of the Graduate School of International Studies and director of the Institute for Development and Human Security. It was her generous support for my research pursuits, even those that were unrelated to the institute's mission, that enabled me to conceive this project in the first place. The Korean Association for the Study of Popular Music, of which I am a founding member, has been a nurturing place for networking and the exchange of ideas for this book project, and I would like to thank Changnam Kim, Aekyung Park, Jung-Yup Lee, and Eujeong Zhang in particular. Chung-hoon Shin, one of my old comrades from the Seoul Institute for Social Sciences years, introduced me to the photography and writings of Young June Lee, who turned out to be an even older acquaintance of mine; both were instrumental in securing some of the stunning color plates in this book. I am also grateful to Korea's premier photojournalist Chŏn Minjo and the estate of O Yun, the great *minjung* painter, for giving me permission to use their iconic pieces of art.

It almost sounds like a cliché to thank family members and personal friends for inspiration and comfort. But in all sincerity, they gave me so much in terms of self-reflection and emotional balance. The lived experience I have had in Gangnam is owed to my parents, Pak Youngja and Kim Kwang An, who found a spacious enough apartment for their three boys in Togoktong forty years ago. The kids all grew up and left, two of us living in the U.S. and one in Ulsan. Still, the same old apartment stands as our home base for family reunions and business stays in Seoul. My elder brother, Philip, and his wife, Eunhee, have long been providing an American counterpart to the Togoktong apartment: a place for family gatherings where my niece, Jean, and nephew, Youbin, have come of age beautifully. Jean lent me her hand to produce the maps included in this book. Whether in the American Midwest or in the Korean Southeast, my younger brother, Pilwon, and his wife, Narina Jung, have always been good company. Our wide-ranging conversations about Korean literature and cinema shaped some of the ideas advanced in this book. Having retired to bucolic rural Virginia after decades of work in Manhattan, Aunt Florence gives me plenty of time to reflect on the meanings of the American Dream as I drive long distances to visit her. Inhee Jung and Youngsil Kim are a reminder of the importance of enduring friendships in my life.

The son-in-law is known as a "hundred-year guest" in an old Korean saying. My family-in-law, however, never makes me feel distant despite the short time we spend together over summer stays in Korea. I appreciate their affection and care, and especially admire the strong bond my wife enjoys with her two sisters. Speaking of my wife, Yoonkyung Lee, I must admit that her influence, not just on my life in general but specifically on this book, is nothing short of profound. For one, the title *Polarizing Dreams* came from her suggestion. It has not been easy to complete this journey, and I owe it to her in almost every way.

Finally, there were two mentors who towered over everyone else in my intellectual background as a sociologist. One was Professor Kim Jinkyun (1937–2004) at Seoul National University, whose devotion to the cause of *minjung*, the common people, earned him the honorific "teacher of *minjung*" in South Korea's historical struggles for political democracy and socioeconomic equality. The other was Professor Erik Olin Wright (1947–2019) at the University of Wisconsin–Madison, who made sure that class "counts" in the social sciences and envisioned "real utopias" breaking out of global capitalism. It is my hope that this book will be a small tribute to their legacy.

NOTE ON ROMANIZATION AND TRANSLATIONS

I employ the McCune-Reischauer romanization system for Korean words and names, with two exceptions: first, widely used alternative spellings such as Seoul, Gangnam, and Shin Joong Hyun; second, authors who write in English and spell their names in their own way. I generally follow the East Asian convention of placing surnames before given names, except for those who prefer the Western convention.

All translations from Korean are mine, with a few exceptions noted.

Introduction
Gangnam, the Phantasmagoria of Korean Capitalism

This book is about dreams—sweet dreams South Koreans hatched after the long nightmare of the particularly brutal first half of the twentieth century,[1] dreams that they would be able to enjoy a comfortable life in a modern family dwelling of their own, raising children who would see a better, more prosperous future than they themselves could hope for. If this sort of nearly universal aspiration of the middle class found a hegemonic expression in the American Dream, nowhere in Korea did it resonate more loudly than in Gangnam (Kangnam, literally "south of the river"), the swath of promised land for upward social mobility. Hence *Dreams of Gangnam* (*Kangnammong*, 2010), the title of acclaimed writer Hwang Sŏg'yŏng's novel that follows a multiplicity of historically informed narratives: rags to riches, ill-gotten fortunes, intrigues, betrayals, and survival of disaster. The social critic Kang Chunman has called Gangnam "a strange self-portrait" of the entire country, which has seen itself rise above poverty and obscurity through difficult and often very ugly struggles. Much was borrowed from the American Dream, for the United States appeared as the promised land to many Koreans.[2] But even that dream had to confront the local constraints of the land and its topography. If the postwar American Dream was based on wide, flat suburbia, its Korean equivalent was dreamt up in high-rise plots cutting off hillsides.

From the moment of its conception, Gangnam was designated as Korea's dreamland. Faced with a huge influx of migrants from the rest of the country to Seoul, the top officials and planners of the incoming Park Chung Hee (Pak Chŏnghŭi) administration (1963–1979) decided to build from scratch a new modern city just across the Han River, to the southeast of the old city. After a few scrapped grand plans and false starts, the ambitious urban development project began in earnest in the early 1970s, just as the nation entered a period of heavy industrialization and fast economic growth under the hard authoritarian rule known as Yusin. The actual process of urban planning that created Gangnam was rather impromptu, if not haphazard. In principle, the conceived space—or the "representation of space," as the French urban theorist Henri Lefebvre would put it—would feature a new central business district, with many important state institutions, both at the national and the local level, relocated from the old city core. This plan was only partially carried out as the old core retained top symbols of administrative power, along with major financial institutions and corporate headquarters. Nonetheless, the powerful authoritarian state exerted enough pressure to make the area desirable to the buoyant new middle class or middle strata, which, along with the ruling elites, reaped the major benefits of economic growth. To the astonishment of some foreign observers, a large-scale apartment complex built with gray concrete became the dominant mode of housing for the middle-class families who flocked to the area thanks to the concerted effort of the government, real estate brokers, and the construction business. It was a strange collision of ideas between the American urban planner Clarence Perry ("neighborhood unit theory") and the Swiss architect Le Corbusier ("towers in a park") that forged a new model for urbanity in Korea, namely the "apartment republic" (*ap'at'ŭ konghwaguk*).[3] Anointed as the capital of the newfangled republic, Gangnam was to be the dreamland of new consumerism, especially with the introduction of mass private automobile ownership. More importantly, Gangnam was to be the destination for the college-preparatory education virtually all upper- and middle-class Korean families were preoccupied with.

The representational space, again to borrow from Lefebvre, is not the same as the representation of space drawn up by urban policymakers, planners, cartographers, or architects. It is assembled from the lived experiences of the inhabitants and the visitors of the space. The dreams of Gangnam have been played out in the representational space shared by its privileged insiders and envious outsiders. Even the most strident detractors of the "Miracle on the Han" must acknowledge the gravitational pull of the middle-class dreams that they critique as mass-marketed aspirational fantasies. The story of middle-class dreams has been retold in numerous ways across different media and genres—popular song lyrics, fictional and nonfictional narratives, and film and television dramatizations. It is the representational space of Gangnam that this book is primarily concerned with. The lived experiences and vivid imaginations of those who populate the space of Gangnam provide ample material for literature, arts, and various pop culture genres. It is also in the same representational space that the dreams of Gangnam—economic, social, and cultural progress led by the rising middle class—began turning sour and eventually spoiled. Such a linear narrative of progress is a product of "bourgeois habits of thought," according to the German philosopher Walter Benjamin.[4]

One of the early literary treatments of Gangnam comes from Cho Sehŭi (1942–2022) in his distinctly modernist novel *The Dwarf* (*Nanjang'iga ssoaolin chag'ŭn kong*, 1978). Not incidentally, Cho breaks with the conventional linear narrative tradition by creating a montage of intertwined plots and different perspectives. The novel is highly critical of the Korean capitalist vision as represented by Gangnam, and yet it stands apart from other comparable works based on social realism and *minjung* (common people) populism due to its style, which reaches the level of Benjaminian modernism. In *Time Travel* (*Sigan yŏhaeng*, 1983), the sequel to *The Dwarf*, Cho further develops this modernist view, portraying Gangnam as a phantasmagoria of images and desires that hover around the official representations of space. Cho characterizes Gangnam as a "pavilion on the sand" (*sasangnugak* 沙上樓閣), a classical Chinese expression equivalent to the English "house of cards." Chamsil, the specific part of Gangnam he zeroes in on, had indeed been a sandy beach by the Han River, on top of which highrise apartments were built with reinforced concrete. He speculates that "everything would crumble into the sand and blow away were it not for cement and rebar."[5] It is a representational space of modernity—the modernity that Marshall Berman conjures up contemporaneously: "To be modern is to find ourselves in an environment that promises us adventure, power, joy, growth, transformation of ourselves and the world—and, at the same time, that threatens to destroy everything we have, everything we know, everything we are . . . it pours us all into a maelstrom of perpetual disintegration and renewal, of struggle and contradiction, of ambiguity and anguish. To be modern is to be part of a universe in which, as Marx said, 'all that is solid melts into air.'"[6] About a decade after the flash of Cho's ominous literary vision, the "maelstrom" finally caught up with the reality when two major collapses—first a bridge and then a luxury department store—at the heart of Gangnam killed hundreds of people within twelve months in 1994–1995. At about the same time, Susan Buck-Morss penned an article that encapsulated Benjamin's dialectical image of a modern city in three polarities: "heaven and hell; phantasmagoria and shock; dreamworld and catastrophe."[7] In retrospect, these events were not a mere coincidence but a portentous sign of what was to come. Since the end of the Cold War, twentieth-century mass utopias had crashed around the globe, starting with the socialist ones, from Moscow to Pyongyang. The shock wave soon spread to some of the capitalist urban centers that were prone to disasters: the Los Angeles Riots of 1992, followed by the 1994 Northridge earthquake, Mexico City in the so-called Tequila Crisis of 1994–1995, Seoul in the Asian Financial Crisis of 1997–1998, Moscow again (this time under capitalism) in the Russian ruble crisis of 1998, Buenos Aires in the Argentine Great Depression of 1998–2002.

Devastating as the financial crisis had been, the Korean economy bounced back rather quickly. The recovery was led by Gangnam's prowess in two new "growth engine" sectors: digital high technology and pop culture. The dreams of

Gangnam have since been renewed as well; no longer colored by the middle-class optimism of the bygone century, their potency may have grown even stronger. It is the main contention of this book that the contemporary representational space of Gangnam should be seen through the double vision of utopia and dystopia, or "dreamworld and catastrophe." The new dreams of Gangnam are those of social polarization—a gripping juxtaposition of fairy-tale success and miserable failure, a revamped phantasmagoria; it is a key ingredient for many Korean pop culture products that are manufactured or assembled in Gangnam and sold like hotcakes in the current global media marketplace. By constructing a genealogy of dreams with respect to Gangnam's cultural history, this book will offer an answer to the question of how Korean pop culture has been taken to such global heights since the turn of the century. To sum up, the utopian dream of middle-class capitalism was the impetus behind Korea's prolific spatio-cultural production. Shattered by the economic crisis, it split into polarizing dreams: an elevation to the global elite or a descent into precarious survival. Now, the polarizing dreams are driving Korea's formidable pop culture industries to conquer the global market—by providing ambitious, elite-level talent for the industries on the one hand, and by turning harsh realities into compelling multimedia narratives on the other. As Cho Sehŭi's writings demonstrate, however, there was already a deep suspicion about the utopian dreams of Gangnam from the early years, at least among the minority who were critical of the authoritarian path of development the country took. The disasters in Gangnam in the 1990s were the moments when the masses were rudely awakened from those dreams.

Disaster Capitalism, Land Speculation, Global Spectacles: Gangnam Development, 1963–1988

The bridge and building collapses in the 1990s were deadly consequences of Korea's own brand of disaster capitalism. The fact that these disasters did not occur in some old, derelict area but in shiny new Gangnam underscores the reckless pace of urban development and the lack of scruples among the planners and developers. It took about two decades for them to transform a sleepy rural backwater with fewer than twenty-seven thousand residents into a dense urban hive of more than a million citizens. The first plan to expand the city across the Han River to the south was proposed by Pak Hŭngsik (1901–1994), the richest man in colonized Korea and the first one to be prosecuted in 1949 by the Special Investigation Committee of Anti-Nationalist Activities (Panmint'ŭg'wi) for collaborating with Japanese war efforts. Pak was also prosecuted later by Park

Chung Hee's military junta for corruption, only to be freed to become a full collaborator with the military regime. In 1963, Pak submitted the ambitious South Seoul Urban Planning Project (Namsŏul tosi kyehoek saŏp), which did not materialize but served as the first blueprint for what would be later dubbed "Gangnam development" (Kangnam *kaebal*). The Blank-Slate New Seoul Plan (Saesŏul paekchi kyehoek) was drawn up three years later, under the Seoul mayor Kim Hyŏn'ok, to build an entirely new city in the mold of Washington, DC, presumably to the south of the Han. The reason for southern expansion had much to do with a previous catastrophe: the Korean War. Architecture scholar Jung In Kim characterizes Gangnam development as "defensive urbanism":

> While communist threats to Southeast Asia became more palpable in the late 1960s, state elites began to raise grave concerns about protecting key national institutions in the event of another inter-Korean conflict. The difficulty of defending Seoul at its current location and the strategic availability of the Han River as a defence buffer were used to justify the creation of another city to the south of the river . . . In the process the Han River became a natural line of defence that also demarcated the boundaries for a new round of urbanisation. While the existing city of Seoul was framed as an undesirable riddle of urban sprawl and a bulwark against a possible North Korean attack, Gangnam contrasted as a perfectly fitted security zone that became blueprint for a safer and affluent urban space.[8]

The same Cold War mentality ruled over both Gangnam development and American suburbanization.[9] Furthermore, it was such Cold War exigencies as South Korea's normalization treaty with Japan and dispatching troops to the Vietnam War that provided necessary financing for urban development in terms of economic aid, concessional loans, and military remittances.[10] The construction of the Han River Bridge Number Three (later renamed to Hannam Bridge) and the Seoul-Busan (Kyŏngbu) Expressway in 1966–1970 was the beginning of Seoul's southeastern expansion as the government launched the massive Land Repatriation Project (T'oji kuhoek chŏngni saŏp) on a 6,600-acre plot of land it initially designated as the Yŏngdong District, now known as Gangnam. This enormous space for new urban development triggered a gold rush for land speculators, who were in cahoots with government operatives charged with the task of accumulating slush funds for the Park regime.[11] In nominal terms, the land price of Sinsadong—the entry point of Gangnam from the newly built Bridge Number Three—jumped a thousandfold from 1963 to 1979.[12] The early years of Gangnam development, however, proceeded much slower than anticipated. The land price went up *only* fifty times from the announcement of the expressway construction until its completion, and there was not much investment in either housing or commercial development in the immediate aftermath. The national and metropolitan governments had to introduce a series of policy measures to incentivize businesses and middle-class citizens to move into the new development zone, which included the following:

> *April, 1972*: Special zoning regulations were imposed to restrict new commercial developments in the area north of the Han, now called Gangbuk (Kangbuk) as opposed to Gangnam; new hotels, clubs, bars, and other tourism/entertainment establishments were only allowed in Gangnam; tax exemptions were given for real estate, entertainment, and other businesses located in Gangnam.
>
> *March, 1975*: Establishment of the Gangnam District; expansion of special zoning to discourage new residential developments in Gangbuk; introduction of dedicated "apartment zones" only in Gangnam; announcement of relocation of the Supreme Court, major government ministries, and Seoul City Hall to Gangnam.
>
> *February, 1976*: The middle and high school relocation policy from Gangbuk to Gangnam began with the top-ranked Kyŏnggi High School.
>
> *April, 1977*: The Triple Nuclei Model City (Samhaek tosi) plan raised the status of Gangnam to make it equivalent to Gangbuk's central business district; construction of Subway Line Number 2 began, which would traverse Gangnam and connect it to the rest of the city.
>
> *March, 1979*: Fifty-four entertainment venues in Gangbuk were prohibited from moving anywhere but to Gangnam; construction of the Gangnam Express Bus Terminal began.[13]

In short, the Gangnam promotion policy focused on four aspects—transportation infrastructure, apartment construction, elite high school education, and adult entertainment—which would have significant impacts and ramifications in the coming decades. Still, it required more than just domestic promotion for Gangnam to take off. Anthropologist Laura Nelson correctly points out that Gangnam development accelerated only "after 1981, when South Korea won the privilege of hosting both the 1986 Asian Games and the 1988 Olympics"[14]—a fact Koreans themselves often forget when they consider Gangnam's rise all but preordained. The hosting of these international sporting events allowed Chun Doo Hwan (Chŏn Tuhwan)'s military regime, which had taken power in the aftermath of Park Chung Hee's assassination, to launch the Han River Comprehensive

Development Project (Han'gang chonghap kaebal saŏp, 1982–1986). The riverside expressway named after the Olympics (Ollimp'ik taero) made Gangnam an international gateway to the newly built sports stadium in Chamsil, which became Gangnam's eastern extension. With the population at almost one million residents, the Gangnam District split in two, creating a new district named Sŏch'o in 1988. By the time the Olympic opening ceremony took place in the Chamsil stadium, the country had already been undergoing democratic transition, the end of the Cold War and the beginning of globalization were near, and the original dreams of Gangnam appeared to come to fruition. In a few years, however, disaster capitalism came back with a vengeance as the bridge, the department store, and the whole economy collapsed. The calamities of the 1990s ushered in the alter ego of globalization: socioeconomic polarization.

Global Polarization and the Fractured Middle Class

The political economist Samir Amin (1931–2018) published a remarkably prescient article entitled "The Future of Global Polarization" at the height of global capitalist triumphalism in the early 1990s: "Inequality in the development of human society has been part of known history since antiquity, yet it is only in the modern era that polarization has become the immanent product of global expansion of a system that for the first time in history has included all people of the planet, that system being capitalism."[15] Although Amin was primarily concerned with socioeconomic inequality and polarization across different regions, nation-states, and areas in the world system, his insightful observation that globalization and polarization are one and the same process remains as relevant as ever. I would only hyphenate the two words into a single term, global-polarization, to stress its singular character. Even at the national level, global-polarization makes sense, as integration into the global market economy entails a spike in domestic inequality and social polarization.[16] This is exactly what happened to Korea in the aftermath of the Asian Financial Crisis and the structural adjustment program subsequently imposed by the International Monetary Fund (IMF), colloquially known as the IMF Crisis and the "IMF regime" (aiemep'ŭ ch'eje), respectively. The dream of capitalist progress toward a middle-class utopia hardly recovered from this heavy blow, even though the cold rationality of self-interest would still dictate that Gangnam remain the place to cling to, for aspiring social climbers and suddenly insecure elites alike. Thus, Gangnam has become the epitome of the nation under the snare of neoliberal capitalism, where even dreams are polarizing and leading the shaken middle-class psyche either to a stratospheric rise or an abysmal fall.

Two recent major sociological studies on the Korean middle class, Myungji Yang's *From Miracle to Mirage: The Making and Unmaking of the Korean Middle Class, 1960–2015* (2018) and Hagen Koo's *Privilege and Anxiety: The Korean Middle Class in the Global Era* (2022) see the fault line within the fractured or fragile middle class that lies between Gangnam and the rest of the country. Both authors agree that Gangnam's speculative real estate market and exclusionary private education industry have played a crucial role in middle-class polarization, especially since the IMF Crisis. But their views differ on the dynamics of internal and external forces that have led to the polarization. While acknowledging the impact of neoliberal globalization, Yang puts the emphasis squarely on "domestic policies and a politics of development peculiar to Korea" in the "unmaking" of the middle class. It is notable that the same internal forces were credited for the "making" of the middle class in pre–IMF Crisis Korea.[17] Koo, on the other hand, flatly asserts that "globalization plays a far more important role in shaping the new privileged middle class in Korea than in America and other older advanced economies" because the Korean economy is "newly integrated into global capitalism" and therefore "subject to more changes driven by global forces."[18] Their arguments do not necessarily contradict each other, but both seem to slightly overstate their cases.

Yang is correct that Korea's speculative urbanism began with the economic takeoff in the 1960s, well before the so-called global or neoliberal era. Its single-minded promotion of private homeownership in large apartment complexes and prolonged neglect of public rental housing provisions was indeed peculiar, even compared to Japan's policy, which Korea's authoritarian governments emulated in many other respects. Japan's legendary "bubble-economy" land speculation did coincide with Korea's first housing price crisis during the mid-1980s, but their subsequent paths have sharply diverged.[19] While Japan's appetite for land speculation has largely disappeared because of asset price deflation in the 1990s post-bubble economy, in Korea, along with many metropolitan areas in Europe, North America, Latin America, and the rest of Asia, "speculative urban property markets have become prime engines of capital accumulation."[20] Los Angeles, for example, began its own peculiar path to this global accumulation strategy as early as the 1980s, with significant investments in real estate from Japanese, overseas Chinese, and even Korean capital.[21] Speculative urbanism has thus never been exclusive to Korea, becoming prevalent globally as a bevy of recent studies on "planetary" gentrification confirm.[22] It is now an integral part of global-polarization that deepens inequality in housing and property assets and puts a squeeze on the middle class, not to mention the poor and the working class in urban areas. In that basic sense,

Korea's domestic policies and politics on urban development conform to the global norms of neoliberal capitalism.

According to Koo, the winner of global-polarization is the upper 10 percent—or 20 percent, to be a little more generous—income group chiefly made up of the capitalist elite, corporate managers, high-ranking government officials, credentialed professionals, high-tech and financial sector employees, and so forth. The biggest loser is not the lowest quintile of the income distribution, who had not much to lose to begin with, but the middle half, whose share of the national income fell by about 13 percent from 1996 to 2010. The gap between the upper income group (earning more than 150 percent of the median income) and the rest had been relatively narrow before the IMF Crisis, but by the second decade of the twenty-first century, the upper income group's national share grew to twice that of the middle income group. There is little doubt that Korea's neoliberal globalization has been handsomely rewarding the new upper-middle class while punishing the lower end of the middle strata with economic precarity and downward social mobility. The "new affluent middle class," as Koo refers to the upper 10–20 percent income group, is met with suspicion and resentment by the rest of the declining middle strata because its increasing wealth is largely based on real estate speculation. However, Koo also finds a new layer of the upper stratum, a "global middle class," distinguishing itself from the speculative nouveau riche and justifying its wealth and privilege in terms of meritocratic competence in the knowledge-based, high-tech global economy.[23] The question is if such a "meritocratic" elite group would give up the tried-and-true wealth accumulation strategy of property investments in places like Gangnam. A cursory look at the latest household asset distribution data reveals that the households with the top 20 percent income hold an astonishing 78 percent of their assets in real estate.[24] While a small number of the Korean elite may hold more financial assets than real estate in their portfolios, like their American or Japanese counterparts, they are far from reaching a critical mass to become the new face of Korea's "global middle class." The affluent middle strata are still bound by the territorial space from which they draw or park their wealth. It is this space where they also build the meritocratic credentials of their offspring through private education, distinguish themselves by conspicuous consumption, and aspire to join the ranks of the global elite.

Gangnam is such a privileged space for social reproduction. At the same time, it is also a space for the economic production of commodities that have become increasingly popular in the global market. Beside the high-tech sector, "the formidable entertainment industry has been able to command global attention to Gangnam, building monumental showcases in the area where it first laid the foundation in the early 1980s" and turning it into "the epicenter of K-pop and the Korean Wave since Psy's 'Gangnam Style' took the world by storm in 2012."[25] Gangnam is more than a dreamland; it is a dream factory whose best-known product is a self-referential joke on global-polarization. Phantasmagoric images of Gangnam are not at all flattering in Psy's deliberately gaudy "Gangnam Style" music video. A perfect comic foil for middle-class anxiety, Psy mercilessly lampoons all the dreams Gangnam has represented—and he has personally lived through—for nearly four decades. In particular, the original dream of social mobility appears all but moribund. The satirical poignancy of "Gangnam Style" lies in the fact that it accidentally made the new dream of global ascendancy come true by shattering the old dream of middle-class utopia into pieces; it created polarizing dreams of utopia and dystopia, which decidedly put both Gangnam and K-pop on the global pop culture map. Thus, a formula was born for the Korean culture industry. In the wake of "Gangnam Style," Bong Joon-ho (Pong Chunho)'s film *Parasite* (*Kisaengch'ung*, 2019) and the Netflix drama series *Squid Game* (*Ojing'ŏ keim*, dir. Hwang Tonghyŏk, 2021) mesmerized a large global viewership by projecting their own polarizing dreams of phantasmagoria and shock.

Critical Self-Reflection from Gangnam's Inner Quarters and the New Politics of Contention

Needless to say, Psy's music video was not the first one to raise a critical voice on Gangnam's new dystopian dreams. Much literary and cultural introspection was done in the first decade of the new millennium, to the extent of creating a new subgenre dubbed "Gangnam literature." It discovered new, mostly female voices coming from the inner quarters of Gangnam's middle-class existence. Mun Chŏnghǔi's poems of leaving her longtime home in the prestigious Apkujŏngdong neighborhood reads like a quiet protest of a longtime middle-class Gangnam resident against being squeezed out of her place by polarizing forces and cynical gazes coming from the outside. Novelists Chŏng Migyŏng (Jung Mi-kyung) and Chŏng Ihyŏn also joined the growing new female literary voices, which renewed the tradition of Gangnam's critical self-reflection dating back to the early 1970s. A common thread in this tradition is the fear of displacement—in other words, of losing one's place in Gangnam. First it was the middle class "conquistadores" of the 1970–1980s who displaced "the last of the indigenes" of the pre-development era rural communities, as the poet Yu Ha put it in his scathing *On a Windy Day We Must Go to Apkujŏngdong* (*Parambunŭn narimyŏn apkujŏngdong'e kayahanda,* 1991).[26] Now it is the middle class itself that is being squeezed and priced out of the promised land because of the new type of urban development for the wealthy and the uberwealthy—a process urban studies researchers refer to as "super-gentrification."[27] Tower Palace, Samsung conglomerate's super high-rise apartment complex in Gangnam, signaled the arrival of super-gentrification. For much of the 2000s, the redevelopment boom continued in Gangnam as global capital inflows helped inflate the real estate bubble.

When the global financial crisis put a screeching halt to the speculative drive in 2008, it caused major fallouts for the middle-class residents who were mired in mounting debt just to keep their footing in the dreamland. Faced with such a malaise, bare-knuckle criticisms of Gangnam returned in full force: Yoon Jong-bin (Yun Chongbin)'s film *Beastie Boys* (*Pisŭt'i poijŭ*, 2008), Yi Hong's novel *Christmas Picnic* (*Sŏngt'an p'ik'ŭnik*, 2009), Hwang Sŏg'yŏng's *Dreams of Gangnam*, Yi Chaeik's novel *Apkujŏngdong Boys* (*Apkujŏng sonyŏndŭl*, 2010), No Hŭijun's novel *Orange Republic* (*Orenji rip'ŏbŭllik*, 2010), Yeon Sang-ho (Yŏn Sangho)'s animation *The King of Pigs* (*Twaejiŭi wang*, 2011), Kangyu Garam (Kang-Yu Karam)'s documentary *My Father's House* (*Morae*, 2011), Psy's "Gangnam Style" music video, Mun Hongju's novel *Sampoong: A Night of Festivities* (*Samp'ung: Ch'ukcheŭi pam*, 2012) and its internet cartoon (webtoon) serial adaptation *Sampoong* (2013–2015) by Son Yŏngsu (script) and Han Sanghun (drawings), Kim Sagwa's novel *In Heaven* (*Ch'ŏn'gug'esŏ*, 2013), Yu Ha's film *Gangnam Blues* (*Kangnam ilguch'ilgong*, 2015), Chŏng Aŭn's novel *Residents of Chamsil Neighborhood* (*Chamsiltong saramdŭl*, 2015), Ma Minji's documentary *Family in the Bubble* (*Pŏbŭl p'aemilli*, 2018), Lee Chang-dong (Yi Ch'angdong)'s film *Burning* (*Pŏning*, 2018), Chu Wŏn'gyu's novel *Made in Gangnam* (*Meidŭ in kangnam*, 2019), and Yun Poin's short story "Because I Couldn't Buy an Apkujŏngdong Hyundai Apartment" ("Apkujŏng hyŏndaerŭl saji mothaesŏ," 2022). Many of these works are steeped in a dark, criminal atmosphere not so dissimilar from what the prophetic urban historian Mike Davis wrote about twentieth-century Los Angeles: "It has been also fertile soil for some of the most acute critiques of the culture of late capitalism, and, particularly, of the tendential degeneration of its middle strata . . . The most outstanding example is the complex corpus of what we call *noir* (literary and cinematic)."[28] For those cultural critiques of Korean capitalism in the neoliberal era, Gangnam noir might indeed be an apt term.

While the fear of displacement from super-gentrified Gangnam is very real, there have also been new imaginations and practices emerging as alternative ways of urban development. The irony is that these new practices are producing what looks uncannily similar to the oldest formulation of gentrification. Pioneering gentrifiers, such as artists, artisans, designers, and architects, sharing a kind of bohemian spirit have been moving into old, blighted neighborhoods. Gangnam is perhaps the least likely area for these urban pioneers to settle in, but there are small pockets of space left untouched by the tidal waves of high-rise construction booms. Some small neighborhoods are actually drawing people away from the boring sprawl of high-rise apartments and into the ideal of a tightly woven neighborhood with European chic. Unlike super-gentrification, this new urban culture shows at least some potential for mitigating the impact of social polarization. At the same time, Gangnam's representational space takes a step away from the automobile-driven suburban-style American Dream and seeks its alternative globally in European or other styles of urbanism. A perception of urban change is activated by a new "spatial practice," yet another term originating from Lefebvre's theory of social space. How people in their daily lives interact with specific spatial settings, as well as with one another, matters a great deal in terms of how they envision spatial changes. Even if the new practice causes only a marginal change of perception—whether it is aesthetic, economic, or political in nature—toward the "apartment republic," it might one day scale up to something genuinely transformative.

Gangnam's noirish reputation owes more to corruption and criminality on the business side than discrimination and displacement on the residential side. Not only the sex industry, which has long been entrenched in the area, but the media, entertainment, finance, and even high-tech industries have been embroiled in one scandal after another. Paradoxically, however, the dark side of Gangnam opens opportunities for another kind of spatial practice to vie for social change. It is the practice of new political contention at the grassroots level, first brought by the women's mass mobilization campaign against femicide, and followed by a highly visible labor protest in front of the nation's flagship corporation. Other than self-interested collective action by property owners or anti-eviction struggles at the margins, Gangnam used to be spared from street activism. Even at the height of the 1980s' mass democratic movements, it was a bulwark for middle-class conservatism and a major hindrance to social solidarity with the lower and working classes. But the new politics of contention has flipped the script on the very sense of corruption, criminality, and conservatism associated with the place and raised questions about solidarity—or lack thereof—in contemporary Korean society. The persistence of man-made disasters into the twenty-first century keeps bringing back the memories of Sampoong and the issue of solidarity with the victims as social polarization turns them into an extremely volatile political issue. A new spatial practice of preserving the memories of disaster, and the renewed politics of contention over memorialization, suggest that there may be something more than noir in the dialectical image of Gangnam.

Image-Text Montage of Representational Space: Theory and Method

Although this book covers an extended range of urban and cultural history from the late 1960s until the present, it does not follow a strictly linear, chronological order; its chapters are only loosely organized by intersecting genres (music, poetry, fiction, film, television) and academic disciplines (popular music history, literature, film studies, sociology, urban studies, geography). It deliberately maintains an interdisciplinary approach and attempts to present an annotated montage of Gangnam in an adaptation of Walter Benjamin's method.[29] In order to understand the power of the dreams associated with Gangnam in its proper context, interpretive text analyses are combined with conventional writings based on archival and field research. Benjamin was famously critical of cultural history as an academic discipline that "presents an eternal image of the past." In opposition to such "historicism," Benjamin proposed a "dialectical construction" of history, "whose locus is not empty time, but the particular epoch, the particular life, the particular work."[30] In the same spirit, each chapter of this book chooses some particular works or places, rearranging them into historical constellations from which the dialectical image of Gangnam as capitalist phantasmagoria emerges.

If there is a single work that has inspired this book to embrace the Benjaminian approach, it would be Cho Sehŭi's *Time Travel*. The unfinished novella ends with a dream sequence montage that not only presages the apocalyptic reality of the first global pandemic of the twenty-first century, but also resonates eerily with Benjamin's critique of history as progress: "The fugitive shouted at the malicious diseases that kept persistently chasing after him. 'What we want is progress. Listen to my advice, everyone! Whatever's in your hands, lay it down at your feet. And go away quietly under the darkness that's been giving you cover until now. Pay close attention to my final advice, all of you. Don't ever ignore it!'"[31] The (de)construction of Gangnam as the modern dreamworld may well require something akin to Benjamin's unfinished magnum opus, *Das Passagen-Werk* (*The Arcades Project*), in terms of method, if not of volume. This book considers his specific method, "literary montage," widely applicable to various texts from poetry and fiction to self-help books and personal memoir. As Benjamin stated, "I needn't say anything. Merely show. I shall purloin no valuables, appropriate no ingenious formulations. But the rags, the refuse—these I will not inventory but allow, in the only way possible, to come into their own: by making use of them."[32] The method of montage, of course, is even more appropriate for spatial/architectural "texts," not to mention visual and cinematic ones, to be reconfigured into representational space.

14   Introduction

Readers must have noticed by now that this book also relies heavily on Lefebvre's conceptual triad of spatial practice, space of representation, and representational space in *The Production of Space*. The notoriously elusive definition of each term in his triad is well appreciated among specialists: "Unfortunately—or perhaps fortunately, he sketches this out only in preliminary fashion, leaving us to add our own flesh, our own content, to rewrite it as part of our own chapter or research agenda."[33] However, Lefebvre's profound notion of space being a social product as well as a means of production is indispensable in understanding the modern city as a capitalist product/production. Table 1 provides a synopsis of how the three concepts are understood and deployed in this book. Lefebvre's spatial theory imposes a loose structure on Gangnam's urban history from the objective perspective of scientific conception (representation of space) and physical perception (spatial practice), while allowing for fragments of texts, images, and sounds to be juxtaposed and coalesced into a historical constellation (montage) in the representational space of lived experience. Taken together, Benjamin's method and Lefebvre's theory provide a critical tool for cultural historians to analyze the social production of an urban dreamworld like Gangnam with all its spectacles, disasters, and struggles.

The double vision of utopia and dystopia haunting contemporary Gangnam is ultimately a consequence of the changing social-class configurations I refer to as global-polarization. It is worth noting that Pierre Bourdieu, whose masterpiece *Distinction: A Social Critique of the Judgement of Taste* opened a new way of understanding capitalist class hierarchy and its cultures, defined social

Table 1.   Henri Lefebvre's conceptual triad

	Spatial practice	Representation of space	Representational space
Phenomenological character	Perceived (physically sensed; acted upon)	Conceived (measured; planned)	Lived (experienced; imagined)
Expressive activity	Daily routine; specific social/physical relations	Scientific, political, administrative	Symbolic, literary, artistic
Concrete examples	Urban routes and rhythms; sense of place	Maps; urban designs; policy plans	Literary narratives; film and visual representations

Source: Based on Lefebvre, *Production of Space*; Stuart, *Understanding Henri Lefebvre*; Merrifield, *Henri Lefebvre*.

class in terms of space. Granted, Bourdieu's usage of "social space" points to an abstract, geometric sense of the term, in which class positions are determined by three-dimensional coordinates of economic, social, and cultural capital.[34] But he was keenly aware of the significance of geographical space as well: "To account more fully for the differences in life-style between the different fractions—especially as regards culture—one would have to take account of their distribution in a *socially ranked geographical space.*"[35] The geographical space does not mean a natural space but a socially produced one in the Lefebvrean sense, hierarchically ranked to maintain the class order: "The distribution of a class or class fraction—in particular its distance from the economic and cultural 'centres'—almost always manifests also its internal hierarchies" as many "cultural properties are acquired by virtue of position in geographical space, partly through the quality of the social contracts favoured by spatial proximity."[36] Bourdieu's three-dimensional model of capital accumulation therefore superimposes an abstract geometric space of social class upon concrete geographic space, or "place" as human geographers would prefer to call it. Since Gangnam's rise as the economic and cultural center, the vicissitudes of Korea's middle class have been tied to their relative proximities to the place. This book's focus on the accumulation of cultural capital—whether it is in the form of popular music, literature, cinema, or other visual cultures—from Gangnam's representational space is intended to highlight the affective dynamic of global-polarization, which exacerbates the anguish of the fractured middle, further polarizing their double vision of capitalist phantasmagoria.

Looking Ahead: Chapter Previews

Chapter 1 begins with Psy's "Gangnam Style," a textbook case of postmodern bricolage in music video format. Throughout the video, Psy is able to make such a poignant mockery of this Gangnam history because his immaculate Gangnam pedigree gives him an air of authenticity, which makes it convincing to read this music video as a consummate carnival act. Taken apart and carefully reassembled, it starts to give a surprisingly coherent narrative akin to Hwang Sŏg'yŏng's novel *Dreams of Gangnam*. The reassembled narrative of "Gangnam Style" therefore serves as a bird's-eye view of the place. This music video is also singlehandedly responsible for putting the name "Gangnam" on the global cultural map, and, in doing so, it has hollowed out the locality of the place. Thus, it takes a kind of reverse engineering to map out a cultural geography of Gangnam and find how Korean popular culture has become a global force since its resettlement in the area. In tracing the musical origins of Psy's "Gangnam Style," this chapter gives a historical account of the music and entertainment industries' relocation to Gangnam since the early 1980s, touching on a wide variety of genres: adult-oriented trot and disco medley, trendy ballad influenced by Western and Japanese styles, working-class rock and roll, club dance music, and hip-hop. Contemporary K-pop would be unthinkable without Gangnam having been the main space of production, distribution, and consumption of popular music. In this sense, Psy's music video pays a sincere tribute to the musical tradition of Gangnam behind the raunchy carnival act.

In chapter 2, the juxtaposition between Gangnam and the rest of the country takes on a poetic quality as Kwak Chaegu's poem "Songji: Marketplace" (1985) locates a bottle of Coca-Cola in many disparate places, including at Hyundai Apartments, Apkujŏngdong, the crown jewel of 1980s' Gangnam, and the traditional marketplace of a rural backwater named Songji. Chŏn Minjo's photograph "Apkujŏngdong" (see figure 2.1) reveals that these two settings may not have been that far apart from each other since there used to be farmland right in front of the Apkujŏngdong high-rise apartments just a few years back. But it was the distance in terms of the Bourdieusian social space that was already there and growing rapidly. Even in the early years of Gangnam development, such literary luminaries as Ch'oe Inho and Pak Wansŏ wrote scathing stories about the new urbanization project. When Gangnam firmly established itself as an Americanized middle-class "paradise" in the mid-1980s, the voices of critique from the likes of Cho Sehŭi, Kwak Chaegu, Hwang Chiu, and Ch'oe Sŭngja (Choi Seungja) grew even louder. Yu Ha's vocal denunciation of Gangnam's excesses ironically made him a pop culture icon in the early 1990s. When the new century rolled in, female writers like Mun Chŏnghŭi, Chŏng Migyŏng, and Chŏng Ihyŏn offered more nuanced introspection about Gangnam and its residents, all of whom were not satisfied with where they had arrived. With global-polarization sweeping across the area, the stories of Kim Yun'yŏng, Yi Hong, and Kim Sagwa revealed how the intricate class dynamics played out as the myth of middle-class society was undermined from within.

Chapter 3 expands on Cho Sehŭi's ominous vision in "There Are as Many as Two Lakes in Chamsil." This short essay-style narrative serves as the key piece of an image-text montage illuminating the pitfalls and traumas of the dreamland, starting with the ecological destruction the Han River Comprehensive Development Project brought about. Cho's class-conscious ecocriticism has found its worthy successor in Bong Joon-ho, whose globally acclaimed films dramatically point out the fundamental link between social stratification and environmental degradation. The river and the bridges in Cho's and Bong's works represent, respectively, the border between and the crossings over the ever-deepening class divide. When the Sŏngsu Bridge connecting opulent Apkujŏngdong to working-class neighborhoods north of the river snapped in 1994, the cause was a catastrophic structural failure in both the physical and the social sense. The commemoration of this tragic event was muted, then overshadowed by larger-scale disasters that followed. Only recently has an independent film by Kim Bora (Kim Pora) reconstructed the traumatic memory through the eyes of a teenage girl. For all the hardships she had to endure while growing up as a working-class child in Gangnam, the girl's story intimates the possibility of mending a bridge across the class divide, giving a long-overdue sense of healing and a glimmer of hope for the future.

The theme of disaster and solidarity continues into chapter 4, focusing on the collapse of Sampoong Department Store in 1995—the single-largest civilian disaster in Korean history, with 502 dead, 30 missing, and 937 wounded. The owner's reckless decisions that resulted in the unprecedented number of casualties were not an aberration. Rather, indifference to human safety has been a systemic feature of Korean capitalism, especially in the construction sector. Construction companies routinely flirted with disaster in foreign war zones before and during Gangnam development, giving a new meaning to the notion of disaster capitalism. Nevertheless, Gangnam's sudden transformation from a metaphorical paradise to a literal disaster zone came as a shock to many, including writers. Compared to the immediate outpouring of political and social commentaries on the systemic failure, literary reflections came slowly and sporadically since people still found it difficult to process the traumatic experience years or even decades later. Once Chŏng Ihyŏn published a story based on her bittersweet personal memories, Hwang Sŏg'yŏng, Mun Hongju, and others followed to memorialize the collapse not as a one-off incident but as a complex series of events set off by disaster capitalism. Their voices were up against the overwhelming force of public amnesia, but the message was clear: such a disaster might well happen again. When it did eventually, victims and survivors of the old disaster came out of oblivion to extend their solidarity to those of the new disaster.

Sense of place is a concept refined by human geographers to understand the affective qualities of a given socio-physical space. Chapter 5 dwells on this concept, in conjunction with Lefebvre's theory of the social production of space, to understand Gangnam's noirish sense of place. Since the very beginning, a plethora of official corruption, political collusion, and organized crime has taken roots in and around the area. The sex industry has also developed along the main business thoroughfare and entertainment districts. An aspect perhaps less sinister than the criminal underworld or the sex industry but profoundly more troubling is the concentration of a massive private education industry as well as elite prep high schools in Gangnam. Given that its long-held status as the promised land for social mobility has been critically dependent on the prowess of college-prep education, Gangnam is never free from controversies over the cutthroat competition on the inside and the lopsided advantage on the outside. Gangnam's sense of place, associated with such "social evils" as organized crime, sex work, and overheated educational competition, has helped create compelling villain characters in cinema. Moreover, Gangnam often makes the evil contagious to other characters, who become complicit either in evil acts perpetrated by villains or in corrupt social institutions. Yeon Sang-ho's *The King of Pigs* and Yoon Jong-bin's *Beastie Boys* are two main visual texts that illustrate the depth of moral issues involving the school system and the sex industry, respectively.

Bloom and Goûte was a European-style café that pioneered the classical pattern of gentrification in Gangnam in the early 2000s. When the British urban sociologist Ruth Glass coined the term "gentrification," she focused on upgrading residential buildings in dilapidated inner-city areas in London, pointing out that the process was essentially the middle-class takeover of working-class neighborhoods. While the historical context is obviously quite different, the neoclassical gentrification in some Gangnam neighborhoods proves that the bohemian, cosmopolitan segments of the middle class are dreaming of a much different urban environment than the sprawl of high-rises. These urban pioneers look out for pockets of space left untouched by the suffocating uniformity of the apartment complex. In chapter 6, an ethnographic investigation spells out how their urban cultural taste has diversified beyond the old model inspired by the Cold War–era American Dream. It further probes into their grassroots activism to assess the potential for the new spatial practice transforming the representation of space, if only on a local, municipal scale. Drawing on the extensive literature on global gentrification, this chapter explores new urban dreams that envision a far less polarized social space even in a place like Gangnam.

The conclusion opens with Lee Chang-dong's film *Burning,* a fantastically bleak portrayal of contemporary Korean youth, which offers an exemplary cultural critique of the polarizing dreams of global capitalism. The complex love-hate relationships among the three main characters are visually represented in stark contrast by their living spaces in different geographic locations, including a Gangnam mansion. The film thus serves as a starting point for recapitulating the main arguments in this book: the utopian/dystopian double vision of modern urban space, global-polarization and the breakup of the middle class into the rising and falling substrata, the pop culture industry's exploits in selling these polarizing dreams, and, finally, a sliver of hope for new spatial practices and social solidarity.

Plate 1: Hwang Mansok, *GangNamStyle* (2016): bronze statue near the World Trade Center, COEX. Source: author's collection.

Plate 2: O Yun, *Marketing V: Painting of Hell* (*Mak'et'ing o: Chiokto*, 1981, mixed media on canvas). The caption at the bottom of the painting reads: "The creation of consumption: is it science or art?" Source: O Yun Estate, reprinted with permission.

Plate 3: Desolate beauty: the concrete piers of Hannam Bridge. Source: Young June Lee, reprinted with permission.

Plate 4: An aerial map of the Teheran Valley sex industry clusters. Escort bars are represented as pink dots, massage parlors as azure dots, *noraebang* bars as green dots, and inns/spas as orange dots. Source: *Han'gyŏre* 21, November 22, 2011, reprinted with permission.

CHAPTER 1

Boomtown Songs on the South of the River
The Origins of "Gangnam Style"

> You believe in a palace of crystal that can never be destroyed—a palace at which one will not be able to put out one's tongue or make a long nose on the sly . . . The palace of crystal may be an idle dream, it may be that it is inconsistent with the laws of nature and that I have invented it only through my own stupidity, through the old-fashioned irrational habits of my generation.
>
> —Fyodor Dostoevsky, "Notes from Underground"

"Gangnam Style," the 2012 music video by Korean pop artist Psy, had a meteoric and unexpected rise to global fame. The reasons for the event's sudden popularity are obscure, and beyond the scope of this chapter. However, it is worth briefly reviewing how others have attempted to do so. In some Korean academic circles, substantive audience survey research found that the comedic aspects of the music video had the greatest appeal among Korean and non-Korean viewers.[1] Still, the near-universal comic effect remains largely inexplicable. Some interpretations cite the dance, the beat pattern, the power of YouTube, social media, and internet memes as contributing factors. Sure enough, a combination of all these elements somehow managed to strike a chord with the global audience, spawning innumerable parody versions made by people from all walks of life.[2] Among the participants were two prominent dissident intellectuals of our time representing the East and the West, respectively: Ai Weiwei from China and Noam Chomsky from the U.S.[3] How did Psy's music video become a versatile stage for sociopolitical parody?

Digital Carnival: Gangnam Boy's Self-Mockery

My theory is that "Gangnam Style" was effective as a double parody, in which Psy's original satire of Gangnam may have lost its locally specific significance but instead found a global resonance because of the carnivalesque atmosphere it conjured up. Indeed, the whole Gangnam Style phenomenon aligns with Mikhail Bakhtin's description of carnival as "a pageant without footlights and without a division into performers and spectators . . . everyone is an active participant, everyone communes in the carnival act."[4] The target of carnivalesque parody, according to Bakhtin, is replaceable; what really matters in carnival is the function of change and shift, not the precise substance. For the majority of non-Korean participants, therefore, "Gangnam" is the most interchangeable part in this assemblage of digital carnival. By contrast, the dizzying speed of shifts that "liquefies" linguistic signifiers,[5] the irresistible "eccentricity" of the move known as horse-trot,[6] and the toilet jokes that need no translation are all essential components for parody to work almost anywhere and everywhere.

More than two billion hits on YouTube, however, generated enough curiosity about the mysterious signifier of Gangnam. Eventually, some knowledgeable foreign observers, like this one, who wrote a magazine article "dissecting Gangnam Style," investigated further: "Gangnam is a tony Seoul neighborhood, and PSY's Gangnam style video lampoons its self-importance and ostentatious wealth . . . the video is rich with subtle references that along with the song itself, suggest a subtext with a surprisingly subversive message about class and wealth in contemporary South Korean society."[7] The reporter and one of his sources, a Korean American blogger, are mostly on the mark in terms of Psy's satire of Gangnam. As the blogger points out, one glaring absence that would render the poignancy of his lampooning is that the music video is a kind of self-mockery for Psy: "It's like he's shouting, 'Look at me! I'm a true Gangnamese but don't I look really tacky and pathetic?'"[8] Psy has impeccable credentials as a Gangnam boy: he is the scion of a wealthy family who grew up in Gangnam and witnessed its spectacular rise from the very beginning. At the same time, he was a foul-mouthed class clown who did not fit the mold of a respectable businessman. He got into all kinds of serious trouble and yet turned his fortune around at critical junctures with his street smarts and talent as a musician and entertainer. In other words, he is the ultimate Gangnam insider who can authoritatively ridicule the superficiality of Gangnam culture. Psy's history of mischief and his personal upbringing were well-known to Korean audiences long before "Gangnam Style."[9] Thus, while the music video might have been made as little more than a tongue-in-cheek insider joke, its success beyond anyone's wildest dreams indicates a much deeper insight and resonance.

Beneath the wildly carnivalesque textual surface of the music video is the bite of the original satire. In working through the layers, one finds multiple subtexts embedded in the makings of Gangnam as the land of dreams. Such a reading turns "Gangnam Style" into much more than just a lampoon, but rather a serio-comic snippet, a Menippean satire in the digital age. This kind of satire "always parodies itself," and the "element of self-parody is one of the reasons for the extraordinary vitality of the genre."[10] While the comic element of this satire explains its near-universal appeal, the serious element reveals how it dishes out a poignant, if not subversive, critique of the socio-economic order. Furthermore, the video opens a pathway to understanding Gangnam's historic rise as the center of the music entertainment industry, which started long before Psy's "Gangnam Style" and continues on a global scale to this day.

The Carnivalesque Subtexts of "Gangnam Style"

While the video sequences frenetic jump cuts among several locations and spaces, it can be rearranged into a handful of key scenes that allude to Gangnam's past and present. The first scene starts with a high-rise office building that is the phallic symbol of Gangnam's economic power, the World Trade Center. The building itself is part of the COEX, a gigantic convention center complex that also includes the five-star Hotel Intercontinental, a sprawling underground shopping mall, a casino for foreign guests, and the K-pop Plaza, which opened in 2018. Initially named the Korea Exhibition Center (KOEX), the convention building can be regarded as a Korean equivalent to the Crystal Palace. With its glass-and-metal facade and ceiling, the COEX Mall is reminiscent of the nineteenth-century London landmark both in form and function. Just as the Crystal Palace had engrossed Dostoevsky, so much so that it became the symbol of the rapacity of Western capitalism in everything he wrote since his visit to London,[11] while Benjamin devoted sixteen "convolutes" of *Das Passagen-Werk* to it, the COEX has been garnering much attention from the mass of consumers and critical scholars alike (figure 1.1). One such scholar goes so far as to resurrect Korea's first fictional flaneur, Kubo the novelist, from the Japanese colonial period of 1934, and have him lament the glass "wall of the neoliberal empire."[12] Thus, the opening images ground the viewer in solid monuments to Korean neoliberalism before Psy commences on his escapade across Gangnam and beyond.

Figure 1.1. The Crystal Palace (left) and the COEX Mall (right). Source (left): Philip H. Delamotte, "The Crystal Palace During Its Re-erection at Sydenham, London" (c. 1854, public domain); (right): author's collection.

Once Psy establishes the authenticity of locale in a flash, the scene then quickly moves to the underground parking lot. Built in 1979, the COEX was one of the first structures that featured such a subterranean parking space. This spatial transition in the video gives a sense of continuity to the viewers that they are still in the same location, only underground—though in fact, the scene was shot nowhere near the COEX or, for that matter, Gangnam.[13] In stark contrast to the glitz of the above-ground tower, the underground is portrayed as a foreboding, seedy place filled with flying garbage and a white foam of unknown origin. In this particular underground scene, Psy acts like the underground man in Dostoevsky's famous novella, sticking out a metaphorical tongue at Korea's Crystal Palace. Visitors may see only a superstructure made of inviolable crystal, but Psy the mischievous Gangnam boy can easily unearth a dirty hen house buried underneath. Later in the video, the underground parking lot reappears, but this time it is a much brighter, rather showy space where Psy does a dance duel with another Gangnam man driving a red Mercedes convertible, played by the popular reality TV show host Yu Chaesŏk. This duel scene constitutes the primary carnivalesque act of "mock crowning and subsequent decrowning of the carnival king" as Psy squares off against the sharply dressed newcomer and is soundly bested.[14] The ritual of humiliation—crawling between the legs of a cowboy-clown—follows.

The yin and yang of Gangnam is a recurring theme as the viewer is taken to other spaces representing the "Gangnam" style, both imaginary and real. Some of the imaginary spaces seem to portray an upscale sports complex or fitness club with sauna, spa, indoor tennis courts, and even an indoor equestrian training ground. While the video was shot in different sites, they appear to constitute a common theme: a space of leisure and sports cherished by the aspiring upper middle class that has been residing in Gangnam since the early 1980s. The tattoo-ridden yakuza types in the sauna scene allude to organized crime's ties with some of the early Gangnam entertainment establishments, hotel nightclubs and spas in particular. One might say it is Psy's slight dig at Gangnam's original sin—that much of the city was built by well-connected real estate speculators, some in concert with organized crime.[15]

The most puzzling vignette of the video, at least for newcomers to Korean popular references, takes place under a Han River bridge. Psy is sitting on a wooden bench with two elderly men playing Chinese chess (*changgi*). In contrast to the clean, modern-looking riverside park that appears later in the video, this dumping ground represents the early years of hasty urban expansion that displaced much of the rural, elderly, native population on the south bank of the Han. Then the scene suddenly jumps to the interior of a tour bus, decorated like a discotheque, with some elderly women enjoying a jaunt. The tour bus does in fact function as a mobile disco for middle-aged or elderly women (*ajumma*) of lower- and working-class backgrounds, a popular recreation that was featured in Bong Joon-ho's film *Mother* (*Madŏ*, 2009). The film's hauntingly beautiful final scene is shot in a tour bus on a highway, where the protagonist joins the crowd of ladies dancing in trance-inducing frenzy. In contrast to Bong's artistic rendition, the mobile disco Psy joins is practically campy. After showing all that old-time fun related to Korea's underdeveloped past, Psy literally blows it all up and moves on to Gangnam's upper-middle-class present. In a concrete-paved riverside park, he rides an air horse following two middle-aged women who appear to be very health- and beauty-conscious residents of Gangnam. The women wear large visors that completely block their faces from the sunlight while briskly walking backwards, likely in response to health programs on television recommending the practice as superior to normal walking. Next, Psy visits another riverside park, this time on the northern bank of the Han, where young women stretch in a yoga pose that is framed in a suggestive closeup. In the blurred background across the river, the World Trade Center tower comes into view. With the phallic COEX structure behind him, Psy erupts into a scream among the women in a collectively submissive position. Is it a scream of joy or a yell of frustration? It is left ambiguous.

The latter part of the video continues where the parking lot scene left off; after schooling Psy with his fancy dance moves, the yellow-clad Gangnam man drives away in his red Mercedes, leaving the humiliated Psy in the underground. Without a car, let alone a Mercedes, Psy is forced to take the subway. It is certainly a humbled state for a Gangnam "playa" like Psy's music video character, despite the critical function of subway lines in Gangnam development, as will be discussed later. Unlike at any other moment in the entire music video, in the subway scenes, Psy appears somewhat sincere and serious. He desperately reaches out for the girl played by HyunA (Kim Hyŏn'a), a female K-pop idol superstar in her own right, as if she were a true object of his desire. The camera cuts back and forth between them at an increasingly rapid-fire pace as Psy slowly walks out of the subway car door. In such a frantic moment, one can barely catch a glimpse of a poster on the glass barrier behind Psy. In a still frame from this scene, the text of the poster reads "employment placement service" (*ch'wiŏp chŏngbo*). Although the poster is likely a coincidence, the subliminal occurrence of these words presents a parapraxis, a Freudian slip of the camera. It begs another lingering question: Does the girl symbolize a job, the affordance of stable employment so desperately sought after by many young Koreans, particularly those who have no other means of transportation than the subway? Considering that the main political function of carnival is to release the dissatisfaction of the downtrodden masses, the unemployed or underemployed, unsatisfied, and disaffected youth of contemporary Korea are a paradigmatic carnival crowd. This audience would readily discern such a subliminal message while reveling in K-pop fueled fantasies. Psy's quasi-populist knock on Gangnam makes even more sense in this carnivalesque context. Even if the subliminal message is not communicated to the viewer, the digital carnival still works its magic of self-parody: every viewer has the right to their own interpretation and adaptation of Psy's Gangnam narrative as asserted by countless parodies of "(replace 'Gangnam' with whatever you want) Style."

It is also significant that the music video comes to an end with a flash-mob dance in a large underground space, which can be construed as a symbolic re-creation of the communal "carnival square": "The main arena for carnival acts was the square and the streets adjoining it . . . Other places of action as well (provided they are realistically motivated by the plot, of course) can, if they become meeting- and contact-points for heterogeneous people—streets, taverns, roads, bathhouses, decks of ships, and so on—take on this additional carnival-square significance."[16] Indeed, Psy's Gangnam phantasmagoria runs the whole gamut of contact points—under the bridge, old ladies' disco bus, subway, yakuza-ridden bathhouse, and even a paddleboat on the Han River—before returning to the underground for a final, grand congregation. That is where the carnival act's imaginary subversion ends, and the symbolic restoration of the existing social order begins. Seeking to capitalize on the windfall from "Gangnam Style," the music entertainment industry and municipalities drove headfirst to create physical spaces in commemoration of the transient digital culture phenomenon. They ended up with not one but two "Gangnam Style" carnival squares, so to speak, when digital carnies had long left the town. Despite the apparent tackiness of these physical spaces, there is no better choice of location. One readily sited landmark near the COEX Complex—Korea's Crystal Palace—is a giant bronze sculpture of two hands making Psy's horse-trot gesture (see plate 1). The other is a small stage located on the northwest corner of the Gangnam Station Intersection, the central point of Gangnam where the vertical axis (Gangnam Boulevard) meets the horizontal axis (Teheran Road/Subway Line Number 2).

A truly memorable achievement of "Gangnam Style" is its interweaving of historical (development, corruption, polarization) and geographical (streets, buildings, public spaces) narratives of Gangnam into the audiovisual texture of popular music. Its global success, in turn, had a significant impact on both the physical and the symbolic status of Gangnam. In short, Psy's music video and live performances of "Gangnam Style" transformed the entire district into a "main arena for carnival acts." From a historical perspective, Psy belongs to the long line of popular music acts who have capitalized on the rise of Gangnam as the new urban center since the late 1970s. Thus, a genealogy of Gangnam's carnival spaces must retrace narratives that existing analyses of "Gangnam Style" have either elided or presented only in fragments. The second part of this chapter will trace a genealogy of Gangnam through a composite of historical, geographical, and musical narratives.

The Vertical Axis: Trotting Down Gangnam Boulevard

As noted in the introduction to this book, the Gangnam of today was built on the winds of development and real estate speculation that traversed the Han River currents. Many commentators have pointed to the 1970–1980s' top female singer Hyeŭn'i's disco hit "The Han River Bridge Number Three" ("Chesam han'ganggyo," 1979) as the first song dedicated to the heady days of Gangnam development.[17] However, this song establishes that the actual Gangnam era began not even a decade after the bridge and highway constructions: in the lyrics, the lands south of the bridge still had only "nameless streets" that people went through in the "early morning" hours. The crowning of Gangnam, so to speak, took place during the 1980s, the decade of "great ambition" (*taemang*)—a propaganda slogan the Park Chung Hee administration chanted ad nauseam even though Park himself failed to see its arrival. The Hotel Riverside, which would become the new showcase of adult music entertainment in Gangnam, opened its doors only in December 1981. Even the ironfisted military regime of Park Chung Hee at the time did not have an easy time convincing the old money of the north to move down south, where there was nothing more than some big roads cutting through farmlands and hillside forests. The government took pains to promote Gangnam through various policy measures through the 1970s and 1980s (see the Introduction). In terms of the genealogy of Korean popular music, one of the most consequential such measures was the relocation of the adult entertainment industry to Gangnam.[18] Along with the relocation, new licenses and license renewals were stopped for adult entertainment businesses north of the river. Consequently, venues such as hotel nightclubs, cabaret dancehalls, and hostess clubs and bars emerged near the south end of Bridge Number Three. This was the neighborhood of Sinsadong, made famous by Chu Hyŏnmi's 1988 hit song "The Man from Sinsadong" ("Sinsadong kŭ saram").

Chu's style was firmly rooted in trot (*t'ŭrot'ŭ*), an earlier-generation adult music genre heavily influenced by Japanese *ryūkōka* from the colonial period.[19] Chu's music was thus a fitting anthem for the adult entertainment industry with a main customer base of middle-aged men. But in this song, Chu's delivery is a bit unorthodox, the tempo a little faster than the typical trot; Nam Kug'in, the song's composer, referred to it as "post-trot." It was actually Nam himself and his lyricist wife, Chŏng Ŭn'i, who sensed an opportunity to exploit Gangnam development by crafting songs about it. The songwriting couple continued their success with Chu and other trot singers. Among their collaborators was Mun Hŭiok, whose hit song "The Street of Love" ("Sarang'ŭi kŏri") unmistakably identifies Gangnam with a street, presumably the vertical axis of Gangnam Boulevard. If one follows Gangnam Boulevard southward to where it intersects with Nambu Ring Road (Nambu sunhwanno), one finds the home of the so-called Legend of Malchukkŏri (Horsefeed street), the origin of the land speculation frenzy just prior to the start of Gangnam development. As the humble name suggests, this area was nothing more than a rural hinterland before the speculative "legend," and there long stood Ŭn'gwang Girls' High School. Founded all the way back in 1946, Ŭn'gwang was the only high school in the area prior to the speculation and urban development. Thanks to its location, it also just happened to join the privileged Eighth School District (P'arhakkun), drawn up for the schools that were either founded or relocated during and after the development. Thanks to its rural origin and proximity to the underdeveloped outskirts, for quite some time Ŭn'gwang held the reputation of being the most un-Gangnam-like school in Gangnam—that is, the least assuming, nonprivileged high school in the area. Sure enough, Ŭn'gwang did what was completely inconceivable to any other Gangnam high school and shocked the test score–obsessed parents and students of the Eighth School District. In 1987, they held a trot song recital for a third-year senior student named Mun Hŭiok.

In addition to being her route to school and the inspiration for the hit song title "The Street of Love," Gangnam Boulevard had additional significance for Mun Hŭiok. Farther north along the boulevard, just before the southeastern corner of Sinsadong, there was the office of Ant'a Production, where the renowned trot music producer An Ch'ihaeng transformed Mun's school-age raw talent into adult trot stardom. Mun thus began her musical career commuting up and down Gangnam Boulevard between An'ta in Sinsadong and her school in Malchukkŏri. Her commercial debut, *Dialect Disco* (*Sat'uri tisŭk'o*, 1987), was a surprise hit especially among tour bus drivers and passengers on the Seoul-Busan Expressway, similar to the mobile discotheque in Psy's "Gangnam Style" music video. Two years later, "The Street of Love" made her a mainstream popular act:

> Here I'm in South Seoul [Namsŏul] Yŏngdong,
> It's a street of lovers
> Hot winds blow all four seasons
> Anyone who feels sick of loneliness
> Take a walk on the street just once
> A-ha, this is where love blossoms
> South Seoul Yŏngdong
> The street of love.

In the lyrics quoted above, apparently "the street" becomes a synecdoche of the entire area of "South Seoul Yŏngdong," the two old names for Gangnam that have dropped out of favor since.[20] While South Seoul had never been used too frequently, Yŏngdong competed with Gangnam for some time as the official name of the entire area. A shorthand for "the east of Yŏngdŭngp'o," the name remains in vestigial form, such as Yŏngdong Boulevard and the Yŏngdong Bridge. The latter was the subject of Chu Hyŏnmi's breakthrough hit, "Raining on the Yŏngdong Bridge" ("Pinaerinŭn yŏngdonggyo," 1985). The same year she also released "Yŏngdong Blues" (Yŏngdong purusŭ), claiming Gangnam as her lyrical territory well before "The Man from Sinsadong," her biggest achievement.

According to the Korea Music Copyright Association's online database, a total of thirty-five song titles released between 1979 and 1993 contained references to Gangnam, Yŏngdong, and other well-known places in the area. Eighteen of the songs were credited to the composer Nam Kug'in, with Chŏng Ŭn'i writing lyrics to seven of them, making the couple a driving force behind the Gangnam-themed trot music boom in the 1980s. Interestingly, Yŏngdong appears in sixteen different song titles, outnumbering Gangnam four-to-one.[21] Considering that a large majority of these songs are trot, one may surmise that the old-school genre preferred the old-fashioned name.

From "The Han River Bridge Number Three" to "Raining on the Yŏngdong Bridge" to "The Street of Love," the frequent use of bridges and roads to symbolize Gangnam through the end of the 1980s suggests that development was still "under way," not quite finished yet. The influx of the so-called new middle class rode on the real estate boom and "education fever" (*kyoyungnyŏl*) into Gangnam. As they were still adjusting to their new environs, the middle-class Gangnam residents had not yet developed a Gangnam cultural vernacular. At this juncture, those who promoted Gangnam in popular culture were mostly nonresident outsiders who worked for the adult entertainment industry located in Gangnam. Chu Hyŏnmi hailed from Gangbuk, and so did Kim Suhŭi, whose nickname "Yŏngdong sister" (*ŏnni*) alludes to her appeal to the women working in Gangnam's adult entertainment establishments in the 1980s. As mentioned earlier, the high school Mun Hŭiok attended is technically located in Gangnam, but she too was originally an outsider who came from another Yŏngdong—the provincial region east of the T'aebaek Mountains—to become a singer. In other words, the regional and social backgrounds of these early Gangnam singers are a far cry from today's artists who represent Gangnam, including Psy. Perhaps more than anything, trot music's outsider status to Gangnam is proven by the composer-lyricist power couple of Nam Kug'in and Chŏng Ŭn'i, who lived in Gangbuk for four decades and had no apparent connection to Gangnam other than writing many hit songs about it. The main audience for their trot songs were also outsiders to Gangnam. As it was then and is now, trot is generally regarded as working-class or lower-middle-class music. For the majority of these folks, the scenery of adult entertainment in this newly developed district was just as familiar yet exotic as Chu Hyŏnmi's voice. Born and raised in the Chinese-Korean enclave of downtown Seoul, her lilting voice possesses a slight Chinese intonation. "The Man from Sinsadong" especially highlights her unique vocal technique.

By the time Chu and Mun were at the peak of their popularity, the adult entertainment industry had outgrown Sinsadong, stretching farther south along the boulevard. As opposed to Gangbuk, all sorts of development promotion policies were mobilized in Gangnam to form new entertainment districts around the main intersections of Gangnam Boulevard that lead into Sinsadong, the Yŏngdong Market (Nonhyŏndong), and Gangnam Station (Yŏksamdong-Sŏch'odong). Glitzy bars and nightclubs dotted the boulevard, behind which was a dense network of back alleys lined with "love hotels," massage parlors, and other such establishments. Mun's "Street of Love" may well have served as another theme song for this new nightlife district. The song lyrics feature suggestive and opaque references to "hot winds" and "anyone who feels sick of loneliness." Prior to their Gangnam-themed hits, both Chu and Mun gained popularity with trot-disco medleys that were played in heavy rotation at the tour bus discotheque. Psy's "Gangnam Style" borrows not only the visual theme of the disco bus but also a rhythmic device from the trot-disco medley: the offbeat exclamation of "huh, huh" that sounds and functions similarly to Psy's stuttering refrain: "Op op op op, oppan Gangnam style."

For those who are familiar with the area's history, the nightclub in Hwang Sŏg'yŏng's novel *Dreams of Gangnam* clearly refers to the Hotel Riverside Nightclub. The novel's protagonist, Pak Sŏnnyŏ, originally ran a "room salon" (*rum ssarong*)—a Korean-style "escort bar" or hostess bar with female sex workers—as a madam somewhere in Gangbuk. Then she earned a fortune from speculating over Gangnam land and moved her business south to the Hotel Riverside. The five major "tourist hotels" soon came one after the other: Yŏngdŏng Hotel in Nonhyŏndong, Namsŏul Hotel (currently the Ritz Carlton), and the Samjŏng Hotel in Yŏksamdong, and the Palace Hotel in Sŏch'odong. Beginning with the "theater-style cabaret" of Tokyo Hall, in the vicinity of these brand-name hotels, small and large entertainment establishments were also added to the landscape. The number of such business establishments, recorded as 110 in 1980, jumped to more than 250 in just two years, and according to a newspaper headline at the time, Gangnam became the destination of "the Great Escape on the Han River Bridge Number Three" for Gangbuk office workers' second round of after-work drinking. The apartment complexes that were built in the surrounding area became famous for being the residences of "women working in the hospitality industry," as the media reported rather dramatically.[22]

While the river crossing from north to south was a characteristic feature of Gangnam development, there was a cultural flow running in the opposite direction along the vertical axis, from south to north. Here "south" refers not to Gangnam but to the southern part of the country that was joined to Seoul by the Seoul-Busan Expressway. Some southern-born rock musicians who had come to Seoul in search of stardom achieved success with music that reflected the hopes and despairs of the migrant working class. The most prominent example would be Yoon Soo Il (Yun Suil), whose masterful blend of rock and roll and trot created a massive hit song, "Apartment" ("Ap'at'ŭ").

Crossing the Starry Bridge: From Trot to Working-Class Rock and Roll

With no definite plans, Yoon Soo Il moved from the industrial city of Ulsan on the southeastern coast to Seoul in 1973 to pursue a career in popular music. The biracial child of a white American GI father and a Korean mother, Yoon graduated from Ulsan's prestigious Haksŏng High School and was "smart enough to attend college in Seoul," but he gave that dream up because of his mixed-race identity.[23] When Yoon arrived in Seoul, it had been only three years since the completion of the expressway, and the Seoul Express Bus Terminal in Gangnam was still several years from opening. The only apartment building in Gangnam was the five-story structure in Nonhyŏndong, completed in December of 1971. The twenty-year-old Yoon first settled in a northeastern corner of Seoul called Mang'uri. It has become somewhat of a legend that he lived in a mud hut inside a vineyard while working as an assistant to a rock band named the Golden Grapes. Led by the brothers Ham Chung'a and Ham Chŏngp'il, the Golden Grapes were a group of young people from the Pearl Buck Foundation, which supported war orphans and multiracial children. The band had been active for two years, since its founding in 1971, under the tutelage of the "godfather of Korean rock," guitarist and composer Shin Joong Hyun (Sin Chunghyŏn), when they won first place at a rock band contest and made their name.[24] After initial success with the Golden Grapes, Yoon's musical career started to take off when he signed a contract as a solo act with Ant'a Production. This was of course the same Ant'a that was run by An Ch'ihaeng, a hitmaker in the trot music world who would later work with Chu Hyŏnmi and Mun Hŭiok, the aforementioned trot divas of 1980s Gangnam.

But Yoon's career with Ant'a began well before the Gangnam trot divas' time, when the company was still located in Gangbuk. Ant'a's foresight to turn Yoon into a solo act was a successful gamble, as he reeled off a series of trot hits, such as "Anything but Love" ("Sarangmanŭn ank'essŏyo," 1977), "Reed" ("Kaltae," 1978), "Nana" (1979), and "Wanderer" ("Yurangja," 1980), among others. By the time Ant'a showed another flash of foresight and relocated its office to Gangnam, Yoon had already declared his independence from Ant'a and launched his own namesake agency. He also formed his own namesake band and released *Yoon Soo Il Band the First Album* (1981), which signaled a transition from trot back to his musical origins in rock and roll. The next year, Yoon released the band's second album featuring the anthemic "Apartment"—a song that needs no introduction to the Korean audience as it has enjoyed national popularity, been used as a sports fight song, and frequently topped karaoke charts. Thanks to the smash hit "Apartment" and other such rock-style songs as "The Second Hometown" ("Cheiŭi kohyang," 1981), "Beautiful" ("Arŭmdawŏ," 1984), and "Fantasy Island" ("Hwansang'ŭi sŏm," 1985), the image of Yoon Soo Il from the 1980s was that of a slender, fit rocker dressed in aviator sunglasses and a leather jacket, holding a mic and shaking his legs. The swagger Yoon exuded behind dark shades appears to be what Psy channels in "Gangnam Style" three decades later, despite marked contrasts between their body types and music styles.

"Apartment" came to be a song that embodied the spirit of the times—massive urban development in Gangnam and elsewhere in Seoul that filled up the space with high-rise apartment towers. Speculations abound concerning which specific apartment complex was the basis for the song lyrics.[25] In fact, Yoon had a long history of apartment living, having resided in one of the oldest apartment complexes in Hoehyŏndong, near old downtown Seoul, and then in another old five-story complex in Tongbuich'ondong on the northern bank of the Han River before eventually moving to the Gangnam area. Whenever Yoon is asked which apartment the song refers to, he avoids a straight answer and speaks about a beautiful apartment building he once saw during an overseas trip. Evidently this did not keep people from guessing about the apartment being located on the riverside of Gangnam, where one can arrive "crossing the starry bridge" and "passing by the windy field of reeds," as the lyrics go. "Reed bed" would be the precise translation of *kaltaesup* in the original lyrics, but the coincidence is just too tempting to ignore—the "Field of Reeds" (Aaru) being the heavenly paradise in ancient Egyptian mythology.

Another early-1980s rock and roll hit by Yoon, "The Second Hometown" includes vague references to Gangnam development. Reminiscent of the *Born to Run*–era Bruce Springsteen, Yoon plays a straight-up blue-collar rock sound. As for the lyrics, Yoon describes them thusly in an interview: "[It] is a song I wrote on my way back from a month-long tour through the local provinces. As we crossed the Hannam Bridge [off the Seoul-Busan Expressway from the south], I looked upon Namsan's night lights and thought to myself, 'Why does Seoul feel so warm? Oh, this is my hometown now.'"[26] In other words, with these lyrics, Yoon intended to convey the emotions of the provincial migrants, as he himself had once been, arriving through Gangnam via the expressway, then over the Hannam Bridge to the poor and working-class neighborhoods of Gangbuk. Phrases like "the new moon hanging on top of the skyscrapers at night" or "the stars gathered at my window" portray a young man wistfully looking out from a tiny room in a hilltop shanty over the city night lights. They would evoke scenes from the popular TV drama series *Moon Village* (*Taltongne*, 1980–1981) for the listeners who lived through this period. In "Apartment" and "The Second Hometown," Yoon Soo Il managed to capture the emotional toll on both sides of rapid urbanization: the isolation and loneliness of the urban middle class living in the apartment complex and the alienation and homesickness of the rural migrant worker living in the moon village.

The Sinsadong Circuit: The Music Industry's Gold Rush to Gangnam

According to both Nam Kug'in and An Ch'ihaeng, the name of Gangnam or Yŏngdong did not have much practical significance for the people actually making and singing these songs, aside from symbolizing development and the adult entertainment industry. This was also the case for An Ch'ihaeng when he moved his Ant'a Production office to a building at the Yŏngdong Market Intersection in Nonhyŏndong's "Furniture Alley." Aside from the "wide and well-laid roads," they did not state any other reason for moving to Gangnam.[27] However, other small record labels, talent management agencies, and recording studios soon followed Ant'a, laying the groundwork for Gangnam's transformation through the 1980s. Gangnam grew from a symbolic place representing consumption and the adult entertainment industry into an actual hub for music production.

Soon after, recording industry offices clustered around the area where Yŏngdong Hotel and Haktong Park are located. This area is now surrounded by intersecting subway lines and stations: Sinsa (Line 3), Nonhyŏn (Line 7), and Haktong (Line 7). To the south on Furniture Alley were Ant'a Production and the recording studio Modern Sound. Following along Tosan Boulevard (Tosandaero) to the north was Ssang'yong Production, which produced many hit songs collectively known as Pangbaedong ballads (discussed in the next section) under the leadership of Ŏm Yongsŏp, and other small label offices such as Han'guk Records and Hyŏndae Sound. Ch'oe Pongho, the éminence grise of Gangnam adult entertainment who ran the Hotel Riverside Nightclub, opened his own label named T'aeyang Sound in Ch'ŏngdamdong. While the label office was somewhat distant from his famous Sinsadong nightclub, Ch'oe's entertainment empire was rich and powerful enough to stretch from the Hotel Riverside to the west, following Apkujŏng Road, through the luxurious Apkujŏngdong-Ch'ŏngdamdong area.[28] Consequently, a grid circuit of Gangnam's music entertainment industry formed around Sinsadong as Apkujŏng Road, Tosan Boulevard, and Haktong Road cut across the area between the Seoul-Busan Expressway to the west and Yŏngdong Boulevard to the east. In the 1990s, recording studios equipped with the latest technology, including Lead Sound (Sinsadong), New Bay Studio (Nonhyŏndong), and Ch'ŏng'ŭm Studio (Apkujŏngdong)—along with two music cable TV channel studios, Mnet in Ch'ŏngdamdong and KMTV in Nonhyŏndong—joined the premises. With the country's largest K-pop music entertainment companies, SM and JYP, also having been established in the area, the center of gravity in the music entertainment industry completely shifted from Gangbuk to Gangnam by the mid-1990s. Since then, both companies have grown to become representatives of the global K-pop phenomenon, while YG Entertainment, one of the Big Three along with SM and JYP, remains outside Gangnam even though it produced Psy's "Gangnam Style" (see figure 1.2).[29]

As noted, those involved in the early Sinsadong Circuit did not at first consider Gangnam as the new locale for music business, other than for the convenience

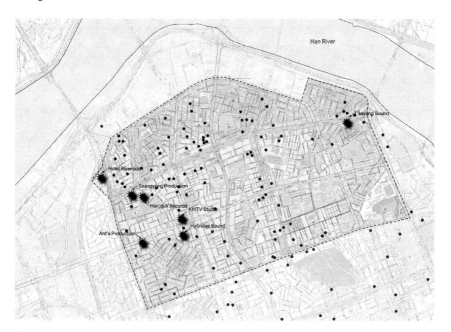

Figure 1.2. The Sinsadong Circuit: the music business network in Gangnam. Spiked dots represent the old music industry establishments that formed the original Sinsadong Circuit in the 1980s–1990s; small black dots represent contemporary music businesses registered with the Ministry of Culture, Sports, and Tourism since 2015. Data source: author interviews and Seoul Metropolitan Government (https://data.seoul.go.kr/dataList/OA-17214/S/1/datasetView.do).

of transportation. However, as Ssang'yong Production's Ŏm Yongsŏp recalled, "those who were fed up with Korea Records would go across the street and sign a contract with Hyŏndae Sound."[30] Such anecdotes show the impact of geographical proximity in the music industry at the time. In some cases, there was a close collaboration among the companies within the Sinsadong Circuit. For example, Ant'a Production frequently borrowed the label name of nearby Hit Records to sell copies and produced some of Yoon Soo Il's albums released by Hyŏndae Sound. Even Ch'oe Pongho's T'aeyang Sound took one of its brightest stars, the 1980s' dancing queen Nami, to Hyŏndae Sound for her fifth album in 1987. In hindsight, therefore, it is clear that the Sinsadong Circuit was generating a synergistic effect thanks to the concentration of music businesses in this area. Furthermore, the nightclubs and adult establishments of Sinsadong and its vicinities served as a test market for the music produced by the Sinsadong Circuit. In other words, a certain feedback mechanism between music production and consumption began to emerge in Gangnam. Although Nam Kug'in cast doubt about the existence of a feedback route for marketing and distribution of trot music, in the case of ballad and dance music, such a feedback circuit had indeed formed through the direct connection between recording studios and club venues. For example, it was none other than An Ch'ihaeng's Ant'a Production that discovered and trained Pak Namjŏng, who went on to become arguably the best solo dance music artist in the late 1980s, regularly performing at the Riverside Nightclub. The obvious main beneficiary of such a direct connection was Ch'oe Pongho's T'aeyang Sound. The company's female superstars could use the Hotel Riverside Nightclub, run by Ch'oe himself, as their personal stage, and the result was such dancefloor hits as Yun Si-nae's "Let's Study" ("Kongbu hapsida," 1983) and Nami's "Round 'n' Round" ("Pinggŭl pinggŭl," 1984).

The Horizontal Axis: The Subway, the Pangbaedong Corridor, and Elite High School District

If the vertical axis and the Sinsadong Circuit represent trot and the old-school musical influences from Gangbuk, the horizontal axis represents new styles of music associated with the residential high-rise apartment boom in Gangnam. The horizontal axis was built with the intent to relocate powerful government offices: the Supreme Court and the National Prosecution Service were moved to the western side (Sŏch'o District). On the opposite side (Gangnam District), plans were made to relocate Seoul's new city hall and a number of central government ministries, but they never materialized. Still, it had the nation's biggest convention center, the COEX complex, which figures prominently in Psy's "Gangnam Style" video, as well as the Olympic Main Stadium in adjacent Chamsil. These important buildings were surrounded by residential high-rises. The underground route that completed this horizontal axis was Subway Line Number 2, and at the ground level it was matched by Teheran Road, which has developed into a major business-finance district over the years (see figure 1.3).

Geographically, Pangbaedong bears some similarities with Sinsadong. It is another gateway area to Gangnam, connected with Gangbuk through Tongjak Bridge over the Han River and underground through Subway Line Number 4. As for the entertainment culture, the Café Street (Kkap'e kolmok)

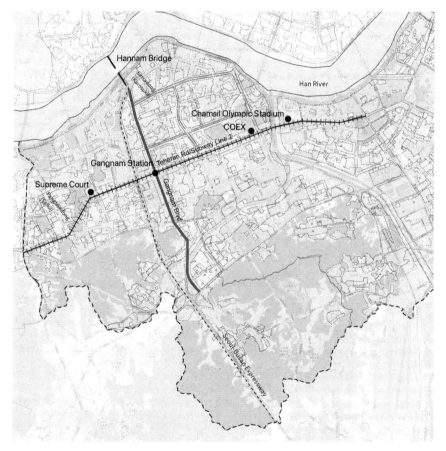

Figure 1.3. The axes of Gangnam: vertical (Gangnam Boulevard/Seoul-Busan Expressway) and horizontal (Teheran Road/Subway Line 2).

in Pangbaedong used to be at the forefront of cool, exotic foreign trends years ahead of Apkujŏngdong. To the north of Café Street is the Old Panp'o (Kubanp'o) Chugong Apartment Complex; to the east is the Pangbae Samho Apartment Complex, and farther south are blocks of restaurants, bars, and storefronts surrounding Pangbae Station of Subway Line Number 2. According to multiple personal and journalistic accounts, the cultural scene of Pangbaedong began in 1978, when the Italian restaurant Forest of Roses (Changmiŭi sup) opened on the northern end of the rather empty street then known only by its official name, Pangbae Central Road (Chung'angno). The restaurant soon became a magnet for writers, artists, scholars, politicians, and celebrities, raising the neighborhood's profile considerably:

> If you didn't know about this place [Forest of Roses], you wouldn't have been considered one of the dandies in Seoul. There weren't many places to hang out in the cold and dreary 1980s, and this was the gathering place for them to talk about literature and arts, debate about life, and whisper secret words of love. The list of celebrity patrons includes novelists Kim Chuyŏng and Kim Hongsin; classical singer Pak Insu; the late avant-garde artist Chŏng Ch'ansŭng; painter Kim Pyŏngjong; sculptor Sin Hyŏnjung; cartoonist Ko Uyŏng; pop singers Patty Kim, Kim Chun, and Cho Yŏngnam; TV actor Yi Tŏkhwa; politicians Cho Sun and Ch'ŏng Taech'ŏl. It goes to over a hundred in total.[31]

By the mid-1980s, Café Street was a major attraction in Gangnam, with a more upscale reputation than the Sinsadong nightlife district. Although the heyday of the Café Street scene barely lasted a decade, it left an important mark in popular cultural representations of Gangnam, especially as the birthplace of the Pangbaedong ballad. Cho Tŏkpae's "My Old Story" ("Naŭi yennal iyagi," 1985) and Ch'oe Hosŏp's "As Time Goes By" ("Sewŏri kamyŏn," 1988) still conjure the ambience of the 1980s Café Street, drawing a sharp contrast to the excitement Chu Hyŏnmi's trot songs delivered for Sinsadong. The Pangbaedong ballad was the first musical trend that actually originated from within Gangnam. The Pangbaedong Café Street in its heyday was dotted with a number of posh Western-style restaurants, bars, and cafés that catered to well-to-do clientele in Gangnam. As opposed to the Sinsadong area, which formed a circuit, with several blocks of residential and commercial buildings surrounded by major road networks, the Pangbaedong neighborhood was a corridor—a narrow strip of land around one small street. Among the crowd who frequented this sort of cosmopolitan, nouveau riche neighborhood were musician types that also came from higher social backgrounds. Some of the cafés had live stages or open mic sessions, where this gang of would-be singers showed off their talents in the after-party hours to end nights of heavy drinking and club-hopping. In more than one way, the Pangbaedong corridor closely approximates gentrification in its classical sense (see chapter 6). A 1987 news story depicts this area at the peak of its popularity: "More than one hundred cafés line both sides of the narrow alley in the Café Village of Pangbaedong. Twenty-something youth are its main clientele, and the early morning hours are more popular than evenings. Cafés serve coffee during the daytime and drinks at night. The street traffic is jammed with personal vehicles driven by the young patrons . . . They follow cutting-edge fashion trends such as 'punk-style hair,' and there are hot young celebrities among the regulars, creating gossips from time to time."[32]

The musician who best personified this atmosphere was Cho Tŏkpae, the first star balladeer to emerge from the Pangbaedong Café Street scene. Cho is the nephew of a construction business mogul who made much of his fortune by speculating on the Gangnam real estate market. Thanks to his family's wealth, Cho grew up with exposure to a variety of Anglo-American pop and other foreign ballad styles, such as the French chanson and the Brazilian bossa nova. He absorbed these genres and created his own ballad style that sounded gorgeous and exotic to the 1980s Korean pop aesthetic. Cho Tŏkpae may have been the first, but he was hardly the last star to rise from the Pangbaedong ballad scene. The scene hosted a bohemian creative community of sorts, including some of the "beautiful people" of the media entertainment industry. Chi Ye, a prominent female character from this scene, won a beauty pageant contest and had a brief television acting career. While she was a recording artist in her own right, Chi Ye was most famous as the lyricist for Pyŏn Chinsŏp, who went on to become a top balladeer and celebrity during the late 1980s–early 1990s. Ch'oe Hosŏp, who once competed with Pyŏn Chinsŏp over ballad supremacy, is a widely acknowledged authority when it comes to the Pangbaedong Café Street, as he frequented Café Street since high school and played a key role in bringing people to the area, using his deep entertainment industry connections. In a personal interview, Ch'oe conveys the feelings he had about the Pangbaedong scene in its formative years: "Young, fearless, ambitious talents gathered together there. I was always the baby there, the youngest one. But soon I became the center of attention because of my musical talent on stage, without which these places wouldn't make ends meet . . . Pangbaedong Street is not long, so once you get in there, you can easily meet people. There's always a scene like that. Naturally it became a cultural street, and back then [in the early 1980s] the street was more about culture than about drinking and partying."[33]

The Pangbaedong ballad was definitely a product of Gangnam, and unlike trot or dance music from the Sinsadong Circuit, it also reflected the upper-middle-class lifestyle and culture of the resident population in Gangnam. Yet the makers of these polished ballads were still technically outsiders, not those Gangnam "natives" who were either born or grew up in the area. The key migration that established Gangnam on the cultural map was not that of the already wealthy. Rather, it was the emergent middle class who aspired to achieve upward social mobility by moving to Gangnam for the education of their offspring. The government was aware of these motivations and took full advantage. To promote Gangnam development, the government either cajoled or forced elite college prep high schools in the north to migrate to Gangnam. The top two such schools were Kyŏnggi and Seoul High. First, Kyŏnggi moved to the heart of the Gangnam District (at the center of the eastern part of the vertical axis). Then Seoul High matched it by moving to the western center, located in the Sŏch'o District. They were followed by a host of lower-ranked elite schools in the old downtown. Consequently, as shown in figure 1.4, the government managed to establish the Eighth School District along the horizontal axis of Gangnam. High schoolers in Gangnam, with more resources from their well-to-do families and

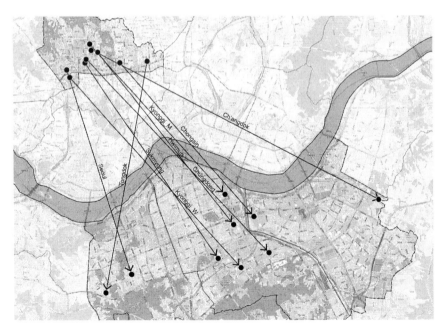

Figure 1.4. The migration of Seoul's elite high schools from Gangbuk to Gangnam.

more exposure to Western and Japanese cultural flows, emerged as the driving force of youthful pop music culture. They explored new, distinct musical genres that proliferated from the mid-1980s into the 1990s, ranging from heavy metal to fusion jazz to hip-hop and dance. This first generation of Gangnam boys led these developments in Korean pop music since the early 1990s, such as the pioneering hip-hop duo DEUX, or the comedic dance duo Clon, which prefigured the arrival of Psy. There is a lengthy roster of pop musicians who came of age in Gangnam during the 1980s.[34] Born in 1977, Psy was one of the younger members of this new Gangnam generation who received their K-12 education in the elite school district. Perhaps not as famous as Psy, but even more important than Mr. "Gangnam Style" himself in the K-pop universe, is Pang Sihyŏk, the head of Big Hit Entertainment (recently renamed to HYBE). Big Hit is known as the professional home of BTS, the K-pop boy band that has become an enduring global pop icon, relegating Psy to a one-hit wonder. A Kyŏnggi High School alum, Pang graduated from Seoul National University and made a successful music industry debut by winning the bronze prize at the prestigious Yu Chaeha Song Contest in 1994. Pang's career has closely mirrored K-pop's global rise since then.

Intersection at Gangnam Station: Cultural Politics into the 1990s

This genealogical venture to 1980s Gangnam concludes at the cross of the vertical and horizontal axes that is the Gangnam subway station, at the heart of Gangnam. Here, adult entertainment meets youth culture. Legendary discotheques, such as Much More, World Pops, Studio 80, Siesta, and Unicorn, drew party-loving youngsters in high schools and colleges. The dance music culture that flourished around Gangnam Station has a pervasive significance that is outside the scope of this study. The veteran club disc jockey Yi Chin, a key witness to Korea's dance club culture history, attests to a "revolution of nightlife" at Much More and other clubs in the Gangnam Station area thanks to the coinciding of the disco boom and the end of the nationwide midnight curfew in the early 1980s.[35] This revolution is clearly linked to the current ascendance of K-pop, and Psy is a personification of this historical link.

The wave of cultural globalization by the new generation from Gangnam, however, would take another decade or so to fully arrive. In the first few months of 1990, the longest-running hit in the pop charts did not come from heart-throbbing dance music or saccharine ballads, as was typical. Rather, this achievement went to a solemn choir that brought protest rally songs to the television screen. It was an unexpected breakthrough of the 1980s' protest song movement led by a collective named Nochatsa (Noch'assa [The Songseekers]). During the first half of the 1990s, the protest folk tradition and its 1980s' incarnation, the People's Song Movement (PSM), inspired music found in mainstream outlets as well as the college underground circuit.[36] While such recognizable names as An Ch'ihwan, Kwŏn Chinwŏn, Kang San'e, and Yun Tohyŏn are connected to this tradition to varying degrees, it was the late Kim Kwangsŏk who became an iconic figure for the 1990s transformation of collective political expression into personal political art (see chapter 4). Besides his original repertoire, Kim reinterpreted many classics of the modern folk and protest songs, introducing them to a new mass audience. Before his unexpected passing at the height of popularity, Kim Kwangsŏk was continuously on the road for over one thousand concerts in small and large venues. His talent was especially celebrated in the intimacy of small theatrical venues. Hakchŏn Theater in Taehangno was the most significant one among them. It was in this theater that Kim Kwangsŏk's mentor, the folk legend Kim Min'gi, launched the fifteen-year run of the musical *Subway Line Number 1* (*Chihach'ŏl irhosŏn*) in 1994. The first actress cast in the main role was Youn Sun Nah (Na Yunsŏn), who later went on to become an internationally acclaimed jazz vocalist.

While Nochatsa, Kim Kwangsŏk, and others were translating protest folk into mainstream genres, another folk musician, Chŏng T'aech'un, worked in the opposite direction. Chŏng had enjoyed significant mainstream success early in his career, but his increasing politicization through the 1980s transitioned him from broadcast appearances to small theater concerts, and then to performances at labor union and student protest rallies. Following the musical *Calf, Calf, Yellow Calf* (*Song'aji song'aji nurŏng song'aji*, 1989), which he wrote and produced in support of the National Teachers' Union (Chŏn'gyojo) struggle, Chŏng released the album *Alas, Republic of Korea* (*A taehanminguk*) in 1990. Full of righteous indignation, he made a scathing, unprecedented critique of Korean politics and society. More significantly, the album was released on cassette tape and distributed through the underground network of college-town neighborhoods and social movement circles because Chŏng refused to submit it to the government censor for approval for commercial sales. This act of defiance was the opening salvo of the long battle he waged against the censorship of popular music. The next album, *In Chongno, the Rainy Spell of '92* (*Kusib'inyŏn changma, chongnoesŏ*, 1993), landed him in the courtroom fending off the charges of illegal distribution and sales. As the Constitutional Court found the censorship unconstitutional in 1996, Chŏng's hard-fought battle finally earned him victory, with major implications for freedom of speech and artistic expression.

Chŏng's righteous stand for justice and democracy may be seen as a carryover effect from the previous decade, but it was much more than that. As mentioned earlier, Chŏng was going against the grain when everyone else in the social activist circle was moving closer to the mainstream. All the while, he remained true to his countryside roots, maintaining skepticism toward urbanites taking advantage of rural folks in the name of celebrating their culture. Two songs best represent Chŏng's music in the 1990s. One is "Insadong" (1990), a merciless satire of this fast-gentrifying tourist district in downtown Seoul since the 1988 Olympics. The other, "Setting the Prairie on Fire" ("Chŏ tŭre purŭl noa," 1993), is a hauntingly beautiful ballad about an old farmer's silent protest against the crushing hardships of rural Korea. Ironically, it was not Chŏng T'aech'un but Seo Taiji (Sŏ T'aeji), the 1990s' golden boy, who took major credit for standing up against censorship. Seo's high-profile defiance was publicized widely when his proto-K-pop group, Seo Taiji and Boys, released "Regret of the Times" ("Sidae yugam," 1995) as an instrumental track after the censors demanded he tone down the "bleakness" of its lyrics. The lyrics were promptly leaked to the public anyway, and the enormous pressure from millions of Taiji Boys fans undoubtedly helped to turn the tide against the censors. However, the abolition of censorship would not have been possible without Chŏng T'aech'un mounting a political and legal challenge to the system. Regardless of style or genre, Korean popular music is greatly indebted to Chŏng's relentless fight for the freedom of expression since 1996 and even earlier.

The censorship controversy also underscored the historical reality that popular expression was political, and that "popular" culture was a politically contested terrain. Korean popular musicians were certainly no strangers to political repression, manipulation, and regulation during the censorship era. With the opening of political space, however, the 1990s witnessed an inversion of sorts. Suddenly, the political was popular. Protest songs were playing on the radio and even on television. "Entertainers" began providing serious, and often foreboding, social commentaries without the fear of being muzzled by the system or losing their fan base. Seo Taiji was not alone in witnessing the world "going crazy" and "going wrong" ("Regret of the Times"). The heavy metal band Sinawe (Sinawi) screamed about "battered children following orders" from those who inflicted pain on them ("Battered Kid" ["Maemannŭn ai"], 1995). The progressive rock band N.EX.T (Neksŭt'ŭ) described the "city life" as "gray buildings, gray skies, and people's gray faces" ("Urbanite" ["Tosiin"], 1992).

Postmodernism, New Generation, Debacles

Korea's political and economic breakdowns of the 1990s were in part compensated by sociocultural breakouts that made this decade all the more compelling. Breaking out of the restrictions on global mobility and communications is probably the most important development of this decade. The global horizon was suddenly wide open to the public hitherto unable to step outside the national borders without going through background checks by the intelligence agency first. The liberalization of overseas travel of 1989 saw a sixfold increase of international travelers by the end of the decade, sending nearly one out of every ten Koreans off to see the outside world. The propagandistic nature of the state-led *segyehwa* (literally, "becoming the world") campaign notwithstanding, globalization became something ordinary Koreans could experience and understand in a very tangible manner. Korean society has been a giant experimental lab for the many revolutionary breakouts of ICT (information and communications technology) since this decade, and the so-called Teheran Valley (T'eheran baeli) in Gangnam has been at the center of the ICT revolution. Whether it is wireless telecommunications (from beepers to cellular phones), computer networks (from the text-based BBS on dial-up networks to the broadband internet on fiber optic cables), or social networking services (from Cyworld to Kakaotalk), Korean youths have been at least a half step faster than the rest of the world in adopting the new technoculture. All these changes point to what the geographer David Harvey called the "condition of postmodernity"—the "time-space compression" in the organization of capitalism that gave rise to postmodernist cultural forms.[37] When postmodernism arrived in Korea as a philosophical-cultural trend, it took much more than the material condition Harvey accounted for. The end of the Cold War shook the core of the modern political ideologies and thoughts held by those on the Left in particular. The triumphalist global capitalism of the late twentieth century pushed them scrambling for answers, of which the umbrella term "postmodernism" offered a hodgepodge.

Moreover, "postmodern" was also widely used to sensationalize and/or advertise various pop culture offerings and tie them to the changing social milieu. At the center of the raging postmodern discourse was Seo Taiji, whose thrilling hybrid musical act sparked the new generation (*sinsedae*) debate of the 1990s.[38] In hindsight, neither postmodernism nor the new generation discourse held much water as the mirage of the 1990s prosperity and its hedonistic slogan, "Do whatever you want,"[39] were instantly dissipated by the economic meltdown of the IMF Crisis. Nonetheless, Seo Taiji's brilliance was postmodern in the sense that he took full advantage of the condition of postmodernity—time-space compression—before anyone else did so as successfully. During the five-year stint of Seo Taiji and Boys, Seo was digesting as well as introducing the latest trends of Anglo-American popular music on an almost real-time basis. In some cases, to preempt charges of being a copycat, Seo even openly talked about what style of music he had borrowed from which musician. For example,

Seo kindly explained that his "Come Back Home" (1995) was "gangsta rap" inspired by the American rap group Cypress Hill. This "educating the public" approach was not to last very long. The globalization of the popular music market soon made it easy for ordinary music fans to access English-language music magazines and imported CDs. And, of course, the widespread use of the internet empowered them even further in catching up with latest global trends. Since Seo came out of retirement as a solo artist in 2000, he has been unable to achieve a similar level of success to the Taiji Boys years, partly because the new styles he has brought in, such as industrial, nu metal, and emocore, are not so strikingly new to many serious music fans anymore.

Another emblematic figure in the new generation pop music was the group 015B (Kong'irobi), whose sleek, danceable pop made a perfect soundtrack for the so-called orange tribe (*orenjijok*)—rich, spoiled young males driving their expensive imported cars around the affluent neighborhoods of Gangnam to pick up girls.[40] However, 015B also made a sober point in their song "The Fourth Branch" ("Chesabu," 1993) that the orange tribe was "an illusion that newspapers, adults, and society at large have fabricated" to stir up moral panic. Thus, the new generation was self-conscious about the criticism of excessive consumerism and hedonistic behavior, and in turn pointed out the hypocrisy of the grown-ups engaging in essentially the same activities, only with less style. In light of the debacle visited upon Gangnam shortly thereafter, their askance look at the older generation's dreams and achievements was proven justified. Whereas the old, middle-class dreams of Gangnam hinged upon the progress of industrial capitalism, the new dream had to be reinvented in the postindustrial society on a global scale. Once again, Gangnam emerged as the land of dreams thanks to the heavily concentrated economic and cultural capital accumulation in the area over a quarter century.

In the meantime, the dark forces of Gangnam development spilled over into the 1990s and beyond. First, the construction boom that made Gangnam so very visible ended up in the spectacular crashes of 1994–1995 with the collapses of the Sŏngsu Bridge and Sampoong Department Store. These gruesome scenes of carnage were replayed in Yun T'aeho's comic book series *Yahoo* (*Yahu*, 1998–2003) and Park Chan Wook (Pak Ch'an'uk)'s global hit film *OldBoy* (*Oldŭboi*, 2003). Both are tales of ultraviolent revenge by antihero characters who were afflicted by these spectacular bridge and building collapses in Gangnam, among other things. The incredibly grim picture they paint is in stark contrast to the rebounding fortunes of South Korean society at the time: democratization, quick economic recovery from the IMF Crisis, a thawing relationship with North Korea, and the soaring popularity of Korean pop culture in Asia. While the skyrocketing Gangnam real estate market spread hopes once again, these dark forebodings somehow resonated with the uncertainties and doubts people felt about the dreams of a brighter future they had believed in. The image of Gangnam as a disaster zone is seared in the memory of those who came of age during the 1990s. Their literary and cinematic recollections indicate an inflection point where dreams turn into nightmares. Despite its fabulous wealth, Gangnam was not a zone safe from disasters, especially man-made ones. After a torrential rainfall in July 2011, there was a huge landslide from the southern foothills of Gangnam, which destroyed many apartment buildings in the Pangbaedong area, killing eighteen people, including the wife of a large department chain's CEO. It also flooded Gangnam Station, paralyzing traffic and business activities for days. In fact, Gangnam Station has always been prone to flooding due to its low-lying location. When Samsung moved its corporate headquarters from Gangbuk to the Gangnam Station area, the Sŏch'o District Office made a controversial decision to allow Samsung to build a direct underground passageway from its headquarters to the subway station, despite objections that it would exacerbate the flooding issue and accusations of granting undue privilege to the corporate giant.

The shoddiness of Gangnam construction might have been rectified after these epic disasters, but the sleaze of Gangnam entertainment has continued unabated since the beginning. Sinsadong today may not be what it used to be, as in Chu Hyŏnmi's song, but now adult entertainment has transposed itself from the vertical axis to the horizontal axis, dotting so many red lights around the glitzy skyscrapers of Teheran Road (see plate 4). Psy's hypersexual "Gangnam Style" carnival may not look so outlandish, given this reality. It is all the more interesting, therefore, that the latest protest against rampant sexism and violence against women launched its campaign in Gangnam, and more specifically in the Gangnam Station area. It was sparked by the harrowing murder of a young woman nearby the station. The killer's misogynistic motive shocked the entire Korean society, and soon the walls of Gangnam Station Exit Number 10 were covered with thousands of anonymous sticky notes commemorating her tragic death as well as criticizing misogyny, violence, and discrimination against women (see chapter 5). This was perhaps one of the most remarkable symbolic transformations a space has gone through in Korean society. The hedonistic carnival of Gangnam has reached a certain limit, and a time for solemn reflection has arrived.

CHAPTER 2

Paradise across the River
Gangnam in Literature

Kwak Chaegu's poem "Songji: Marketplace" is regarded as an exemplary piece of militant protest literature of the 1980s—*minjung* (common people) literature—that denounced both American cultural imperialism and Korean industrial capitalism.[1] But the poem is not overly subversive or caustic in its tone; rather, it is pensive and even melancholic at times:

> One bottle of Coca-Cola
> delivered to a room in Building Number Seven
> of Hyundai Apartments, Apkujŏngdong.
> One bottle of Coca-Cola
> carelessly rolling around on the forehead of the stone Buddha
> at the venerated Kyŏngju Museum.
> One bottle of Coca-Cola
> carefully stored inside a limousine,
> awaiting the lady emerging from a luxury gym.
> One bottle of Coca-Cola
> wrapped neatly together with chocolates in a gift box
> for soldiers on the frontline.
> One bottle of Coca-Cola
> at the Tong'il Textile factory, Kuro Industrial Complex,
> keeping factory girls awake on the night shift.
> One bottle of Coca-Cola
> luring vendors at Songji Marketplace, Haenam County:
> "Wow, fizzy and sweet—it's really something!"
> At the close of market,
> two pounds of rice's worth of Coca-Cola dances in their bellies.[2]

When the poem was quickly adapted into a protest song entitled "Coca-Cola," however, the sardonic commentary on class divide and American cultural imperialism came to the fore with punchy lyrics and mocking sound.[3] By this time, "Hyundai Apartments, Apkujŏngdong" became the symbolic residence

45

of Korea's new, morally questionable moneyed class, where the consumption of Coca-Cola meant the fondness for all things American.[4] But a bottle of Coca-Cola traveled everywhere, enticing anyone from a solder guarding the DMZ to the female textile worker in Kuro to the country bumpkins of the southernmost county of Haenam.

A Coca-Cola Bottle at the Border Crossing: The Beginnings of Gangnam Literature

Kwak's poem, along with Cho Sehŭi's *Time Travel,* published two years prior, can be considered early works of Gangnam literature. Gangnam development finally rounded into shape with the completion of Subway Line Number 2, establishing the horizontal axis of Gangnam in 1984. It had taken roughly fifteen years since the opening of the Seoul-Busan Expressway, the vertical axis. To be sure, Gangnam—then more frequently referred to as Yŏngdong or South Seoul (Namsŏul)—made its appearances in 1970s' literature as an object of poignant social critique. Not surprisingly, it was Ch'oe Inho (1945–2013), arguably the most astute observer of Korea's rising urbanity and hyperurbanity throughout his illustrious career, who first produced a critical story about Gangnam development. Ch'oe's oeuvre is bookended by two major pieces—"A Stranger's Room" ("T'ainŭi pang," 1971) and *Another Man's City* (*Natsŏn t'aindŭrŭi tosi,* 2011)—written thirty years apart yet resonating with each other in terms of their critical approach toward the hyperreal urban life of contemporary Korea.[5] Along with "A Stranger's Room," he published a remarkably prescient short story titled "Savage" ("Migaein"), one year before the Gangnam Boulevard construction was even finished. In "Savage," Ch'oe describes the early landscape of S-dong, a thinly veiled reference to Sinsadong, thusly:

> In a word, it was a raucous place. The land was always sloshy with mud; people walked the streets wearing long rubber boots as if they were fishmongers. On one side, bulldozers rumbled around flattening the ledge of a slope for a future apartment complex site, while a stench of composted manure came from the other side as the vestige of countryside. On both sides of the street were buildings like makeshift barracks, some of which had teahouses with creaky chairs and kerosene-selling stalls. In between them were unusually prim gas stations, along with some motels and massage parlors.[6]

"Savage" is based on a news story from 1969 about a group of parents at the local elementary school who kept their children at home to protest the school's decision to accept students from a nearby community of people with Hansen's disease, disparagingly referred to as a "leper colony" (*mundung'i ch'on*).[7] "Civilized people cannot mingle with lepers" was the slogan the parents used, which the protagonist, a newly appointed teacher, finds ironic because of the savage violence the parents unleashed upon the stigmatized and shunned minority. This area back then was a far cry from today's or even 1980s' Gangnam, yet the dynamics of social exclusion have endured. Sensing the strange air of madness surrounding the town, the teacher attributes their reactions less to the traditional fear and loathing of leprosy but more to the land development frenzy that gripped the minds of the S-dong residents. Watching bulldozers flattening unclaimed tombs in order to build a new housing complex, he concludes that the madness comes from "the living who raise themselves up by knocking down and stomping on the dead"—the mindset of land speculators in a modern capitalist society.[8]

Pak Wansŏ (1930–2011) was another prominent writer who focused on modern urban life and apartment living in particular. Both Ch'oe Inho's "A Stranger's Room" and Pak Wansŏ's "Identical Apartments" ("Talmŭn pangdŭl," 1973) focus on human alienation in the apartment space from their respective gender perspectives. Ch'oe's protagonist is a husband who returns to his apartment only to find out about his wife's absence under false pretenses; Pak's is a housewife who grows tired of mimicking her neighbor's lifestyle in the identical apartment next door.[9] When it comes to Gangnam specifically, Pak's short story "Kids in Paradise" ("Nakt'o ŭi aidŭl," 1978) reads like a sequel to Ch'oe's "Savage." In seven years, the manure-smelling backwater became a shiny new urban district that was "strictly yet conveniently divided into an apartment complex area, a high-end housing area, a commercial area, and a school and public administration area." Surrounded by barren hillsides "except to the north, where it faces the old downtown across the putrid river," this fictional Gangnam was named "Murŭng" by Pak in an allusion to the classical Chinese utopia of Wuling (武陵) in Tao Yuanming's *Peach Blossom Spring* (427 CE).[10] It is "indeed an earthly paradise [*nakt'o*]. The soil here does not breed worthless stuff like rice straws or potato bulbs; it breeds straight-up gold. The gold is not earned by the tiller [*p'anŭn saram*] of the land but by the seller [*p'anŭn saram*] of the land."[11] As literary historian Song Ŭn'yŏng observes, the story's cynical tone is directly articulated through the narrator, an adjunct university professor who relies on his wife's large income from real estate speculation. Representing a kind of paradigmatic critical intellectual of the period, he mockingly acknowledges the "meritorious service" of realtors and speculators to Gangnam development.[12]

Ch'oe and Pak are two definitive predecessors of Gangnam literature from the ensuing decades. A notable feature of both writers' works is their use of made-up names for actual locations and places. One possible reason is that Gangnam, Apkujŏngdong, Sinsadong, and other places were not yet recognizable household names at the time. For example, the official district name of Gangnam was established about four years after Ch'oe's story. As Chŏn Minjo's emblematic photograph illustrates, the famous Hyundai Apartment Complex in Apkujŏngdong still looked like an island in a sea of farmland by the time Pak's story was published (figure 2.1). Apkujŏng Primary School, the presumed model for Pak's fictional Murŭng Primary, had opened only a year prior. Thus, Pak's classical reference to paradise was probably more effective than the unfamiliar real name in conjuring up the image of real estate El Dorado. The masking of real places in Ch'oe's and Pak's work hardly diminishes their importance, while it serves as a clear demarcation between the precursors from the 1970s and the main body of Gangnam literature from the 1980s onward.

Compared with these predecessors, Cho Sehŭi emerges as a transitional figure in Gangnam literature who combines real names and fictionalized

Figure 2.1. Chŏn Minjo, "Apkujŏngdong" (1978). Reprinted with permission.

variants in his writing. He masks or unmasks the actual places as he sees fit. His magnum opus, *The Dwarf* (*Nanjang'iga ssoaolin chagŭn kong*, 1978),[13] for example, incorporates specific place details in describing the origins of one of the novel's major villains, a real estate speculator: "His office, like his apartment, was in Yŏngdong . . . His advertisements appeared in the paper every day: 'Everyone's interested in Chamsil. Call now for free consultation on Chamsil apartments. Ŭna, a real estate agent you can depend on—Ŭna Realty.' Advertisements for residential complexes also appeared: 'New Ch'ŏnho Bridge, Chamsil area, fast-growing location along First Gangnam Way. Bargain-priced units for your dream home. Don't miss this opportunity—Ŭna Home Realty.'"[14]

On the other hand, Cho relies on made-up names to mask those places that are associated with the dwarf, his family, and their friends and allies: "Felicity Precinct" (Haengboktong) in "Eden District" (Nagwŏn'gu) is the slum the dwarf family resided in as squatters; the dwarf's children grow up to become workers in the industrial city of Ŭn'gang, a fictional composite of Inch'ŏn and Ulsan. This masking strategy continues in the sequel, *Time Travel*, as Cho studiously avoids naming any real place except for two essays on Chamsil. Then, in the eponymous main story of the book, a middle-class housewife, Sin'ae, who once saved the dwarf's life in the very first installment of the dwarf saga ("Knifeblade"), is moving from her old house to a large, brand-new apartment, "built by a well-known construction company along the bank of the Han River" in the spring of 1979.[15] A reader who picked up the book in 1983 or later would have easily guessed that Sin'ae's new residence must be located in Apkujŏngdong, and likely a Hyundai Apartment as in Kwak Chaegu's "Songji: Marketplace." The elitist image of the Apkujŏngdong Hyundai Apartment Complex was set from the beginning by a massive corruption scandal involving the upper echelons of the political and business world.[16] If Cho has no qualms about explicitly tying Chamsil to a disreputable speculator, why does he refrain from naming Apkujŏngdong when it is all but obvious? Is this masking perhaps a sign that Sin'ae still remains an ally of the dwarf and what he stands for—the oppressed, exploited Korean working class—despite her family's soaring socioeconomic status? That Sin'ae's family has not yet gone over to the side of speculators and oppressors? After all, the most remarkable line in Sin'ae's narrative appears in a dialogue with her husband, declaring the move to Gangnam is "not just a simple move":

[Husband:] "What is it then?"
[Sin'ae:] "I feel as though I were crossing a national border."

When the eminent literary critic Kim Pyŏng'ik characterizes Sin'ae's border-crossing remark as "a decisive break [*kyŏlbyŏl*] from the painful past," he seems to take the author's explanation at face value, that Sin'ae breaks away from "the old life; she left behind her mother's, grandmother's, mother of mother of grandmother's, all those old lives" in Korea's tormented early modern history of colonialism, national division, and war.[17] If so, Sin'ae would have failed at such a border crossing since she actually had to relive those painful old lives herself through time travel to the past in the final installment of the saga ("Time Travel").

However complex Sin'ae's—and, by extension, the author's—feelings might be, the border she crosses while moving to Gangnam is primarily a class border. Literary scholar Youngju Ryu accurately observes that the dwarf saga unfolds "as so many variations on the central theme of class antagonism," and "the text persistently explores class issues in terms of neighbor relations." In this context, Sin'ae's relationship with the dwarf family is portrayed as an "attempt at neighbor love [that] ultimately ends in failure."[18] If we reverse engineer Ryu's notion of "neighbor love" in terms of social class, the story would turn into an allegory of class alliance. In fact, allegory is key to understanding the political explosiveness of the dwarf saga—how it translated the abstract concepts of class and class alliance into affective relations. Building on Walter Benjamin's theory of allegory, Gilles Deleuze expounds on how "allegory uncovers nature and history according to the order of time":

> It produces a history from nature and transforms history into nature in a world that no longer has its center. If we consider the logical relation of a concept to its object, we discover that the linkage can be surpassed in a symbolic and an allegorical way . . . the object itself is broadened according to a whole network of natural relations. The object itself overflows its frame in order to enter into a cycle or a series, and now the concept is what is found increasingly compressed, interiorized, wrapped in an instance that can ultimately be called "personal."[19]

The dwarf's stunted "nature" and his family history from premodern chattel slavery (*nobi*) to modern wage labor are intertwined in Cho Sehŭi's stories, which broaden the narrative cycle to the dwarf family's neighbors, to their co-workers and allies, and even to some members of the capitalist elite. The concept of class becomes deeply personal, as in the flashback where the dwarf's little daughter asked her older brother to "kill those devils who call Father a dwarf." And it is Sin'ae, the loving neighbor, who has to relay the heartbreaking news of the dwarf's passing to his now-grown daughter.[20] The dwarf saga begins and ends with these two neighboring families, the dwarf's and Sin'ae's, closing an allegorical cycle that can be reconstructed in the following manner: there are two knives in the old kitchen cupboard Sin'ae wants to throw away on moving day. One is an old "large knife," like a cleaver, handed down from ancestors, and the other a sharp, menacing sashimi fillet knife. It is these knives that Sin'ae brandished frantically to ward off the thug who would otherwise have beaten the dwarf to death in her own yard ("Knifeblade"). Thus, the knives symbolize her solidarity with the dwarf in the struggle against hardships and violence in their decrepit neighborhood, ironically named Eden District. Only a few years later, however, their fortunes diverge sharply. The dwarf's family is evicted from their squat house and falls apart ("A Little Ball Launched by a Dwarf"), whereas Sin'ae's takes a bright turn toward abundance and prosperity, culminating in their departure to Gangnam ("Time Travel"). Sin'ae and her husband, both from the generation that spearheaded the April Revolution of 1960, are deeply conscientious about the political situation, yet not about to extricate themselves from this polarizing class dynamics created by the so-called economic miracle of the 1970–1980s.

As early as 1983, therefore, Cho Sehŭi was foreshadowing a breakup of the democratic alliance between the white-collar middle class and the blue-collar working class that would become painfully clear in four years. Not unlike the April Revolution of 1960, when the student "vanguard" joined forces with the disaffected urban underclass to overthrow the corrupt autocracy of Syngman Rhee—only to part ways shortly thereafter[21]—the democratic alliance of the 1980s soon dissipated, after forcing the military dictatorship into key political concessions in June 1987. Historian Bruce Cumings offers a tart observation: "South Korea's middle class has been growing rapidly with industrialization and urbanization, but it remains difficult to specify its political tendency. Elements in it gave critical support to youthful dissidents in the June 1987 mobilization, but also faded from the streets once the elections terminated . . . The absence of effective political representation in the Park and Chun regimes was a basic issue for many middle-class citizens, and once they got it, they did not rush back into the streets to help the working class achieve the same thing."[22] The June Democratic Uprising (Yuwŏl minjuhwa hangjaeng) of 1987 was immediately followed by the Great Workers' Struggle (Nodongja taet'ujaeng) in July and August. The striking workers did not find much support from the middle class except for the student vanguard, who had opened their eyes to the plight of *minjung* since 1970.[23] Adding insult to injury, a split within the opposition political establishments cost them the presidential election and gave away the victory to the military regime's successor. While the dispiriting denouement of 1987 did not deter the outbursts of political energy from the downtrodden masses of *minjung*, it also nudged the middle class further toward political conservatism, deepening the class divide in the coming years.

The political awakening of *minjung* through the 1970s–1980s demonstrated that the border did not exist only between the new urban classes. The deeply entrenched poverty and the maddening drive toward industrialization put all kinds of pressure on the traditional rural community, prompting a great migratory outflow across the rural-urban border and thus reinforcing the urban class divide in turn. Kwak Chaegu's "Songji: Marketplace," the poem cited at the beginning of this chapter, provides a panoramic view of this social class landscape ranging from high life in Apkujŏngdong to hard labor in Kuro to bittersweet trade in Haenam. Projecting this urban-rural phantasmagoria of twentieth-century Korea, the poet places a Coca-Cola bottle as a final touch to each scene. Coca-Cola was often castigated as a symbol of American neocolonial rule over South Korea by *minjung* left activists, as illustrated in the artist O Yun's visceral paintings (see plate 2);[24] Kwak's poetic treatment of Coca-Cola sounds almost tame by comparison. However, the poem distinguishes itself from 1980s' garden-variety anti-Americanism in two interrelated respects. First, Coca-Cola is not simply presented as an isolated symbol of American imperialism or consumer capitalism; it becomes an allegorical object entering into intimate personal relations with a series of neocolonial subjects across the class divide: Gangnam parvenues, female textile workers, frontline soldiers, and poor farmers. In this Benjaminian/Deleuzian allegory, Coca-Cola emerges as a unifying emblem of neocolonial South Korea: regardless of their social status, everyone is beholden to American cultural hegemony. Second, as Susan Buck-Morss points out, Marx "had used the term 'phantasmagoria' to refer to the deceptive appearances of commodities as 'fetishes' in the marketplace," and Benjamin extended it to modern urban spectacles.[25] Taking Marx's and Benjamin's visions together, the poem illuminates how the fetishized Coca-Cola bottle traverses from the urban spectacle in Gangnam to the rural marketplace in Haenam. "Capitalism concentrated in a bottle," as China's *Rénmín Rìbào* (*People's Daily*) once memorably put it, Coca-Cola is a reified American Dream that has gone global in the truest sense of the word.[26]

Torn between the Dwarf's Dream and Kirin's Mom's Dream: The Middle Strata in Gangnam Literature

The dwarf never gets to be the narrator of his own story. Scattered around Cho Sehŭi's books in fragments, it is always told in someone else's voice or described from other people' perspectives. His last days on earth can be pieced together thusly: "In the name of urban renewal, the city takes away the only space where the dwarf had been just a father and not a dwarf, offering him as compensation the right to purchase a unit in a new apartment complex that he cannot afford. So the dwarf dreams. Standing on the roof of the factory where his sons were exploited for their labor, he dreams of other worlds, a utopia to be found perhaps on the moon. He launches paper airplanes, then a little ball, and finally his small body."[27]

The dwarf's pipe dream emerges as a sheer expression of despair and a forceful denunciation of social polarization at the same time. The early period of Gangnam literature was dominated by such critical voices as we have heard so far; they tended to see in Gangnam little more than a "cannery of desire engineered by the regime" or a "graveyard of all kinds of pleasure," to borrow from Yu Ha's characteristic hyperbole.[28] There was, however, another compelling dream on the part of the would-be border crossers, a dream much closer at hand than the dwarf's colony on the moon. While no heavyweight comparable to Pak Wansŏ or Cho Sehŭi openly championed it, some traces of their dream can be found in the nooks and crannies of 1980s literature. To wit:

> Again today on the riverbanks of Yeoui Island [Yŏŭido], wings were sold as if they'd grown balloons, and in the night sky above Golden Bells Apartments on Dogok Street [Togoktong], dear moon sits dear stars around and treats them each to a glass of beer, and yellow tulips giggle on the retinas of Kirin who falls asleep nibbling a Bon-Bon cracker and in the dream of Kirin's mom a Pinto[29] runs on with no gas and now from the armpits of Kirin's tired dad centimeter-long wings grow secretly.[30]

The above stanza from Ch'oe Sŭngja's poem "Merry Diary" ("Chŭlgŏun ilgi") draws an idealistic vignette of middle-class family life in Gangnam. Rather than the gilded riverside quarter of Apkujŏngdong, the up-and-coming inland neighborhood of Togoktong is presented, where apartment complexes were named after such unassuming wildflowers as golden bells (*kaenari*) and azaleas (*chindallae*). The family car in Kirin's mom's dream is a modest yet unmistakable status symbol, just like the apartment.[31] These attributes give symbolic wings to the family's aspirations, wearily shouldered by Kirin's dad.

The lure of this middle-class dream was a major product of the economic "miracle." For the residents of Gangnam, the Park Chung Hee regime's slogans throughout the 1970s, "the era of the family car in every household" (*maik'a sidae*) and "the ambitious '80s" (*taemang'ŭi p'alsimnyŏndae*) seemed achievable. Precisely because of such a dreamy buildup, the rude awakening delivered in the next, final stanza is truly devastating:

> Uncle Su-young, Uncle Star, thank you thank you again. Owing to your immense love, we, your nephew, dreamed big again today and had a grand spree under this everlasting blue sky of Korea.
> Assa-rabia, doro-amitabul! [Yay! Back to square one!][32]

While the last line's colloquialism renders it difficult to comprehend, let alone translate, Ch'oe Sŭngja's well-known penchant for dramatic reversals leads me to interpret it as Kirin's family waking up to the reality that looks nothing like the dream they have had. Even that sharp emotional turn, however, does not negate the dream's potency she captured so vividly; on the contrary, Ch'oe is able to accentuate despair, one of her signature poetic affects, precisely because of the dream's liveliness. The "middle (propertied) strata" (*chungsanch'ŭng*) was the name given to aspiring families like Kirin's by the mass media and mainstream academia. In the repressive public discourse of Cold War South Korea, class (*kyegŭp*) was a controversial and potentially dangerous term that few used outside of their close circles—for example, with radical activists, sociologists, or academics in related fields. Even the politically neutral term "middle class" was used very cautiously, although in substance it was little different than the middle strata.[33] Many political commentators and academics noted that the middle strata, in Gangnam and elsewhere, were increasingly leaning against military dictatorship and toward civilian democracy, which was corroborated by their consistent support for the liberal opposition parties in the 1980s.[34] On the other hand, the middle strata were considered risk averse, and expected to make a conservative turn in the face of a systemic crisis that could potentially hurt their socioeconomic prospects. They were supposed to provide a middle ground, a buffer, which would slow down class polarization and hold the capitalist system together. To borrow from a neo-Marxist class theory, the middle strata were to be affected by their "contradictory class locations."[35]

The poet Ch'oe Sŭngja occupied a unique position in the Korean literary establishment, which was divided along ideological as well as stylistic lines by the time of her debut in 1979. With no particular allegiance to either left-leaning committed literature (*ch'amyŏ munhak*) or conservative pure literature (*sunsu munhak*), Ch'oe offered a keen perspective on the collective psyche of the rising urban middle strata.[36] Unlike dissident, antiestablishment contemporaries, she did not try to rationalize her critique of the middle strata. Free of any ideological burden, Ch'oe unloads a barrage of condemnation upon them in a fiery, and often grotesque, poetic language. The brief reference to Gangnam in "Merry Diary" shown above is but a prelude to the fire and brimstone she brings to Yŏŭido, which was initially developed to become a "Manhattan of Seoul" before being overshadowed by Gangnam development.[37] In "Yeoui Island Rhapsody" ("Yŏŭido kwangsigok," 1984), she thunders:

> —Awake!
> The flood is advancing
> that will engulf your dreams.

There is no land for you to return,
no land to inherit.
. . .
In the deepest spot of Yeoui Island's empty air
one giant black mouth in God's image
crunches and munches the leftover bones of this world.[38]

One of Ch'oe Sŭngja's left-leaning contemporaries was Hwang Chiu. His early poems constitute another interesting case study for the literary treatment of the middle strata by one of their own: "Major figures in his poetry are white-collar employees—office workers, journalists, professors, teachers, public servants, etc. His poems reanimate the daily lives of the new middle strata."[39] A former radical activist who was tortured and imprisoned by the Park regime, Hwang is sympathetic to the working-class despair and eager to stand in solidarity with them. At the same time, he finds trappings of middle-class conformity and discriminatory behavior toward the working poor all around him and even in himself. Compared to Ch'oe visceral denunciation of the middle strata, Hwang's approach is reflective and self-conscious.

Hwang's poetry takes only a very small dose of Gangnam, and it rarely extends beyond Old Panp'o, the very first large-scale apartment complex of Gangnam development.[40] The five-story apartment complex built by the state-owned Korea Housing Corporation (Chugong) in 1973 holds a special significance for the poet and his fellow writers, who had frequent gatherings at a fried chicken restaurant in the neighborhood, drinking, singing, and discussing literature and politics together. Among them was the late Kim Hyŏn (1942–1990), a celebrated literary critic and leader of the Munhakkwa chisŏng (Literature and Intellect) coterie, of which Hwang is a member. In a poem published a year after Kim's untimely death, Hwang fondly recalls the deceased mentor softly singing a love song at their Old Panp'o hangout ("Depressing Mirror 1"). The poet's Old Panp'o has been a place for reminiscence, where he has been contemplating his middle-strata existence since the early years. For example, the poem entitled "A Seagull Flying over the Han River Bridge Number One" ("Cheil han'ganggyo'e naradŭn kalmaegi," 1983) contains the following lines:

In this time of patience, obedience, tolerance, indifference, resignation,
    and resilience
in this time of arrearage
war refugees headed south in the year 1950
marine troops headed north in the year 1961

they'd all moved up and down the Han River Bridge No. 1, where I saw
   a seagull cruise over the steel arches toward Tongbuich'ondong and
   Panp'o Apartments,
the bird wasn't anticipating its own demise with the wind direction;
in its struggle for survival it had ended up here, so I thought even
   though
it was flying the wrong way
it had flown to the wrong place
it was flying the wrong way
it had flown to the wrong place.
Ah, in such a frozen moment, the Han River may look like a sea, from
   the bridge toward Panp'o Apartments,
upon closer inspection, it is a fake sea.[41]

Stuck in a crowded bus crossing the Han River during rush hour, the poet watches a seagull flying south over the bridge toward Panp'o Apartments. As the long file of vehicles crawls in the opposite direction, he experiences a series of flashbacks, not unlike Cho Sehŭi's middle-strata heroine Sin'ae does in "Time Travel." These flashbacks bring him harrowing collective memories of the Korean War and Park Chung Hee's military coup of 1961. Born in 1952, when the war was already at a stalemate, Hwang cannot personally claim the war refugee memories—unlike Sin'ae, who is supposedly about ten years older. Still, it does not stop the poet from recalling such traumatic history when he ponders his own sociopolitical existence in a claustrophobic space, again in parallel with Sin'ae's situation. The real-life poet Hwang and the fictional housewife Sin'ae have two things in common as conscientious members of the middle strata. First, their fondness for Gangnam has to be tempered with historical memories. Second, they both see a yawning gap between Gangnam and the rest of the city, and by extension the country: for Sin'ae, it is a "national border"; for the poet, it is a "sea," no matter if it is real or fake.

American Murŭng: Gangnam Literature at the Outset of Global-Polarization

After a four-year hiatus, Hwang Chiu revisited his familiar Old Panp'o with a semi-epic poem, "A Camel Walking by the Old Panp'o Arcade" ("Kubanp'o sanggarŭl kŏrŏganŭn nakt'a," 1987), which reads like a long, grisly coda to Gangnam literature of the 1980s. It follows a thirty-one-year-old woman's fatal walk from an Old Panp'o bus stop to the riverbank. She asks, "Is disillusionment the only way out of a magic spell?"—a pointed question quite possibly directed at Gangnam's middle-strata residents like the poet himself. Hwang's disgust at his own neighborhood is palpable throughout the text, as he goes on trashing the aforementioned fried chicken joint as "an abattoir scraping out human guts." At first, the anonymous woman seems to be waiting for a bus to the Express Bus Terminal, just a few stops away in New Panp'o (Sinbanp'o), which is closer to the heart of Gangnam. From there, her final destination would be the United States, but the departure date is still two months away. She hears an inner voice questioning her:

> *Where are you going?* America! Ameeeeeeerica!
> *Is that your terminal?* No, doesn't a terminal mean a place for departure?

She looks up the bus schedule posted at the stop and finds one of the lines going to Murŭngdong—here Hwang may or may not be making an intentional reference to Pak Wansŏ's fictional Gangnam neighborhood Murŭng, itself an ironic allusion to the classical Chinese utopia.

After a moment of thought, the woman gives up the plan to go to the New Panp'o Terminal, walking back where she came from. On the way, she hears footsteps following her steadily. Turning around, she finds a glowing golden camel, a phantasm, standing there. She says:

> Amazing, how can you be in space without occupying space?
> Look at that apartment building. Out of thin air people create a space, make it a private property, and put the sacrosanct price on it. You're just passing through it without hurting anyone or breaking anything.

With the camel by her side, she reaches the riverfront next to the Old Panp'o apartments, feeling exhausted. She takes one final look at the buildings:

> Fighting vertigo, she caught the sight of the soaring chimney of the heating plant in the Old Panp'o Apartment Complex Number Two. A sore throat connected to heaven, a sewer pipe for keeping warmth. Penis envy of the residents who want a good night's sleep, she thought.

And she enters the dark river, "the river that allows for only one crossing in a lifetime," hoping to cross it on the imaginary camel's back.[42] Border crossing, a recurring theme in Gangnam literature of the 1980s, has taken an even more drastic turn than ever before.

Korea's middle strata, and even those who crossed the river and landed in Gangnam, were not entirely immune to disillusionment and desperation, since the magic spell did not always work for all of them. One could say that theirs was nothing compared to the dwarf's despair, yet middle-class disaffection was very real. A significant number of people wanted out. Following the U.S. Immigration and Naturalization Act of 1965, applications dramatically increased among the well-educated, professional middle strata of Korean society to immigrate to the real promised land, the United States, crossing the real national border over the real sea of the Pacific Ocean. Gangnam development apparently did not slow down this trend. Since 1972, more than thirty thousand Koreans immigrated to the U.S. annually, more than 80 percent of them well educated and with a professional background (see figure 2.2). When U.S. immigration reached its peak of nearly 36,000 in 1987, about half of them were still from the solid middle strata.[43] This probably should be considered the early onset of globalization in Korea, although the world was still divided along ideological lines, and Koreans were severely restricted from traveling outside the country and around the globe. For the majority of Koreans at the time, "outside" was America.[44]

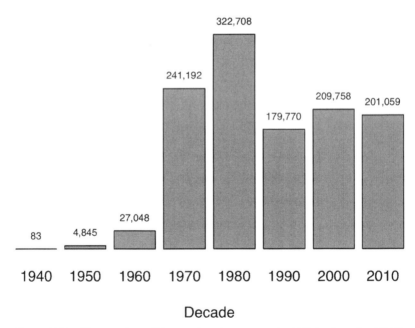

Figure 2.2. The number of Korean immigrants to the U.S. by decade, 1940–2019. Data source: U.S. Department of Homeland Security Immigration Data and Statistics (https://www.dhs.gov/immigration-statistics).

No wonder then that Gangnam strenuously chased symbols of Americanism in the quest to present itself as a Murŭng. This sort of postcolonial "mimicry" was sometimes not even close to the real thing, especially in 1980s' Gangnam.[45] Walking down the street of Old Panp'o, for example, Hwang Chiu's anonymous woman "sees the 'McDonald Donuts' restaurant with an acrylic signboard promoting 'Pure American Style' written in Korean." Authentic or not, the appetite for American pop cultural artefacts continued unabated through the next decade, and nowhere was it more voracious than in Apkujŏngdong. Its famous Rodeo Street was named after Rodeo Drive in Beverly Hills, California. With much fanfare, Korea's first McDonald's chain restaurant opened there in 1988 (figure 2.3).

Yu Ha's Apkujŏngdong poem series uses a host of kitsch references to American pop culture of the 1970s–1980s: *Penthouse* magazine, Sylvester Stallone, Richard Gere, the TV show *MacGyver*, the film *Dead Poets Society* (dir. Peter Weir, 1989), Wendy's restaurant, Clint Eastwood, the sprinter Carl Lewis, and the Steven Spielberg movie *Jaws* (1975). Like Hwang before him, Yu criticizes the trend of kitsch Americanism in Gangnam. In this respect, Yu's homage

Figure 2.3. The grand opening of Korea's first McDonald's in Apkujŏngdong. Source: *Han'guk ilbo*, March 29, 1988, reprinted with permission.

to Hwang Chiu in the Apkujŏngdong series is a sincere one, for all the tongue-in-cheek parody it makes out of Hwang's deadly serious protest poem "From Winter-Tree to Spring-Tree" ("Kyŏul-namurobut'ŏ pom-namuero," 1984). For Yu, it was his way to protest American Murŭng rising on top of all the pear trees cut down and buried under the asphalt of Apkujŏngdong:

> A café named From Winter-Tree to Spring-Tree has opened in Apkujŏngdong
> It's made of wood all around, with a flawless wooden interior.[46]
>
> Café From Winter-Tree to Spring-Tree has a frequent guest, this chick who looks like Sim Hyejin; she asks me, *who is Hwang Chiu?* A great poet, I answer. *Greater than Sŏ Chŏng'yun?* I gag in response.
> *What does it mean, "With its whole body a tree becomes a tree"?*
> Ah, Hwang Chiu's poem in this place, a society of dead poets. No, it's not a poem but
> a propaganda flyer, a requiem for mass-murdered pear trees, in this sexualized street playing sexed-up Christmas carols. I hear
> at freezing temperatures, beneath the brick-layered sidewalk, the roots of countless pear trees moaning wooo-ooo-oooh.[47]

Yu Ha's pointed critique of Apkujŏngdong created such a sensation that it catapulted him to instant stardom. It was also a richly ironic turn of events that one of the fiercest critics became a huge beneficiary and an unwitting promoter of American Murŭng in the go-go 1990s. Although his directorial debut with the film based on the Apkujŏngdong poem series was a flop by his own admission, Yu made a successful return to the silver screen a decade later.[48] At the time his second Gangnam film premiered—this time based on his high school memories—it was well into the twenty-first century, and the disasters of the previous decade had already changed the public's mood surrounding Gangnam.

Millennial Gangnam: Bipolar Dreams and the Middle-Strata Reality

From the "economic miracle" of the authoritarian 1970s–1980s through democratization and globalization of the go-go 1990s, Gangnam was portrayed as the dreamland for upward social mobility. Soon, however, the dark side of the 1980s' Gangnam development spilled over into the 1990s as the construction boom that made Gangnam so very visible ended with a spectacular crash with the collapses of the Sŏngsu Bridge and Sampoong Department Store. They were followed by the IMF Crisis, a meltdown of the national economy that split the dreamland into "phantasmagoria and shock."[49] Whereas the old, middle-strata dreams of Gangnam hinged upon the progress of industrial capitalism, the new dreams had to be reinvented in the coming postindustrial society on the global stage.

In those turbulent fin de siècle times, the literary world was largely silent about the excesses and disasters of Gangnam, unlike other media and art forms like journalism, academic studies, film, music, and theater. Since the publication of Yu Ha's Apkujŏng poem series in 1991, Gangnam literature had been fading away, just as the prominence or notoriety of Gangnam had only been growing in every other respect. By the mid-2000s, new literary introspections appeared on the horizon. Some astute newspaper journalists branded them as "Gangnam realism" or simply as "Gangnam literature," as if the previous century's literary works critical of Gangnam were not worthy of merit or even mention.[50] Be that as it may, there were new, mostly female voices coming from the inner quarters of Gangnam's middle strata existence. Mun Chŏnghŭi's poetry, and novels by Chŏng Migyŏng and Chŏng Ihyŏn stay clear from taking overly harsh or moralizing tones, giving a sympathetic look at the characters who struggle to come to terms with the reality of widening socioeconomic gaps in their daily lives. For instance, Mun bitterly protests against the stereotypical image of Apkujŏngdong residents in the first two stanzas of "Leaving Apkujŏng" ("Apkujŏng'ŭl ttŏnamyŏ," 2007):

> Possessed nothing but an axe in hand
> Snuck in like a young robber
> Settled in Apkujŏng for ten-odd years, now leaving
>
> I'm packing for a move
> Some call this place a wealthy neighborhood
> Some dismiss it,
> As a lowbrow symbol of pariah capitalism
> But here, there are neither elites nor outcasts
> Just a dazzling thirst, commonly found anywhere.[51]

Mun's observation of flattened social hierarchies ("neither elites nor outcasts") echoes some demographic realities. Not all residents of Gangnam are wealthy homeowners who have seen their apartment prices skyrocketing over decades, notwithstanding the stereotype. In fact, an analysis based on the 2003 economic survey data shows that the social class composition of Gangnam was distinct from the other areas of Seoul in terms of its high concentration of the upper middle class (corporate managers and professionals) and a strong wealth advantage based on real estate value, but it also confirms the substantial presence of working-class and lower-middle-class residents in Gangnam.[52]

Yi Hong's depiction of Apkujŏngdong in the novel *Christmas Picnic* amplifies this point through grotesquerie. This is the story of a poor working-class family on the outskirts of Seoul striking gold: they win the lottery, buy an apartment in Apkujŏngdong, and move in quickly. The windfall, however, has failed to push them into the upper echelons of Korean society, and their struggle for acceptance only causes them deep, disturbing troubles while also exposing the underbelly of Apkujŏngdong highlife in much more intimate ways than Yu Ha ever did. Literary critic Kim Mihyŏn states that the protagonist family are only allowed temporary "residency" in Gangnam, not a permanent one, and wonders about its "restricted permeability" to people like them. Worse still, the Apkujŏngdong apartment they managed to move in has already been going out of shape after merely three decades of existence, presenting with all kinds of problems—insulation, heating, water supply, sewer, you name it—that could be addressed only by wholesale demolishment and reconstruction (*chaegaebal*). And yet, "for the protagonist family, this place is a utopia and a dream palace."[53] Why? Because of the social-class distinction attached to this place: "It didn't matter if the house was cold because the heat failed. Once you said you were living in the Apkujŏng Han'yang Apartments, schoolmates would envy you, and the parents of the kids you tutored would treat you differently. No matter how sad and difficult things became, this house provided consolation."[54]

By the new millennium, it became clear that the class border existed not only between Gangnam and the rest, but also within Gangnam itself. As the financial crises of 1997–1998 and 2008 attested, globalization has been inseparable from polarization in every respect—economic, political, social, and cultural—since the very outset. Once again, the focus was put on would-be border crossers, but this time within Gangnam: Who is getting in and who is left out in the ever-tightening social class network of the uber-rich? Chŏng Ihyŏn's "Romantic Love and Society" ("Nangmanjŏk saranggwa sahoe") is another story of an outsider's desperate attempt to get into Gangnam's elite inner circle. While its depiction of Gangnam life is more realist than *Christmas Picnic*, it is no less discomforting to observe the starkly rational calculation based on her desire to move up the social ladder in a young woman's choices about dating:

> A boy without a car is a drag. First of all, it gives you a bad look. It'd be an embarrassment, during one's junior year of college, to still be meeting your date in front of the New York Bakery at Gangnam Station or the

Apkujŏngdong McDonald's . . . Even if he were a medical student, having no car would be a serious flaw . . . the only reason I spent months dating this clueless guy who went to a regional college and didn't kiss very well was, after all, his sports car. Blaring music through the open window so loud that the whole apartment complex seemed to tremble, the silver car was waiting for me! Words couldn't express my feelings when I walked out the apartment building entrance, moving as slowly as I could, and finally pulled the door open to hop into the car that had been waiting for me.[55]

Here Chŏng adopts the popular "chick lit" style, cleverly deploying such technics as annotated illustrations of luxurious consumer goods mentioned in the text, in order to give the main character an authentic voice. It is as though one of the Apkujŏngdong women, whom Yu Ha dismissed out of hand as a "chick" for comparing Hwang Chiu to Sŏ Chŏng'yun, started speaking for herself, clapping back, and laughing at "dudes" like Yu who did not have much to offer her other than libidinal aggression and/or moralistic outrage.

If the above stories are from the perspective of the outside looking in, there are also stories of insiders looking out. Chŏng Migyŏng's My Son's Girlfriend ("Nae adŭrŭi yŏn'in") provides arguably the most sophisticated and elegant narrative from the perspective of the Gangnam elite.[56] The narrator, a middle-aged mother whose college student son is dating a female classmate from a dirt-poor family, feels a bit conflicted about the situation at first but decides to put a good face on it. She goes out of her way to befriend her son's girlfriend and finds herself genuinely fond of the girl, although she senses all along that her son's romance would not last. Setting aside the plausibility of this fictional setup, the mother's narrative feels highly realistic in terms of her psychological dynamic oscillating between bourgeois guilt and feminine solidarity. Furthermore, the story goes into granular details of class distinction in the Bourdieusian sense, and how "cultural capital" creates a mundane yet potent barrier against an alliance—whether it is romantic or political—between members of different classes in a polarized society.[57] In the following, the narrator takes her son's girlfriend, Do-ran (Toran), to a luxury department store:

People say that when shopping at a department store, you should be carefully made up and dressed up . . . but the atmosphere of this particular department store is way over the top. This realization hits me again after I take Do-ran to a young casual brand boutique and see her standing there. If two women with no makeup were to stand side by side, the complexion of the woman from this neighborhood would be different from the one from a different area . . . How do I put it—the difference seems to emanate from deep within, from their very bones. Do-ran is of an age where she looks pretty and radiant even when she wears something bought from a vendor at Namdaemun Market, but this is not the case here, not in this place. Do-ran stands awkwardly, suddenly giving off the impression of a girl who isn't well cared for, who fails to dress fashionably.[58]

Another distinct aspect of this story is the gap between first- and second-generation Gangnam residents. Before getting married to a wealthy businessman who owns several apartments in Gangnam, the narrator had, as a first-year college student, briefly been romantically involved with a young man she nicknamed Ch'op'in, an apparent mispronunciation he had once made of the classical composer Frédéric Chopin. It was this memory of Ch'op'in from a presumably poor, unsophisticated social background that triggers her sympathy toward her son's girlfriend, Do-ran. Her children, the second-generation residents who were born and grew up in comfortable wealth, lack such lived experiences of poverty and hardships the first generation like her had. As a result, they have different reactions and attitudes toward Do-ran than she does. The narrator's daughter Myeong (Myŏng) has been openly cynical about her brother's relationship from the beginning, accusing Do-ran of "busy calculating behind the mask of innocence" without knowing "a thing about her social standing."[59] Her son Hyeon (Hyŏn), on the other hand, is obviously much more open-minded than his sister, but the narrator knows him all too well to miss the subtle signs of bourgeois habitus in him as well. When Do-ran points it out to Hyeon's mother, she realizes a kind of feminine solidarity between herself and Do-ran coming from their shared experience of non-bourgeois life:

[Do-ran:] "Hyeon, he's a narcissist."
A laugh slips out of my mouth.
"Do you mean that he's full of himself, despite the way he looks?"
"I don't mean that. His self-love is extraordinary, but it doesn't come off as offensive. How can I put it? It seems that he was raised that way."
She's right, quite observant for her age. He doesn't mind eating at a tacky joint, but his appetite disappears at the sight of a roll of toilet paper lying on the table in lieu of napkins. A bourgeois youth through and through—that's my son.[60]

If Chŏng Migyŏng's fiction can be widely considered a crowning achievement of Gangnam literature in the 2000s, it is not because she turned away from the thorny class issue that haunted Korean literature in the previous century—as some conservative critics have suggested. On the contrary, she embraced, internalized, and wedged it into the innermost quarters of the middle-strata life. This shows that Gangnam literature has ever more deeply embedded itself into the residents' real lives and various experiences without necessarily compromising its critical perspective. The poet Mun Chŏnghŭi, who has reminded us of the struggle Gangnam residents like herself had to go through to reconcile the external perception of Gangnam and their internal reality, turns a critical eye to the rise of the new, super-gentrified Gangnam in "Rainbows of Seoul" ("Sŏurŭi mujigaedŭl"):

> Pushing aside the forest of buildings, a rainbow rises
> Is it a genetically modified rainbow?
> It's more than one or two
> Fearsome like massive weapons
> I-Park, Tower Palace, Acroville, Platinum
>
> Lined up like foreign troops
> They erect at a brand-new angle
> It is happiness, parceled out on a large scale
> Garden-variety style love and classiness
> Dignified life turning into counterfeit
> Notifies the delivery of quick dreams.[61]

As Mun rattles off the corporate brand names of the newly built super-highrise apartments in Gangnam and elsewhere—I-Park (Hyundai), Tower Palace (Samsung), Acroville (Daelim), Platinum (Ssang'yong)—her tongue grows sharper and sharper against these "massive weapons" in the guise of rainbows. Mun's poetic expressions evoke those of the preeminent colonial-era resistance poet Yi Yuksa (1904–1944), who once famously compared the season of winter, a thinly veiled metaphor of Japan's colonial rule over Korea, to a "rainbow made of steel" (*kangch'ŏllo toen mujigae*). Channeling Yi Yuksa's fighting spirit against imperial dominance, Mun boldly proclaims that these "genetically modified" weapons are like "foreign troops" invading Korea. Elsewhere in the same poem, she even uses the term "comfort woman" (*wianbu*) to make her intention clear. One may question the wisdom of conjuring up the dark colonial past to justify her misgivings about the present, but it dramatically captures the anger and resentment of those who have left Gangnam behind, of their own volition or otherwise.

While there is a rather wide spectrum of socioeconomic statuses among the resident population of Gangnam, the authors discussed in this section so far have focused on the middle strata, whether they are aspiring new entrants, barely clinging to their good status, forced out of competition unceremoniously, or rising to the level of the global elite. On the opposite pole of the class divide is Kim Yun'yŏng's "Operation Tracking Metalcase" ("Ch'ŏlgabang ch'ujŏk chakchŏn"), a story about students from a low-income rental apartment complex built on the fringe of Gangnam as a part of a "social mix" policy experiment by the government:

> The "remote island" or "dark side" of Gangnam, as it was called, the Susŏ Rental Apartment Complex remained as an eyesore to other residents in the area . . . The quibbles over its negative effect on the area's property values were past debate. There were PhDs, professors, and medical doctors among those school parents who treated kids from the rental apartment complex like lepers. The worse the kids were mistreated, the tighter they stuck together . . . Money was the engine that drove the kids. If they had money, they would go to the video arcade or the game parlor. Otherwise, they gathered to conspire, and attending school took a backseat. Some of the students there couldn't read a book or recognize the alphabet even in the ninth grade. Sitting next to the students who had mastered English during primary school and were solving high school math problems, these kids couldn't catch up with the school curriculum, staring blankly all day before going back home. They had gradually become invisible. Teachers started teaching visible students only, believing it was the right thing to do. So the kids dreamed a different dream and anticipated for themselves a different future. Not all of them had a plan to escape, but they would certainly be willing accomplices for any who dared to.[62]

Similar to Chŏng Migyŏng's novella, the narrator of Kim Yun'yŏng's story is a solid member of Gangnam's middle strata, a teacher at a middle school near the Susŏ Apartment Complex. While Kim's story is more heavily focused on the disadvantaged poor than Chŏng's, both aim at exposing the vicious class prejudice of the middle strata when they are forced to live in proximity or come in close contact with the poor and the working class. To this end, both stories employ a literary strategy that has the main character or narrator from the middle-strata background feel empathetic toward the downtrodden. In fact, this strategy harkens back to the early Gangnam literature of Ch'oe Inho and Cho Sehŭi. Ch'oe's "Savage" and Kim's "Operation Tracking Metalcase" bear two striking similarities with each other. First, the protagonist in both stories is a teacher shocked by the harsh reality of school segregation. Second, both refer to the discriminated minority as lepers, although leprosy is only a metaphor for poverty in Kim's story. The bourgeois lady narrator in Chŏng Migyŏng's novella bears a strong resemblance to Cho Sehŭi's middle-strata heroine, Sin'ae, in terms of their social backgrounds and attitudes to other classes. Three decades apart, these works still grapple with the guilty conscience of Gangnam's middle strata confronting the poor and marginalized.

Gangnam Style sans Gangnam: Kim Sagwa's Stories of Global-Polarization

This chapter has traced the chronology of Gangnam-focused literature from the early days of development into the formation of Gangnam as a distinct geography and brand identity. Literary works that came in response to the Sampoong disaster, most notably Chŏng Ihyŏn's "Sampoong Department Store" ("Samp'ung paekhwajŏm," 2004), Hwang Sŏg'yŏng's *Dreams of Gangnam*, and Mun Hongju's *Sampoong: A Night of Festivities* deserve a separate treatment in chapter 4 because of the disaster's singular impact. In addition, there have been various kinds of genre fiction, coming-of-age stories, and other works that could be included in the category of Gangnam literature if it is defined as any literary writing making references to Gangnam. In this book, I limit the scope to the works that significantly touch on the issue of global-polarization of Korean society, arguing that the formation of the middle strata in the twentieth century and the dissolution of it in the twenty-first century are the overarching themes of Gangnam literature.

However, I must admit that in terms of literary style, what Gangnam represents could be much wider, and not necessarily bound to one or another topical issue specific to Gangnam as a physical location. A major source of Korean urban pop culture "cool," Gangnam seems to have affected the style of writing as well. One of the most notable writers in this regard is Kim Sagwa, whose flash fiction entitled "SF" gives off just a touch of sleekness of her style: "We're lying in the shade beside the pool. The deep blue sky shines in the dark mirrors of your eyes. What could be more beautiful, I wonder, as I look into those eyes. You sit up and find your glass of Coke. The ice whispers as it melts. I look beyond our feet at the city below. Its paleness is heavenly. You ease yourself into the pool and glide through the heated water. The air is cool and brisk."[63] From the quoted passage above one cannot tell exactly where—it may well be a penthouse on Tower Palace, Gangnam's new uber-rich residence supplanting Apkujŏngdong Hyundai Apartments. If so, the glass of Coke by the poolside has come a long way from the bottle of Coca-Cola that used to entice the vendors at Songji Marketplace, Haenam County. In fact, Kim has written much more glowingly about new dreamlands for the globally oriented Korean youth—such as New York, London, or Berlin—than about Gangnam through the voice of the main character in her long-form novel *In Heaven*. But as Kim herself seems to admit in the same novel, the gap between these cities is closing fast in this age of "planetary gentrification."[64] A conversation between two old friends, former schoolmates in Chamsil, is as mundane as it is revealing in Kim's *In Heaven*:

> When K arrived at a Karosukil café [in Gangnam] for the meet-up, Chaeyŏng had already been there. Sitting by the window and looking down at her coffee mug, Chaeyŏng was perfect as always—her thick, lush brown hair was neatly flowing over the shoulders, and a slim, luxurious gold necklace was draped over her apricot blouse. From underneath the table shined the golden logos of Torry Burch shoes on her feet.
> . . .
> "Did you buy a new bag? It's pretty," Chaeyŏng remarked.
> "Yeah, in New York. It was on sale."
> "I'm jealous. What brand is it, by the way? Alexand—" Chaeyŏng was muttering the letters on the buckle.
> "It's called Alexander Wang, an up-and-coming brand in New York."
> "Is that so? Alexander Wang? I think I've heard about it . . ."
> "Maybe not available in Korea yet. By the way, long time no see, Chaeyŏng. How've you been?"
> . . .
> While K was placing her order at the counter, Chaeyŏng took out her smartphone as if something had occurred to her. Once K came back, Chaeyŏng started talking with a wide smile.
> "Alexander Wang, turns out their products have been available in Korea for quite some time now. Would you take a look?"
> "Really? When?" K said, ignoring the phone screen Chaeyŏng stretched out to her. "But it's very expensive in Korea . . . and pretty ones are hard to come by here . . ."
> "No, look here, they're on sale at the Shinsegae Mall, including yours. Isn't this the same as yours?"[65]

It was Kim Sagwa's own generation, having grown up in Gangnam, who lived through global-polarization taking place right at the center of Gangnam's middle strata. The two characters of *In Heaven*, K and Chaeyŏng, illustrate how this polarizing dynamic plays out at both the macro- and micro-level social relations.

Predictably, their beginnings had been nearly identical until the watershed moment came in the form of the IMF Crisis:

> Walking in the direction of Tosan Park [in Ch'ŏngdamdong], Chaeyŏng thought about K. This was only the first time they got together since K's return from New York, but she had changed for sure. Chaeyŏng had known her since primary school days, and K's occasional weird turns had shocked her before. This was by far the worst, though. Why? Because of New York? But Chaeyŏng had been there as well. In terms of overseas experiences, as a matter of fact, Chaeyŏng had more than K. But that didn't change Chaeyŏng too much at all . . .
> Chaeyŏng was one of the "Chamsil friends" of K . . . Most of the residents in their apartment complex were young couples with more or less similar socioeconomic backgrounds. Their kids grew up becoming friends with one another naturally. This peace was broken when the IMF Economic Crisis broke out. Chaeyŏng's family was fortunate. Her father survived at his company, and even earned a promotion to become a member of the board of directors.[66]

The breadwinner's survival in the economic crisis was obviously a crucial part, but not the only one in the entire story. The kids of Gangnam's middle strata also faced a struggle they had not quite expected. The increasing distance between friends who grew up in the same environment, unlike their parents, who moved to Gangnam as adults, had to feel quite different for them. Kim describes it as sitting in different "theaters," presumably watching different movies, which evokes the original meaning of "phantasmagoria" as horror theater:

> Meanwhile, her mother had hardly slowed down investing in Chaeyŏng's future since her early years, and the returns were better than expected. She went to a prestigious foreign-language high school and then to the [top-ranked] Seoul National University. Those Chamsil friends who rode out the crisis followed a similar life trajectory, if not as successful as Chaeyŏng's . . . Korean economy was already well onto a path of endless polarization as the future of the middle strata had been blown into smithereens back then [during the IMF Crisis]. The ever-more-sophisticated urban landscape was no longer theirs. It was like a movie theater, planted with a time bomb, screening the longest, most flamboyant movie in the world. The spectators were still enchanted by the fascinating narrative despite their impending doom. In that respect, K and Chaeyŏng were the

same. On the other hand, though, they were totally different in the sense that they had parted ways to different theaters at some point in the past.[67]

The diverging paths between old friends is one of the recurring themes of global-polarization played out in the phantasmagoric theater of Gangnam.[68] But it is even more brutal to any aspiring entrants to new Gangnam's inner circle. In Yi Hong's story *Christmas Picnic*, the character Ŭn'yŏng is the eldest child of the poor family who won the lottery and moved to Gangnam. She excelled at school and entered the prestigious X University, thereby taking one step further into the coveted upper-middle-class status Gangnam represents. Even with her impeccable academic credentials and Gangnam residency, however, she keeps failing at securing a well-paid job. As a last resort, she tries to make a personal connection with a network of scions of the privileged in her university by ingratiating herself with one such scion, Min'u. Ŭn'yŏng's desperation leads to a sexual encounter with Min'u in a motel room near a resort area. It is in the aftermath of this sordid affair that Ŭn'yŏng comes to realize the dividing line of bourgeois habitus between herself and a thoroughly Gangnam boy like Min'u:

> Min'u put a palm over his lower belly above the underwear and pressed hard. He furrowed his eyebrows and stood up from the bed abruptly. Ŭn'yŏng's body rebounded slightly with the bedsprings. Min-u rushed toward the bathroom, stopped at the door, and then slammed it without entering. Instead, he hastily put on his clothes. With a blushing face, he left the room, saying he'd be back soon.
>
> Min'u didn't return in thirty minutes. When she picked up the cell phone to call him, the bell rang. It was Min'u, saying, "Oh, sorry. I had to go use a toilet cause it was a big one. By the way, how shall I put it? I've met friends of mine here at the hotel. I'm sorry, but can you call a cab to get here? My friends won't let me go, and I'll tell them you'll come here so as not to surprise them."
>
> This reminded Ŭn'yŏng of a return trip from school she had once taken in Min-u's car. Suddenly, in the middle of the road, Min-u started looking for a hotel to relieve himself. He had driven with his face severely contorted, continually wiping away sweat. He had passed by all the public restrooms even in such a moment of urgency. He needed a hotel restroom.[69]

Ŭn'yŏng reflects the reader's astonishment at the degree to which a Gangnam habitus determined the lifestyles of people like Min'u. An example of a parallel character depiction is the son in Chŏng Migyŏng's *My Son's Girlfriend*, who loses appetite over toilet paper in a dingy eatery. This bourgeois notion of hygiene was certainly inculcated in these Gangnam boys from an early age to trigger such automatic responses. This brings us all the way back to Pak Wansŏ's "Kids in Paradise," where she makes a critical connection between personal hygiene and social-class distinction during the formative period of Gangnam:

> In any case, the Murŭng families had to instill fear in place of curiosity about the river to keep their children from playing by the riverside. They told their kids that factory waste and raw sewage from the poor folk's latrines in the old city up north had poisoned the river. They taught them repeatedly that dipping their hands or feet in the river was as unsanitary as washing them in a shit bucket. It is likely for that reason that I have never seen any children out playing in the sandy beach or the green patches of the riverbank.[70]

This is the level of contempt Gangnam's middle-strata residents harbored against the river and the people living across it. With this lesson in mind, we move to the next chapter to see how the putrid river figures into the disasters that plagued Gangnam.

CHAPTER 3

Two Lakes in Chamsil
Ecology, Class, Disaster

Chamsil was an island on the Han River. In the premodern Chŏson Dynasty era (1392–1897), this area was known for mulberry trees, grown there to be used by the royal sericulturists to raise silkworms. In fact, the name "Chamsil" denotes a sericultural chamber. Before Gangnam development, the Han River split into two streams around the island of Chamsil—Sinch'ŏn to the north and Songp'a to the South—before merging again to flow westward to the old city of Seoul. Gangnam development changed the entire area by turning Sinch'ŏn, once a dry stream, into the main river and reclaiming land from Songp'a to attach Chamsil to the Gangnam side. This gigantic undertaking of civil engineering, followed by the construction of the 1988 Olympic Games main stadium and massive apartment complexes, completely changed the landscape of Chamsil to the point where its original form was no longer recognizable. The days of mulberry trees and silkworms were long gone, and so were the beautiful sandy beaches by the river where people would enjoy swimming on the hottest days of summer.

Sandy Land and Putrid River

Cho Sehŭi bluntly describes Chamsil in the beginning passage of "There Is No Dandelion" ("Mindŭllenŭn ŏpta"), a short cautionary tale about environmental conservation in *Time Travel*:

> Chamsil is a neighborhood made of sands. A sandy land full of sandy apartments. Flooded river waters would strike and sweep across Chamsil in the summer until they built an embankment and poured asphalt on top. Residents of the sandy neighborhood remain unaware. They think of Chamsil as a land for apartment buildings, and they live there because the apartments are there.
>
> What holds Chamsil together is cement and rebar. Remove the ferroconcrete, and everything would collapse, and only grains of sand would remain to drift everywhere. Sand grains cannot stick together no matter

how desperately they may try. What a sad situation. It is not just the sand. Even with this, Chamsil residents are not grateful for the cement and rebar. But if you meet anyone living in Chamsil, do console them first. They deserve your consolation because they are sand-like people, living in sandy apartments on a brutal land of sands.[1]

In his subsequent story, "Chamsil Has as Many as Two Lakes" (hereafter "Two Lakes"), Cho softens his criticism of Chamsil, if only for the promptly ensuing ironic twist:

> But it's not all brutal through and through; Chamsil has as many as two lakes. There used to flow a stream. When they poured dirt over the stream and erased it off the official map, a part of it was spared and turned into the Chamsil Lake as it stands today. Originally there was only one lake, but they also extracted soil in the middle, splitting it into two.
> The stream disappeared.
> Two lakes appeared.
> In fact, these are inaccuracies. To be exact, the stream only disappeared from the official map. Its flow was just diverted. We don't know where the stream flows under the sands, or under which apartment buildings its waters run. The stream is likely meandering underground after disappearing from the map. Maybe under Building Number 507 or 521, or far away from there, under Building Number 2. The stream has not gone away.[2]

Cho Sehŭi had previously criticized the environmental toll Korea's rapid industrialization had taken. Already in *The Dwarf*, his magnum opus to which *Time Travel* is a sequel, Cho divulges a strong tendency toward social ecology, echoing Murray Bookchin's ideas, as many commentators have pointed out. *The Dwarf* is focused on the destruction of the socio-ecological system caused by industrialization, including labor conflicts, forced eviction, urban redevelopment, class division, not to mention the severe air and water pollution some of the stories depict so vividly.[3] *Time Travel* seems to push this agenda further, urging readers to reconsider the relationship between human and nature on a philosophical level, and touching on the main argument of deep ecology by questioning anthropocentrism itself.[4] The transition from social ecology to deep ecology takes place in the remaining text of "Two Lakes," which is worthy of a close reading in its entirety:

> People would not want to stay for more than ten minutes by the side of these lakes, which were made by cutting off the waterhead of the stream now meandering underground. They are lakes in name only and do not at

all resemble actual lakes. They are too small and pathetic. The surrounding grounds are always barren, no matter when one visits there. Nonetheless, the lakes give Chamsil residents a huge comfort. The reason is simple. They make it possible for Chamsil residents to boast of the fact that "Chamsil has as many as two lakes" whenever someone who doesn't know Chamsil wants to ask. Regrettably, much like the city officials, Chamsil residents are clinging to the quantity, not quality [of living standards], and some of them are even bluffing as if they were living someone else's life. Otherwise, they would know why the stream had to be displaced by the lakes. They don't know the reason. Early last spring, a flock of countless migratory birds came down upon the lakes and then flew away. It was a flock of winter migratory birds making its way back north after flying somewhere south of our country in the fall and staying through the winter. Their mating instincts brought them back north. They breed in the cold region. It's unknown whether the two small lakes were used as an area for feeding or resting. Nothing is known of their migratory route. Nothing is known about their arrival time, departure time, flying altitude, flock size, twittering vocalization, flying patterns, nothing. Had there been an ornithologist, we would have known. The ornithologist observes the moon and migratory birds flying into the moon. It's such a beautiful sight, even just thinking about it. There was no moon hanging over the two small lakes. So the birds that had landed on the two lakes didn't fly into the moon. The birds that flew back in the pitch-dark night sky knew of the two lakes on the corner of Chamsil, away from the apartment complex. They drew the two lakes in their own map. This is the reason that the lakes should now stand there as lakes.

The stream lost its place and departed.

The stream meanders underground.

Two lakes appeared in place of the stream. Now the two lakes have to stand there as lakes.

Had they known this, Chamsil residents would have said it a bit louder, "There are as many as two lakes in Chamsil."[5]

The narrator expresses a clear derision of the two "pathetic" lakes, described as a side effect of rapacious urban planning, and yet acknowledges their essential purpose for the migratory birds, not for the human residents (figure 3.1). This profound shift of perspective was rare in mid-1980s Korea, where the environmental movement had been launched only few years prior, under the banner of antipollution, and remained in its infancy. Cho's ecological outlook began early with

Figure 3.1. Two lakes in Chamsil: The Sŏkch'on Lake and its vicinities, May 15, 1986. Source: Seoul Metropolitan Government, reprinted with permission.

The Dwarf at around the same time as the poet Sŏng Ch'an'gyŏng wrote "Wake Up the Poet inside Your Heart" ("Kŭdae kasŭm sog'ŭi siin'ŭl kkaeura," 1974), the first environmentally conscious poem in modern Korean literature, originally entitled "The Age of Pollution and the Poet" ("Konghaesidaewa siin"). But the rest of the Korean literary world was only slowly catching up. In poetry, environmental themes began to be deployed in the 1980s. For narrative fiction, it took another decade to follow suit.[6] With *Time Travel*, Cho was apparently well ahead of his time as he moved beyond merely criticizing the environmental pollution taking toll on human society to argue for the priority of natural ecosystems over human activity. In his last major literary work, *The Roots of Silence* (1985), Cho takes the reader to the famous migratory bird sanctuary Ŭlsukto on the Naktong River Delta, elaborating his concerns about ecological destruction on an even larger scale than in Chamsil. "Ten years have passed, but nothing has changed" in this regard since *The Dwarf*, he laments.[7] While his feeling of helplessness at the time is understandable, it is not entirely true that nothing had changed during the decade. For one, the environmental movement had since grown in Korea, albeit from humble beginnings. For another, Cho's own understanding of the value of the natural ecosystem deepened as he devoted more of his writings to this issue.[8]

Cho's clairvoyance does not end there either. Observing the wanton destruction of the natural surroundings, Cho notices something ominous afoot—not just near factories and other places where the poor live, but an impending disaster of people's own making, which might happen to middle-class apartment residents like himself, even in places like Chamsil. That is why the Chamsil residents should be thankful for the ferroconcrete, without which their apartment buildings would crumble into sand. He concludes the first of the two Chamsil pieces with a terse verdict: "No dandelion seed would fly as far as Chamsil."[9] What the youth of Chamsil mistake for dandelion parachutes are cottony weeping willow seeds that cover the skies in the spring, causing severe allergies and breeding poisonous moths. This premonition follows wherever he goes: it is not confined just to the "City of Machines" and the ironic Felicity Precinct in Eden District, where the fictional dwarf family in Cho's previous work used to live and/or work. Most disturbingly, he finds it in the city's very aorta, the Han River. In "Dying River," another concise piece on ecological disaster, Cho writes his signature "literature of witness" into practice:

> One morning I saw the river dying away. It had been dying for a while. Always watching from afar, I mistakenly thought it was alive, with its green color intact. From an elevated height, driving on a concrete overpass or a steel bridge, the river looked dark. I thought it was because of polluted air, smoke, or fine dust blocking the green color from shining through.
>
> Up close, the river's ongoing death was starkly visible. The green color was gone. A mining ship was drawing up pebbles from the darkened riverbed. Another one was scooping sand. Here and there, puddles had been dug up.
>
> Filled with polluted water, the river lay groaning on its side. The putrid smell was awful. The heart of our city was rotting away. Big speculators were building a new ruin in our city, leaving even bigger wounds at its heart. That morning, my lips were parched. Re-lacing my worn-out sneakers, I shook off the drops of morning dew from the grass I had stepped on while climbing over the embankment. I didn't want to be suspicious about the purity of the morning dew. We had already killed off a lot of things: we'd killed sunlight, moonlight, and starlight; killed the Milky Way; killed roadside trees; killed flowers; killed butterflies, bees, dragonflies, and even fireflies. On any survivors, we'd inflicted damage.[10]

The list of ecological abuses endured by the Han River is lengthy, spanning more than a half century. The so-called Miracle on the Han dumped an inordinate amount of untreated industrial and domestic wastewater into the river as the city population grew fourfold to ten million between 1960 and 1990. The parents in Pak Wansŏ's "Kids in Paradise" wisely cautioned their children to avoid the river (see chapter 2), which had been an open sewer until the first-ever wastewater facility began operation in 1976. By then the number of residents in Seoul had ballooned to seven million, accounting for nearly 20 percent of the country's entire population. Even when the city was fresh from hosting the 1988 Olympic Games, raw sewage routinely overwhelmed the four treatment facilities,[11] three of which had been built within the previous five years to make the city presentable to international visitors. Under the banner of the Han River Comprehensive Development Project, the river was transformed into an artificial waterway of sorts. It was by far the largest public works project ever attempted to date, with a total of 4.2 million workers, hundreds of thousands of heavy construction equipment pieces, 105,000 tons of rebar, and nearly 700,000 sacks of cement.[12]

The project changed the Han's waterscape in three fundamental ways. First, two underwater barrages were built for the crucial main purpose of flood prevention by controlling the water level and slowing down the flow, since the Han had been prone to disastrous floods for centuries.[13] These barrages, one of them located in none other than Chamsil, have been the focal point of controversy over the Han's relatively poor water quality despite the steady improvement of wastewater treatment. Second, the project eliminated sandy beaches, dunes, and marshes, replacing them with concrete-paved riverside "parks" in Chamsil, Panp'o, and Yŏŭido, among other places, where the middle strata would enjoy easy access to leisure amenities accessible via personal automobiles and in close proximity to the nearby apartment residences (recall Ch'oe Sŭngja's "Merry Diary" in chapter 2). Third, the riverbed was dredged up to provide construction aggregate—sand and pebbles—for the very apartment buildings to be erected in Gangnam and elsewhere. The deepened river not only made the water look cleaner with its dark green hue than it actually was, but also accommodated new leisure activities such as windsurfing, waterskiing, and motor- and paddle-boating. As noted in chapter 1, Psy parodies the enduring legacy of this transformative project in "Gangnam Style": senior men play Chinese chess under the bridge, ladies jog backwards or practice yoga in the riverside parks, and duck-shaped boats paddle the water. Three decades earlier, however, Cho Sehŭi was in no mood for joking as he witnessed the ongoing destruction: "I walked around a small puddle. Out of the oil-covered, decaying grass crawled a few snails, headed toward a tarred sand hill. I couldn't see my apartment from there. It was a concrete apartment building made of rebar mixed with pebbles and sand from the river. Large trucks passed by, making the sandy lot tremble. I was sitting there amidst the earsplitting truck noise, watching the river dying away."[14] Cho realizes that the river's demise and the displaced stream's underground meanderings have gone unnoticed for far too long. A certain doom must await, perhaps in the form of nature's revenge. The author sternly warns middle-strata residents blithely content with their apartment living.

Of Monsters and Middle Strata: Revenge of Nature in Bong Joon-ho's Films

Thirty years after Cho Sehŭi's dire warning, Bong Joon-ho's summer blockbuster *The Host* (*Koemul*, 2006) imagines nature exacting just such a grim retribution in the form of a river monster. *The Host* is somewhat patterned after the archetypal monster movie *Godzilla: King of the Monsters* (*Gojira*, 1954), which allegorizes the U.S. atomic bombings of Japan. Both films invoke the horror of a real-life environmental disaster, albeit on a much different scale, to critically examine the sociopolitical climate of the times.[15] The opening sequence of *The Host* is a fictional reenactment of an actual event at the U.S. Army Yongsan Garrison, where toxic formaldehyde from the morgue was illegally dumped into the Han River in 2000. In the next sequence, two fishermen wade waist-deep in the water near the Chamsil Underwater Barrage and glimpse a strange fry, which grows into a giant mutant fish that kills, kidnaps, and terrorizes people gathered at the concrete-paved riverside park. As the lurking monster attacks from its lair below the huge steel-and-concrete Han River bridge structures, the fate of the city depends on a tenacious working-class family who confront the monster in a final showdown. Bong's sardonic critique of Korea's class divide is formative through the film, a titular counterpoint to his latest internationally acclaimed film *Parasite*. The "host" of Bong's 2006 film is a horribly mutated representation of nature, and the parasite is a wily, dispossessed family of humans. Another parallel between the ecocriticism of Cho Sehŭi and Bong Joon-ho is their unflattering treatment of the middle strata. Cho's critique focuses on Chamsil residents, who are largely ignorant, indifferent, or, worse yet, mistakenly boastful about the environmental consequences while reaping benefits from the Han River development. In Bong's film the middle strata are portrayed, at best, as hapless victims like the picnickers falling prey to the monster at the riverside park. At worst, they are represented by such a conniving, opportunistic character as the white-collar office worker who rats out his old friend, the second son of the protagonist working-class family.

Middle-class complicity in ecological destruction is what Rachel Carson so poignantly decries about American suburbia in her landmark book, *Silent Spring* (1962): "The mores of suburbia now dictate that crabgrass must go at whatever cost. Sacks containing chemicals designed to rid the lawn of such despised vegetation have become almost a status symbol."[16] The chemical she speaks of is the notorious insecticide DDT, the use of which was not banned in the U.S. until 1972 and in Korea until seven years later. As shown in *Parasite,* children in Korea's poor neighborhoods are still delighted at chasing the tail of a fumigation truck. Those who grew up doing that very thing prior to the DDT ban, however, may now well shudder to think about the potential harm from their childhood pastime. These children of the 1970s and 1980s also witnessed a new status symbol for the Korean middle strata rising: apartments in Gangnam, built with the sand and pebbles dug up from the contaminated, flood-prone river. If the neurotoxin-laced lawn in front of a suburban single-family house is the symbol of the American Dream, the Korean equivalent is a high-rise apartment overlooking the stale, concrete-embanked river that routinely caused mass die-off of fishes and had to be flushed of toxic contaminants well into the mid-1990s.[17] This symbolism is alive and well in the age of global-polarization as glyphosate-based herbicides took the place of DDT in American suburbia and Korea's three other major rivers, following the model of the Han, underwent concrete-based transformations. As the controversy over carcinogenicity of glyphosate has been heating up in recent years, so has the debate on the Han's toxic algal blooms. According to the environmentalists, the blooms are mainly caused by the concrete barrages that artificially slow the river current. Today's observer would note the irony that the Han River development was initially promoted to the public as an ecological restoration project by the authoritarian government:

> The construction of a large-scale sewer treatment network will wash off the stain of "dead river flow" by returning clear blue water to the Han, where fish will frolic and citizens can blithely swim. (*Kyŏnghyang sinmun,* September 28, 1982)

> The "healing" of the sick Han River has begun ... The Seoul Metropolitan Government has raised the banner of this [Han River] Comprehensive Development Project that would restore the river's original function and give it back to the citizenry. (*Tong'a ilbo,* September 29, 1982)[18]

Early environmentalists like Cho Sehŭi were having none of it, but they were only a small minority at the time. To the large majority of citizens, and Gangnam residents in particular, the project had some undeniable merits in terms of flood control, sewage treatment, and urban amenities such as riverside expressways and parks.

The Han River Parks (Han'gang kongwŏn), colloquially referred to as highwater sites (*kosubuji*) because they often submerge during the flood season, were the main attraction of the Han River development to those Seoulites who craved urban leisure space commensurate with their ascending economic fortunes. Access to such waterfront amenities was far from socially equitable, however. The architect and critic Hong Sŏng'yong complains that ordinary Seoulites "encounter the Han in their daily lives only by looking at it over one of the bridges" as the "unapproachable waters have been monopolized by the pricy [apartment] houses with the riverview." When the riverside parks opened to much fanfare in 1986, public transit stops were located at a distance and pedestrian traffic could only access the parks "through the tunnel known as the rabbit hole [t'okkigul] that crawls under those pricy houses," whereas private automobiles and taxicabs could get there conveniently via expressway ramps. Despite this preferential access given to the selected few by design, Hong concedes that the parks have since become "playgrounds for the citizenry," as there is precious little urban space for leisure and outdoor activities for the masses.[19] In the twenty-five-year period since the parks' opening, the number of registered automobiles in Seoul has soared by a factor of four and a half,[20] fueling a boom in weekend travels and outdoor leisure activities among the middle-strata families who took advantage of increasingly affordable private car ownership. Even though in the beginning many of these parks looked like anything but natural waterfront or green spaces (see figure 3.2), improvements were made over time as more and more people paid them regular visits.

Figure 3.2. The high-water site overlooking the Panp'o Bridge, February 29, 1986. Source: Seoul Museum of History, reprinted with permission.

Given the historical background, the riverside parks were an ideal location for Bong Joon-ho to set the stage for an epic clash between a chemically polluted nature and a class-divided society. The river monster, whose commemorative statue graces the Yŏŭido Han River Park, turned out to be not just a grim reminder of the toxic dumping incident but also a fictional magnification of a looming ecological plague. In combination with the concrete barrages slowing down the flow, global warming introduced micro-sized monsters, such as harmful algae and ribbon worms, to the Han. When *The Host* set a new box office record with a total of thirteen million viewers nationwide, an algal bloom advisory was issued on the lower stream of the Han flowing through Seoul for the first time since the establishment of the warning system in 2000. It was lifted after nine days. Nine years later, another advisory was issued and then quickly raised to a full warning. This time the warning lasted a total of 180 days, all through the summer and fall of 2015.[21] It looked as though someone had poured green enamel paint into the river, but Koreans opted for a euphemism and called it "green algae latte" (*nokcho ratte*). Meanwhile, ribbon worms started invading the river from the mudflats of the Yellow Sea, their original habitat. Spewing a neurotoxin that kills schools of fish and eels, these micro-monsters have become a scourge on the downstream fishery business ever since. Yet there was little impact on the number of visitors to the riverside parks from these disturbing signs of ecological failure. Rather ironically, the success of *The Host* seemed to have raised the profile of the Han as a filming location—most notably in the Hollywood blockbuster *Avengers: Age of Ultron* (dir. Joss Whedon, 2015). In contrast to the gritty, unflattering depiction of the Han in *The Host*, however, the American superhero flick preferred the ultramodern chic of Gangnam, choosing the glittering artificial "islands" named Some Sevit (Sebit sŏm) at the Panp'o Han River Park as one of the main locations.[22] In the spring and summer of 2015, more than ten million Koreans went to movie theaters to watch *Avengers,* which may have afforded a point of pride for the Seoulites, with the neighborhoods, landmarks, and daily traffic routes being showcased in the global blockbuster film. At the same time, the dying river and its monstrous creatures failed to inspire as much of a public response, perhaps because the problem did not rise to the level of threatening the safety of drinking water as it often had before. The previous public scandal over Seoul's drinking water was prompted by the discovery of waterborne viruses in 1997, and the ensuing controversy dragged on for nearly four years.[23] It would not be a stretch to conjecture that this controversy might have inspired Bong Joon-ho to concoct a narrative of mass panic over a potential viral infection caused by the river monster in *The Host*.

At the time of this writing, the raging COVID-19 global pandemic has cast a new light on various fictional works, including *The Host,* that envisioned similar emergency situations in which mass panic, conspiracies and false information, official incompetence, and authoritarian responses would all come to the fore. Bong's tale is particularly relevant to the current pandemic situation in the sense that the "essential worker"—the main character named Kang-du, played by the inimitable Song Kang-ho—is the one who loses family members in the valiant fight against the monster and exposes himself to the potential viral infection, yet he falls victim to societal discrimination and governmental mistreatment. Once the threat is gone, he remains in the same place as before, running a makeshift corner store at the riverside park once again populated by middle-strata picknickers as if nothing ever happened. It is an ending John Lennon's famous refrain would befit: "A working-class hero is something to be." As Lennon explained in an interview, "it's for the people like me who are working class, who are supposed to be processed into the middle classes, or into the machinery. It's *my* experience, and I hope it's just a warning to people, 'Working Class Hero.'" [24]

At first blush, the working-class family in *Parasite* appears diametrically opposed to that from *The Host* even though both are anchored by the father character played by Song Kang-ho. They are anti-hero figures at best, if not villains (or monsters), who cheat, deceive, conspire, and ultimately kill and are killed. And yet their vice mirrors many of the defects of the middle strata, especially those who aspire to elevate themselves to elite status. In many ways, *Parasite* can be appreciated as a satire of Korea's broken American Dream. Indeed, much online discussion from the (post)colonial perspective has been focused on the significance of the "Cowboys and Indians" games—and their deadly consequences—played through the film, and of the liberal use of English by some of the characters.[25] As noted in chapter 2, for the rising middle strata, Gangnam's initial appeal as an American Murŭng was the possibility of joining an Americanized Korean elite. Bong Joon-ho plays with the hackneyed American Indian trope as though he were telling an inside joke about the Korean elite make-believing themselves as American settler colonists—a postcolonial cosplay, as it were. The same goes for out-of-the-blue English sentences blurted out by the wife of the nouveau riche Pak family, such as "I am deadly serious!" The intended effect is to draw laughs and thicken the irony. However entertaining or enlightening it may be, though, the colonial psychodrama of the Korean elite is but one minor aspect of the compelling look into the class conflict taken at the microscopic level.

Most film reviewers have latched onto another well-worn trope—"the stupid rich versus the smart poor"—and rightfully so; the risible gullibility of the rich Paks (host) in contrast to the clever ingenuity of the poor Kims (parasite) serves as the comedic engine of the film. But then the con job the Kim family pulls on the Paks is not just a clever one; it involves such a high level of sophistication that the viewer may well wonder about the backstory to the Kims (and the Paks to a lesser degree). Known for his meticulous attention, down to minute details, Bong Joon-ho sprinkles subtle clues in the film suggesting that the older Kims used to be solid members of the rising middle strata before being ruined by the IMF Crisis, whereas the younger Paks have been making their fortune in the booming high-tech industry since the crisis. In other words, these two families represent winners and losers, respectively, in a global-polarizing Korea. Seen in this light, *Parasite* is a tragicomedy about the Korean middle strata's worst nightmares: "fear of falling" and a deep sense of insecurity.[26]

Presumably having fallen off the social ladder, the Kims are relegated to the semi-basement (*panjiha*) level in a multifamily housing unit. The elaborate ruse they play in order to live off the Paks, who reside in an architect-designed mansion with an immaculate lawn reminiscent of American suburbia, reaches a breaking point when torrential rain causes a disastrous flood of consequences, literally as well as figuratively. They barely escape one catastrophe in the Pak house only to find another one awaiting them right where they live. To the affluent Paks, the downpour is only a nuisance that made them cut short a weekend getaway. It turns into a devastating flood—a classic revenge of nature—that wreaks havoc on the lives of those who have fallen from the middle strata into the ranks of basement dwellers. The revenge of nature drives them to a bloody denouement in which monstrous hostilities hold sway. Ultimately, *Parasite* is a parable of the middle strata devouring themselves in the face of a catastrophe co-created by natural and social forces.

The monstrosity of the violence fueled by class-based rage came as a shock to many viewers, both foreign and domestic.[27] At least Koreans have long been forewarned, since the early years of Gangnam development, of a brewing animosity between classes and its conspicuous ecological symptom—a putrid smell of sewage from the dying river. Pak Wansŏ could not make it any clearer in "Kids in Paradise":

> From the bathroom toilet seat next to my large study, I look out the small window facing north to see the decrepit, crude old city submerged in a thick haze of foggy or dusty particles. And it's unclear to me whether the turbid river visible below is flowing or still. In spite of the heavy traffic crossing the wide, sturdy bridge that joins both sides of the river, there is little to no friendliness, only a vague hostility. I'm not sure if the river itself, which the Murŭngdong residents call the putrid river, creates such

a distance, or the hatred of the old city makes them look down on the river and call it the putrid river instead of its proper name.[28]

As Song Ŭn'yŏng points out, "the Han River had not become simply a physical border between Gangbuk and Gangnam, but also a dividing line between social classes and cultural distinction."[29] But at that time, Pak believed in the "wide, sturdy bridge"—again, one of the material symbols of Gangnam development. Perhaps not coincidentally, the first of the series of disasters in Gangnam struck a bridge, severing the very physical connection between the two hostile sides.

Silver Stallion Never Goes Away: Two Films on Ŭnma Apartments

In his photo-essay book *Fretful City* (*Chojohan tosi,* 2010), the photographer and critic Young June Lee (Yi Yŏngjun) makes a controversial argument for "class" (*kyŏk*) in ferroconcrete as an example of the "desolate beauty" (*sangmangmi*) he finds in Seoul's urban landscapes. The overabundance of concrete structures—ranging from omnipresent apartment complexes to such iconic buildings as the Sejong Center for the Performing Arts (Sejong munhwa hoegwan, 1978) in the old downtown and the Seoul Arts Center (Yesurŭi chŏndang, 1988) in Gangnam—has been roundly panned as an unsavory legacy of authoritarian-era architecture. Lee sees a certain hypocrisy in the fashionable "disavowal" of concrete for "being dreary, spewing toxin, [and] ruining the environment," among other things, even as it carries the weight of "the modern world on its shoulders."[30] Lee illustrates his point with a series of photographs depicting massive volumes of concrete used for essential urban infrastructure, many of which can be found in the bridges over the Han (see plate 3). Similar to Bong Joon-ho's film *The Host,* Lee's bridge photographs show both the strange beauty of concrete and its embedded traumatic associations:

> Compared to the other Han River bridges, the Sŏngsu Bridge has massively voluminous piers, and a painful backstory attached to them. Needless to say, I am referring to the trauma of the collapse . . . In fact, it was a deck slab that failed, without any connection to the piers. Photographs of the collapse show that only the deck slab fell down. Nevertheless, the reconstruction expanded the bridge, including the piers. It is easy to tell how large Sŏngsu is in comparison with the neighboring Yŏngdong Bridge. Next to Sŏngsu, Yŏngdong's piers look almost like slim

chopsticks. Sŏngsu's fattened piers are to withstand the heavier load from the structurally reinforced deck. It is a bitter irony that the fat, sturdy-looking piers of Sŏngsu came as a result of the traumatic accident.[31]

The bridge that Pak Wansŏ's narrator once deemed "wide and sturdy" from his toilet seat in a Murŭng apartment was probably Yŏngdong and not Sŏngsu. The latter first opened in 1979, a year after the story's publication. The shock of the bridge collapse must have affected public perception dramatically, as the Yŏngdong Bridge now appears miniscule in comparison to the reconstructed Sŏngsu. Even Cho Sehŭi, whose dire warnings were quoted in the chapter introduction ("Remove the ferroconcrete, and everything would collapse, and only grains of sand would remain to drift everywhere"), dared not imagine that concrete might fail. Cho's words came true at least on one count, though: some of the "sand-like people" were dispersed from Gangnam just as the concrete-built land of dreams began to disintegrate. At the time of the bridge collapse, class tensions across the river, as in Pak's story, were already firmly entrenched. Amidst the shock of the disaster, the social polarization within Gangnam became newly apparent.

Morae (sand) is the original Korean title of the documentary *My Father's House* directed by Kangyu Garam. In this autobiographical film, the director reflects on the experience of losing an "apartment game" of real estate speculation.[32] The house Kangyu's father owned is a unit in the Ŭnma (silver stallion) Apartment Complex—a colossal 4,424-unit mass housing complex with 28 towers on a 60-acre plot of land. This largest apartment complex in Gangnam is also one of the most diverse in terms of residents' socioeconomic backgrounds, for the majority of units are leased out to those who move in temporarily to place their children in nearby elite schools and to be in the proximity of the *hag'wŏn* (cram school) private education empire built around Ŭnma. The Kangyu family's resident homeownership in Ŭnma would ordinarily have accorded them prestige, but there was the opposite effect. The film is an intimate introspection of the family's struggle to stay in Gangnam while the proverbial walls were closing in. The original title *Sand* has multiple connotations, each of which constitutes a narrative of displacement on a personal and/or societal level. Taken together, they interlace into a multilayered saga involving the family, the apartment complex, and Gangnam at large.

First, the desert sands. The Middle East construction boom from the early 1970s through the mid-1980s sent many Korean male workers to toil in the desert sands, separating families for many years in the process. The father of the Kangyu family went to Saudi Arabia, missing the birth of his daughter, who would grow up to recount her father's story on film. The petrodollars the father and his fellow workers earned for their companies and remitted to their families back home in turn fueled a domestic construction boom spearheaded by Gangnam development. While there were some major corporations in the construction business, especially the branches of the so-called *chaebŏl* conglomerates—family-controlled business empires—like Hyundai, at the outset there were mostly small- and midsize startups without any name recognition. Once Gangnam development gathered full steam, these smaller companies became household names due to the soaring popularity of their apartment complexes. One of them was Hanbo Group, the builder of Ŭnma.

Second, a pavilion on the sand. The tremendous success of Ŭnma pushed Hanbo to the upper echelons of the newfangled "construction *chaebŏl*" companies that bulked up their size in the booming economy. Hanbo, in particular, aggressively expanded its business to other industries, including iron and steel. Entry into the heavy industry required huge new capital investments, for which private companies routinely greased the wheels of high-ranking officials and prominent politicians through bribes and kickbacks in order to secure credit and loans from the financial sector tightly controlled by the economic bureaucracy of the authoritarian state. Hanbo conformed to the well-established practice of collusion (*yuch'ak*) without realizing the changing political economic climate of the 1990s.[33] Once the collusion was exposed, Hanbo's business empire turned into a classic pavilion on the sand (see introduction) as the founder and chairman, Chŏng T'aesu (1923–2018), went to prison twice on corruption charges. The final bankruptcy of Hanbo Group in January 1997 triggered a domino effect of similar bankruptcies that decimated construction *chaebŏl* in a matter of months, and ultimately led to the devastating IMF Crisis by the end of the year. Concrete and steel, the two main ingredients of Hanbo's magical rise, could not hold the company together as it succumbed to the quicksand of financial crisis.

Third, drifters like sand. The IMF Crisis revealed a fundamental weakness in Korea's "economic miracle" of the twentieth century—debt-financed growth. Debt/credit was the cement of all business activities large and small, while government policy, particularly economic planning and industrial policy, was the rebar that structured the national economy. This metaphorical ferroconcrete structure failed, much like the literal collapses of Sŏngsu and Sampoong, when the weight of concrete (corporate debt) far exceeded the endurance limits of the rebar (policy and institution). Corporate bankruptcies caused mass layoffs and skyrocketing unemployment. Consequently, Kangyu's father joined the ranks of jobless middle-aged men who were drifting like loose grains of sand: "Father was forced to retire due to the IMF [Crisis]. He told me later that he had pretended to go to work proudly every day but actually loitered elsewhere.

Many forced retirees soon opened small businesses with their lump-sum retirement allowance [*t'oejikkŭm*], but he bided his time . . . eventually we were able to buy an apartment house of Ŭnma in Taech'idong. Already more than twenty years old, Ŭnma was showing its age; during the rainy season the surrounding streets were flooded regularly."[34] Going from an unemployed loiterer to a Gangnam homeowner was such a dramatic turnaround of fortune that the family initially celebrated it as "a come-from-behind grand slam home run" (*yŏkchŏn mallu homnŏn*), using a homely baseball metaphor. From then on, their fortunes were carried by the post-crisis speculation frenzy, driven this time by soaring household debt. The Kim Dae Jung administration (1998–2002) decided to stimulate the crisis-stricken economy by easing regulations on the housing market as well as the consumer credit market. At the beginning of the new millennium, Gangnam became once again the epicenter of speculation as the relaxed rules enabled wholesale demolition and reconstruction (*chaegŏnch'uk*) of existing apartment complexes, none of which were older than thirty years. *My Father's House* begins with a montage of news coverage on the apartment reconstruction bonanza. As the largest apartment complex in Gangnam, not to mention its apparent state of disrepair, Ŭnma was a prime target among real estate speculators and government regulators alike. Watching the television news coverage of incredible price hikes on Ŭnma was, however, her father's grim face. From there, the film recounts a familiar story not just to Koreans but also to Americans, Spaniards, and other members of the global lower and middle classes who have experienced similar predicaments since the 2008 financial crisis:

> Father took out a loan of one hundred million won [approximately eighty-three thousand USD at the time] using our home as collateral. It didn't take long for the debt to snowball from one hundred million to seven hundred million won. Father was already deep in anguish when I began feeling odd about the large amount of the loan . . . The interest on the principal was ballooning, but so was Ŭnma's housing bubble.
> . . .
> As I was observing the emotional rollercoaster my parents were on whenever the housing prices went up or down, I became curious about what made my parents so fearful. The Ŭnma apartment was a fruit borne of Father's wherewithal and Mother's dedication to her children's education and desire for wealth accumulation [*chaet'ek'ŭ*]. Little by little, it was eaten away. Ŭnma's real estate bubble began to burst as the economy went downhill in 2008. The confident smiles on my parents' faces were fading; the apartment price was falling.[35]

It was at this point that Kangyu decided to pick up the camera and start documenting the emotional toll the apartment was taking on her family. They barely persevered under the weight of debt that felt like a ton of crumbling concrete. The film is a careful study of family life on the verge of disintegration. All members appear to be keenly aware of the stakes: should the wager on their aging silver stallion—Ŭnma, the father's house—fail, they would be unable to stick together, like the proverbial grains of sand. Kangyu sincerely credits Ŭnma for her family avoiding such a cruel fate, saying, "So many families went their separate ways in the aftermath of the IMF [Crisis], but we were able to stick together for another decade thanks to our ownership of a Gangnam apartment."[36] Some families were relatively lucky, others were not. Regardless, they all fit the profile of Chamsil residents in Cho Sehŭi's stories. Living a stone's throw from Chamsil, Ŭnma residents were also "sand-like people" who might deserve consolation for being stuck "in a sandy apartment, on a brutal land of sands."

Perhaps no one is more deserving of consolation than Eun-hee (Ŭnhŭi), a fictional teenage girl from Ŭnma in Kim Bora's debut feature, *House of Hummingbird* (*Pŏlsae*, 2018; hereafter *Hummingbird*). A story loosely based on the filmmaker's own childhood, *Hummingbird* garnered universal accolades, winning a total of fifty-nine awards from film festivals around the world. This international acclaim was a major achievement for the perennially underfunded independent film industry, contributing to Korean cinema's banner year that culminated with Bong Joon-ho's *Parasite*. *Hummingbird* might have received many more honors domestically had it not been in direct competition with *Parasite*. These two film narratives converge on the themes of social class—hierarchy, conflicts, and solidarity (or lack thereof)—played out at the level of intimate personal relationships, although they cannot be more different from each other in terms of tone and style. *Parasite* is a crisply shot satire with Hitchcockian alternations of humor and suspense. In contrast, the hazy cinematography of *Hummingbird* presents a moving coming-of-age story, with the joys and sorrows of adolescence. As such, they represent contrasting "ways of seeing" the same issue of class divide, one being sardonic and the other sincere. As a caricature of class stratification, *Parasite* limits sympathetic responses toward any character. In contrast, the earnest tone of *Hummingbird* and Eun-hee's emotional honesty renders more humanized albeit imperfect characters in her surround. Consequently, class hierarchy and conflicts in *Hummingbird* are not as overt as in *Parasite*, yet they are powerfully resonant on a personal level.

Eun-hee lives in a 1,200-square-foot apartment—a uniform size for all 4,424 units of Ŭnma—with her parents and two older siblings, a brother and a sister. Her parents run a small rice mill, a traditional business of rural origin, tucked in the sprawling market arcade (*sangga*) next to the Ŭnma Complex. They are people from a working-class background serving the middle-strata residents in Ŭnma and nearby apartment complexes. Long hours of hard work are etched on their tired faces, like the real-life parents in *My Father's House,* who also run a small shop in the old downtown to afford their life in Gangnam. The difference is that Eun-hee's parents work in the same area where they live, though it is not clear whether they own or rent their apartment. For this reason, Eun-hee's position in class hierarchy is readily apparent to local residents even though she does not look or behave differently from her peers.[37] She lives in one of the "identical apartments" in Ŭnma and attends a local all-girls' middle school wearing the same student uniform. Still, Eun-hee is a "daughter from the mill" (*pang'akkan chip ttal*), a lowly working-class kid in status-obsessed Gangnam. It does not seem to affect young Eun-hee much until she encounters the first moment of truth. She has been in a budding romantic relationship with a boy from a neighboring school, and viewers learn that the boy's father is a medical doctor. One day, the teenage couple is out on a date around the apartment complex playground, only to be confronted by the boy's mother. She asks her son, "Is this the daughter from the mill?" Before dragging the boy away, the mother shoots a withering stare at Eun-hee with an unspoken message of bone-chilling disdain: a doctor's son cannot mingle with a miller's daughter.

In the midst of adolescent turmoil with her family, friends, and romantic interests, Eun-hee finds solace in an unexpected place, an afterschool *hag'wŏn* for classical Chinese learning. A newly hired teacher named Yŏngji, a weary-looking female college student appearing older than other students, who enjoys smoking cigarettes alone in a cool, detached manner, forms a surprisingly easy rapport with Eun-hee. When Eun-hee has a serious falling-out with her best friend, who also attends the same *hag'wŏn* class, Yŏngji tries to broker a peace by volunteering to sing for them. In one of the most stunning scenes of the film, Yŏngji then breaks out into "A Severed Finger" ("Challin sonkarak"), a protest song with graphic depictions of the horrible working conditions of Korean industrial labor.[38]

> Looking at my severed finger / I drank a shot of soju at night
> The machine rattles still echoed in my ears / I looked up at the skies
> The night I buried my severed finger / was the night I shed bitter tears
> My youth passed me by in a bloody uniform / I felt such a deep sorrow
> Day by day I consoled my worn-out body / drinking shots of bitter soju
> Reminiscing of the day I'd left / my hometown and my mother behind
> Getting drunk, I wandered around / the hill where I'd buried my finger
> Step by plodding step I roamed / drunk on cold, cold soju.

From the wistful look on Yŏngji's face, even a casual viewer might be able to tell that the song is not really for the girls but for herself, a kind of self-consolation. Furthermore, an informed viewer could deduce from this and other subtle clues in the film that Yŏngji was a left-wing college activist at the time of great political upheavals, when many idealistic youths like her dreamed of building a revolutionary alliance with the working class. Sadly, they were destined to witness the historic downfall of the global Left after the collapse of Soviet communism.

The unlikely yet beautiful bond between Yŏngji and Eun-hee grows stronger when Eun-hee pays a surprise visit to her teacher's office right after the disheartening encounter with her boyfriend's mother. The consolation she receives from Yŏngji leads the teenager to another eye-opening revelation of social polarization and class conflicts. After drinking tea quietly, they set out on a walk past a redevelopment zone slated for eviction and demolition. Looking at the protestors' banners (one reads "Not even death can take us out of here," and another "Oppose redevelopment to death"), they launch into a moving dialogue:

> [Eun-hee]: Why do the people living here hang banners?
>
> [Yŏngji]: So that they don't get their homes taken away.
>
> [Eun-hee]: Why would anyone take away someone else's home?
>
> [Yŏngji]: So many absurd things are happening, aren't they?
>
> [Eun-hee]: I feel sorry for them, their houses look cold.
>
> [Yŏngji]: Don't pity them, though. We shouldn't pity so readily without knowing much.

A life in Gangnam therefore does not shield young Eun-hee from class tensions and polarization in pre–IMF Crisis Korea. Furthermore, *Hummingbird* unflinchingly takes on other difficult aspects of the teenage girl's life, such as domestic violence, parents' marital issues, juvenile delinquency, intra-family gender discrimination, and physical scarring. The film avoids patronizing treatments of its young characters, or oversimplification of the moral complexities of their everyday lives. Eun-hee's emotions may be in frequent turmoil, but the film maintains an even keel—until a disaster upends the tenuous balance.

Just like many other families in Ŭnma, Eun-hee's family lives there primarily for college preparatory education. In their case, it is specifically for Eun-hee's brother, the family's "golden boy" who aspires to enter the nation's top-ranked university. Eun-hee's sister, on the other hand, is the proverbial black sheep who somehow failed to secure a spot in the Eighth School District of Gangnam and instead attends a high school across the river.[39] The cross-river divide in society at large is not only present within Eun-hee's family but also compounded by gender hierarchy. As opposed to the imperious brother, Eun-hee gets along fine with her sister, who only plays a minor role in her life until the day of the disaster. Upon hearing the news of the Sŏngsu Bridge collapse at school, Eun-hee instantly realizes that her sister may have been on her way to school, crossing this very bridge. Eun-hee goes into a panic for that obvious reason, although the association is delayed for the viewer. This fictional crisis is based on the terrible reality that eight students of Muhak Girls' High School perished on that fateful morning, all of whom were commuting daily by bus from Gangnam, just like Eun-hee's sister. The unraveling of events after the shocking moment follows the classic bildungsroman theme of the loss of innocence. From the tragedy, Eun-hee emerges stronger and more clear-eyed about her place in her family, at school, and in society at large. Simply put, she ages.

Teenagers get stronger as they grow older, but buildings do not. Unlike the adolescents who come to shoulder the weight of personal, familial, and societal ambitions, buildings tend to become weaker with age. Some structures may mature gracefully even if they are made of gray concrete, in line with Young June Lee's notion of desolate beauty. However, the concrete buildings of Ŭnma, along with most other apartment complexes built before the IMF Crisis, did not age well, to put it mildly. There is no hypocrisy about disavowing the lack of "class" in the concrete apartments of pre-Crisis Gangnam. The sand mixed in with cement to build the Gangnam apartments was, as Cho Sehŭi lamented, dredged from the "dying river." Environmental damage aside, it was considered excellent construction aggregate, superior to sea sand or artificial aggregate. Hanbo and other construction companies benefited from getting the good material at a low cost, yet the results were poor in terms of building quality and durability. In fact, neither builders nor homeowners were particularly interested in the long-term health of high-rise apartments because of the speculative, short-term orientation of the Korean housing market. When the Kangyu family moved in, Ŭnma was already in such a poor shape ("more than twenty years old, Ŭnma was showing its age") that some residents would joke about downgrading it from "silver" to "bronze" stallion (*tongma*). Barely a decade later, the deterioration was far advanced, as seen in *My Father's House*.[40] If the lifespan of an apartment was similar to that of a horse, what did an Ŭnma apartment look like when it was at fifteen years of age? A gracefully matured building with the desolate beauty of gray concrete that befit the name "silver stallion"? The celebrated cinematography of *Hummingbird* may provide an answer.

In the cold open of *Hummingbird*, Eun-hee is seen mistakenly ringing the doorbell, and then pounding on the door, of an Ŭnma unit that turns out to be just one floor below her family's. This is a common slipup in real life that is almost cliché in Korean literature and film. After throwing a tantrum at her absent mom, she realizes her mistake, finds her rightful place, and disappears into the door opened by the mom. The camera then slowly pans out to rows of shabby, near-identical units on the long corridors of the drab concrete building (figure 3.3), another visual cliché of the Korean "apartment movie" genre.[41] Thus, nothing in this picture should really surprise a Korean viewer. The film's mise-en-scène is realistic, as the filming location and story setting are both Ŭnma apartments. But there is a catch: a twenty-three-year time lapse between the story's setting in 1994 and the actual shooting in 2017. Walls with deep cracks, peeling paint, and discoloration from mold are all disturbing signs of premature aging and disrepair even for the forty-year-old Ŭnma Complex of today. It is hard to imagine that the fifteen-year-old concrete structure as portrayed in the film would have looked just like this. Nevertheless, the film's depiction is an accurate one for viewers familiar with the area. Director Kim Bora, for her part, has underscored the importance of a monthlong location shooting at Ŭnma for "weaving the texture" of the film, leaving no such essential elements to chance.[42] The deliberately unkempt visuals imply that Ŭnma has changed little since the early 1990s, at least in the collective memory of those who lived in the apartment complex or knew it well enough.

Figure 3.3. Identical apartments: Exterior corridors of the Ŭnma Complex. Source: screenshot from *House of Hummingbird*.

Indifference and Ignorance amid Disaster

The Ŭnma Apartment Complex and the Sŏngsu Bridge opened in the same year, 1979. Fifteen years later, the apartments were already seriously geromorphic, and the bridge collapsed amid unheeded warnings.[43] The city officials and construction companies were found responsible, and eventually held accountable, for the bridge disaster. In the aftermath, the government belatedly began load testing all the bridges over the Han and found several to be under similar stress. In general, the majority of Gangnam residents seemed strangely unfazed. They all saw the grave dangers of shoddy construction in Sŏngsu; they were surrounded by visual reminders of such shoddiness in Ŭnma and other apartments where they lived. Nonetheless, few seemed to exhibit a change of behavior, let alone a change of heart. Once again, Cho Sehŭi's earlier words on Chamsil proved prescient: "Regrettably, much like the city officials, Chamsil residents are clinging to the quantity, not quality, and some of them are even bluffing as if they were living someone else's life." Except for those who were directly affected by the disaster, like Eun-hee's family in *Hummingbird,* Gangnam residents did not seem to care, even for the victims. There was minimal public memorialization of the lives lost due to the bridge collapse to begin with, and none existed in Gangnam. The monument for the thirty-two deaths of the Sŏngsu Bridge collapse was established in an obscure rest area off the expressway on the northern riverbank, hidden from public view and accessible only by automobile. Only Muhak Girls' High School, also in Gangbuk, still holds a commemorative event for the victims, who included eight of its own students.

Gangnam's general indifference to the bridge disaster might have been an expression of "vague hostility," as Pak Wansŏ referred to the decades-old class divide over "the putrid river." Or, it could have been, as Cho Sehŭi implied, that Gangnam residents maintained an uncritical belief in their own security, blissfully ignorant of how Gangnam was built ("They think of Chamsil as a land for apartment buildings, and they live there because the apartments are there"). Either way, they were neither attentive to nor appreciative about the quality of ferroconcrete that sustained their land of dreams. The consequences of this unthinking indifference were severe. Awful as it was, the Sŏngsu Bridge collapse was only the first in a series of deadly man-made disasters. The next one could not be ignored by Gangnam residents due to the location, causes, and magnitude of the tragedy, and the numbers of elite residents included in the massive death toll. A Korean-style "disaster capitalism" was about to befall the heartland of Gangnam.

CHAPTER 4

Solidarity amid Disaster Capitalism
The Sampoong Collapse

> Your laughter becomes ocean waves,
> Becomes nightly rainfall on a dark seaside.
> It stays there, under the shade of rocks no one remembers.
> I follow your laughter, follow my dreams,
> Follow white, foamy waves, follow seagulls.
> —Kim Kwangsŏk, "Your Laughter" ("Kŭdae us'ŭmsori," 1989)

It would not be an exaggeration to call Kim Kwangsŏk (1964–1996) the troubadour of post-authoritarian Korea. He was christened *kagaek* (itinerant bard), a moniker that served as the title of Kim's posthumous tribute album by his fellow musicians. There is a popular street named after him in Taegu, the city of his birth, which has claimed the UNESCO "City of Music" title since 2017. Born in 1964, Kim moved from Taegu to Seoul at the age of four along with his family and grew up in the working-class neighborhood of Ch'angsindong, located in the Tongdaemun (East Gate) District of the old city north of the Han. He attended Myŏngji University in the Sŏdaemun (West Gate) District, where an underground music culture had flourished around the area colleges since the 1970s, especially in the Sinch'on area.[1] At college, he was involved in the People's Song Movement (PSM) as a standout singer whose rendition of "Mung Bean Flower" ("Noktu kkot"), a protest song adaptation of Kim Chiha's eponymous poem, became legendary.[2] Kim Kwangsŏk performed "Mung Bean Flower" as a member of the PSM vocal group Nochatsa at a concert on the heels of the June Democratic Uprising of 1987. This collaboration was instrumental to the group's surprising commercial success in the mainstream popular music market into the next decade. In addition to his PSM involvement, Kim befriended a group of amateur college singer-songwriters. Together they recorded two albums under the name Tongmurwŏn (Zoo), both released in 1988 to great acclaim. When he launched a solo career the next year, Kim was in the enviable position of being able to claim two distinct yet interrelated heritages as his own. One was PSM and its political consciousness, and the other was college underground music and its urbane sensibilities. As a legitimate heir to both heritages, Kim became an instant folk hero among young, high school, and college-age audiences, who flocked to catch his performances in the intimate setting of a small-theater concert (*sogŭkchang kong'yŏn*) (figure 4.1).

Kim Kwangsŏk's career cannot be separated from the small-theater concert venue he had mastered. On top of his superb talent as a singer, Kim had a knack for charming audiences with humor and warmth as a gifted storyteller. The spatial proximity between performer and audience in a small-theater setting was conducive to Kim's style of music and performance. While he did have a television and radio presence, his star power owed far less to mainstream media exposure than to the relentless concert touring he carried out throughout his career. Upon completing one thousand concerts in the first six years of solo work, Kim gave a celebratory performance at his familiar venue, Hakchŏn Theater. Hakchŏn is located in Seoul's premier theater district of Taehangno, about two kilometers from where he grew up. After his death, Hakchŏn Theater became a memorial site for Kim's legacy. In 2008, the theater installed a bronze-plaque monument

Figure 4.1. Kim Kwangsŏk in concert at the Hakchŏn Theater. Source: Yodeanso, CC-BY-SA-4.0.

on the outer wall and inaugurated an annual Kim Kwangsŏk cover song contest. Public remembrances of Kim Kwangsŏk are closely tied to Hakchŏn and other similar venues concentrated in Taehangno and Sinch'on, the two theater districts representing the north of the Han (Gangbuk). Although his first solo concert happened to take place in a small theater called the Kyemong Arts Center in Togoktong, Gangnam, Kim was not associated with the boomtown on the south of the Han in any significant way until about a half year before his tragic, controversial death in January 1996.

Your Laughter, Our Loss: Dreams of Kim Kwangsŏk

It was on the evening of June 29, 1995, that Kim Kwangsŏk stepped into the studio of KMTV, a pioneering cable television music channel that had begun broadcasting only three months prior. KMTV was created by the old-school music industry that had been relocated to Gangnam's Sinsadong Circuit (see chapter 1) and eager to tap into the newly emerging youth market for socially conscious singer-songwriters like Kim. The studio in Nonhyŏndong had a capacity of over five hundred, more than double the size of Hakchŏn or any other small theater, which generally had fewer than two hundred seats. Kim noted this difference at the start of the show, but soon he was his usual intimate self, entertaining and playful at times, and pensive and sentimental at others. The live broadcast show billed as the "Super Concert: Unforgettable Blue Light of Youth" went as planned until the 45-minute mark, when Kim was introducing the next song he would play, a Korean contrafactum of Bob Dylan's "Don't Think Twice, It's All Right":

> The next song is "A Car on Two Wheels" ["Tubak'wiro kanŭn chadongch'a"]. In fact, if we look around, many preposterous events are becoming commonplace. Another outrageous incident happened today—the Sampoong Department Store collapsed. Those of you who arrived early haven't heard the news yet, right [laughs]? Nine hundred people are under the rubble, they say. Anyway, I don't know the exact number. I hear some murmuring in the audience [laughs]. Well, why don't you check out the news once the show's over? [Pause] Upon hearing the news, I was worried and called home. My wife told me she'd been in Sampoong today. I asked her what had happened, and she said she had left at 3:30 p.m. [audience laughs]. I don't know. Well, so many absurd things are happening and just unsettling our minds. I hope for minimal casualties. Now, let me start the song.

It is a jarring experience, decades after the fact, to hear Kim's remarks on the news of the disaster and observe the audience's real-time reaction. As Kim shared the story of the department store collapse, to be sure, his eyes showed a flash of outrage. Yet he could not suppress laughter, or rather a sardonic mirth (*hŏt us'ŭm*), as he lamented such events becoming all too familiar. When he wryly mentioned his wife's close call—she had gotten out only a couple of hours before the building collapse—the audience laughed in sympathy, as if it were a minor disturbance that could happen in their own daily lives. There was an implicit consensus that the show must go on.

So Kim moved on to the next song, "A Car on Two Wheels," which was in line with his comments on the unsettling absurdities of the times: "A car on two wheels, a bike on four wheels / A plane traveling under water, a sailboat flying in the sky." Frustration at the upside-down world marred by a series of disasters was weighing on everyone, including Kim Kwangsŏk in particular. Signs of mental fatigue were evident in the singer's facial expression in the waning minutes of the show, which happened to be his last video-recorded performance. Before singing the final song "Rise" ("Irŏna"), he made a stunning admission, which carried a tone of finality: "For some time, I was heavyhearted, feeling gloomy. Really, I thought about not living anymore. But I said to myself, if I was going to live anyway, I should find something to have fun with and enjoy life." Depression was evoked in the song's lyrics—"Standing in the middle of a dark night, cannot see an inch ahead / Where to go, where is it, cried out for answers in vain"—and the title, "Rise," might well refer to one of the most debilitating symptoms of the condition, namely the struggle to get out of bed.

Despite these warning signs, Kim Kwangsŏk's suicide in January 1996 was a shock to his acquaintances and fans, and the larger public. Mental health conditions like depression continue to be stigmatized and poorly understood in everyday Korean public discourse.[3] Actually, there were markers of depression in his early works as well. In "My Dream" ("Nae kkum"), Kim sings:

Buried among people who can't escape
we, too, live our forgetful lives
Unable to look up the skies
everyone's tired, tired, tired, tired
even as the sun rises from the east just like yesterday.

This song was released two years after the Democratic Uprising of 1987, which had once given so much hope for political change and social reform. Despite the palpable tone of disappointment, Kim seemed to keep sight of the goal for social change as he continued to perform select protest songs from the PSM repertoire whenever he could, including on network television broadcasts. Then one day came the news of nine hundred people under the concrete rubble. Kim was merely three kilometers away from the disaster zone, preparing for the show that would begin in about an hour or so. He had to break the terrible news to the unsuspecting audience, which he did with awkward laughter; the audience responded in kind. News of disasters were mind-numbingly frequent at that point. Two years prior, a plane crash had cost sixty-eight lives. Sixteen months earlier, a ferry had capsized, drowning nearly three hundred passengers; eight months back, the Sŏngsu Bridge collapse had caused thirty-six deaths, nine of them schoolgirls on a commuter bus (see chapter 3). Two months back, a gas explosion at the Taegu subway construction site had taken 101 lives, including 42 students from Yŏngnam Middle School. Kim's laugh, more than the sober statement he made or the satirical song he sang, revealed an acute sense of loss—the loss of innocent lives, the loss of shock and outrage at recurring disasters, and perhaps his own melancholic loss of hopes and dreams.

Dreams of Gangnam or the Roots of Korea's Disaster Capitalism

Disaster capitalism is the term Canadian journalist Naomi Klein coined in her bestselling book *The Shock Doctrine*. Arriving between two major shocks originating in the U.S., Hurricane Katrina in 2005 and the global financial crisis of 2008, the book lays out a sweeping indictment of the rapacity of neoliberal capitalism, ranging from General Pinochet's U.S.-supported military coup in Chile in 1973 to the "Shock and Awe" of the 2003 U.S. invasion of Iraq, and beyond. There is no shortage of shocking examples for Klein's thesis on disaster capitalism, which she defines as "orchestrated raids on the public sphere in the wake of catastrophic events, combined with the treatment of disasters as exciting market opportunities."[4] The archetype of shock she establishes is torture, especially the kind developed by psychiatrists and psychologists in collaboration with the coercive state apparatus in the twentieth century. Klein's main argument is that this kind of devastating psychological shock can be mass-produced by a disaster, whether it is military, political, economic, or natural. Once "the original disaster—the coup, the terrorist attack, the market meltdown, the war, the tsunami, the hurricane—puts the entire population into a state of collective shock," disaster-stricken societies behave like severe torture victims curled up in a fetal position, and "often give up things they would otherwise fiercely protect."[5] Klein cites several instances where the shock doctrine was fully operationalized, such as the economic "shock therapy" applied to Russia after the collapse of the USSR and the rise of the American homeland security state after the 9/11 attacks. However, the debate remains on the extent to which the shock doctrine applies to openly premeditated—and therefore not so shocking—events such as the U.S. invasion and occupation of Iraq. Furthermore, one could plausibly argue that (neo)colonial conquest, military coups, or any kind of political violence in favor of capitalist expansion is a manifestation of the shock doctrine: "Capitalism, after all, has always been a shock doctrine of selfish predation, as one can discover from Hobbes and Locke, Marx and Weber," wrote the late journalist Alexander Cockburn in a critical review of *The Shock Doctrine*.[6]

Let us set aside the shock doctrine for the moment and consider the term "disaster capitalism" specifically in the Korean context. The first half of the 1990s was supposedly a golden age of Korean capitalism. Having recently debuted as a host nation for the 1988 Summer Olympic Games, Korea experienced a ten-year boom that culminated in its accession to the Organisation for Economic Co-operation and Development (OECD) in 1996. And yet, it could not extricate itself from disasters large and small, which made the population feel deeply insecure. More often than not, official disaster responses further eroded public trust in the institutions responsible for disaster prevention. The Sŏngsu Bridge collapse, for example, prompted a nationwide emergency audit on major buildings and infrastructure; remarkably, Sampoong passed the audit three times.[7] Twenty days after the Sampoong collapse, the National Assembly hastily enacted the Disaster Management Law (Chaenan kwallipŏp) as a redress for the costly confusion and missteps that plagued the official rescue effort at Sampoong. This legislation was expanded into the Basic Law for Disaster and Emergency Management, which established the National Emergency Management Agency in 2004. However, the wave of disasters resumed ten years later. The Sewŏl Ferry sinking in April 2014 resulted in the deaths of 305 people, including 250 high school students on a field trip. It was the second-biggest postwar calamity after Sampoong, and arguably even worse than Sampoong in terms of official response, since a timely, competent rescue operation at sea could have saved many of the lives lost.[8] Less than a decade after Sewŏl, when all the acrimony it had brought on was still lingering, 151 revelers who came out to celebrate Halloween in 2022 were crushed to death in an overcrowded back street of It'aewŏn, Seoul.

For Korea's predatory capitalists, such disasters are less about creating an "exciting market opportunity" to exploit than about bearing the costs necessary for their business. Put another way, the Korean-style disaster capitalism is a capitalism that invites disaster in pursuit of profit maximization, by cutting all possible corners in wanton disregard of public and workplace safety standards.

The record number of casualties alone would make Sampoong a particularly egregious case, but the coup de disgrace was the owner of the department store, Yi Chun (1922–2003), a paradigmatic disaster capitalist. When reporters goaded him for his apparent lack of remorse, Yi shot back: "The collapse didn't just inflict harm on customers, but also damaged my company's assets!" He strenuously refused to accept any responsibility for the disaster and actively displaced blame onto his own son, the chief executive officer of the department store. In fact, Yi Chun's reckless decision-making provided both the root and immediate causes of the disaster, ranging from illicitly building another story on top of the originally approved four-story design to continuing store operations instead of immediately evacuating the building when the roof was found buckling many hours before the collapse. Despite torrential public furor over his culpability and brazenness, Yi received a relatively light sentence of seven and a half years in prison. He served out his prison term and died shortly after release. One of the line-level prosecutors of the Sampoong trial recalls:

> Mr. Yi Chun, the chairman of the Sampoong Department Store, was an old man . . . We spent a lot of time reviewing and debating legal principles to settle on the charges and sentencing demands . . . "No way to charge for murder"; "How can we recommend only seven and a half years"; "We cannot demand a longer sentence"; "The [murder] charge won't stick"; "Will the public, and bereaved families in particular, accept our decision?"; and so forth. Victimized families and the public wouldn't accept the prosecutorial demand of seven-and-a-half-year prison term. But I had no other choice. It broke my heart. So I had to say at the final court hearing, "We have considered a murder charge, but the legal principles won't allow for it. I sincerely regret to demand only seven and a half years [of prison for involuntary manslaughter]." (Yi Sanggwŏn, Seoul Central District Prosecutor's Office)[9]

Yi Chun's life as the ultimate disaster capitalist inspired at least two super-villain characters in popular culture—one named Cho P'ir'yŏn in the television drama series *Giant* (*Chaiant'ŭ*, 2010) and the other named Kim Chin in Hwang Sŏg'yŏng's *Dreams of Gangnam*. Cho P'ir'yŏn is a composite character of many real-life villains covering the gamut of Gangnam's dark side, from political corruption to organized crime; Kim Chin is a fictional replica of Yi Chun in Hwang's novel built around the Sampoong disaster as the foundational event. Like the real-life figure, the fictional Kim Chin was a creature of South Korea's anticommunist right-wing state security apparatus—spying for the Imperial Japanese Army in Manchuria during the colonial period, then for the Counter

Intelligence Corps (CIC) in the U.S. Army–occupied southern Korea, and launching a military career at the outbreak of the Korean War. After the military coup of 1961, Yi/Kim participated in founding the Korean Central Intelligence Agency (KCIA). The meteoric rise of his business fortunes owed a great deal to his connections with CIC and KCIA, through which he won many lucrative contracts in Korea and wartime Vietnam. Most notably, he was able to secure a former U.S. military warehouse site shortly before a major announcement about Gangnam development that would eventually bring the Supreme Court and the Prosecution Service Office to the area. The luxury department store his construction company had built on this prime parcel of real estate soon became the crown jewel of his business empire, only to crater most spectacularly in just five years. The life story of Yi Chun/Kim Chin illustrates how Korea's crony capitalism transmogrified into disaster capitalism.

Hwang Sŏg'yŏng's literary method with respect to Yi Chun/Kim Chin was to make the character a puppet of the historical master narrative. In the author's afterword of *Dreams of Gangnam*, he explains the rationale:

> I thought about our [traditional] puppet theater, *Kkoktugaksi norŭm*. The puppet's acting and motion is unnatural or exaggerated because it's manipulated by a puppet master. Its voice, also uttered by the master, is as comical as its motion. However, it is this comical distancing effect [*Verfremdungseffekt*] that creates formative types of human lives too complex to sort out.
>
> So I came up with the idea: How about streamlining the breathtaking journey of Korean capitalist modernization and its extraordinary episodes during the past three decades with such simple puppet characters?[10]

It is an intriguing idea, even though Hwang's stated technique is more like classic caricature than Brechtian *Verfremdungseffekt,* and perhaps literary fiction is not the best medium to execute the idea. Hwang's novel was in direct competition with the television drama *Giant,* which had a distinctive advantage in terms of staging exaggerated *kkoktugaksi* characters like Cho P'ir'yŏn—a greedy capitalist, raging militarist, corrupt politician, and shady crime boss all rolled into one Frankensteinian villain. Instead of creating an entirely fictional character, Hwang devotes a good third of *Dreams of Gangnam* to Kim Chin's biography, which roughly parallels Yi Chun's real-life trajectory. The fictionalized biography is full of imagined encounters with real historical figures, such as the military dictator Park Chung Hee and his henchmen. In a sense, Kim Chin serves as a Forrest Gump character for postwar Korea, as he either witnessed or participated in key moments of history during the latter half of the twentieth century, including the Vietnam War. But there is also a crucial difference between the two characters—while Forrest Gump is a good-hearted, innocent American "country bumpkin" type, Kim Chin is anything but. The odious puppet character of Kim Chin is manipulated by the master narrative of collusion (*yuch'ak*) between the state, the capitalist elite, and the criminal underworld. His "business was a near-dominant player in the government-ordered construction projects thanks to the long-standing personal relationships with the power elites and the slosh funds" he offered them; among his major construction projects before Sampoong were Korea's best-known Christian megachurch—Full Gospel Church (Sunbog'ŭm kyohoe)—in Yŏŭido, the Peace Market (P'yŏnghwa sijang) in Ch'ŏnggyech'ŏn, and "ports, roads, bridges, and even American military facilities in Vietnam."[11] Thus, Yi Chun/Kim Chin had been burnishing his credentials as a disaster capitalist since the early 1960s by profiteering from the shock doctrine of the Vietnam War and by building what would become a hazardous sweatshop complex in Ch'ŏnggyech'ŏn.[12]

Sampoong is often cited as prima facie evidence for Korea's "backward" modernity, not capable of rationally calculating and managing societal risks due to its abnormal, "compressed" modernization.[13] Disasters, however, do not seem to spare "risk societies" in the West that supposedly figured out "a systematic way of dealing with hazards and insecurities induced and introduced by" modernization; some of them, most notably the United States, have suffered deadly structural failures similar to Sampoong and the Sŏngsu Bridge in recent years.[14] Would a normal, uncompressed modernization have resulted in fewer such disasters? The Wikipedia entry "List of structural failures and collapses" details many catastrophic structural failures in North America and Western Europe through the nineteenth and twentieth centuries, indicating that Korea's disaster-prone modernization in the late twentieth century is more normative than anomalous. However, the Korean case is distinguished by the intricate system through which state actors and the political elite collude with disaster capitalists like Yi Chun.

Construction has been one of the leading sectors in government-business collusion, and chapter 3 detailed how another well-connected disaster capitalist from the construction business, Chŏng T'aesu of Hanbo Group, ushered in the IMF Crisis. In fact, Sampoong and Hanbo were minor players compared to the construction arms of giant *chaebŏl* conglomerates, such as Hyundai, Samsung, Daewoo, and Daelim. True to the form of Korean-style disaster capitalism, these *chaebŏl* companies aggressively pursued construction projects in the conflict-laden Middle East during the 1970s–1980s.[15] They were working on both sides of the Iran-Iraq War (1980–1988) under the aegis of the Korean government, when all other foreign companies withdrew from Iran for security reasons.

Disaster struck eventually: on June 30, 1988, an Iraqi fighter jet attacked Iran's Kangan natural gas refinery construction site, killing thirteen Korean workers from Daelim Industries (figure 4.2). Undaunted by mounting criticism at home, the Korean government and construction companies were determined to stay in the war zone. Just twelve days after the Kangan attack, Daelim and the families of the deceased workers reached an agreement on the amount of compensation: 190 million won—approximately 588,000 in current USD—for each victim. Three months later, Daelim quietly resumed the construction in Iran, with international attention focused on the Olympic Games in Seoul. In retrospect, the company brags about how it adopted an ethos of "toughing it out" to complete

Figure 4.2. Disaster capitalism: The Kangan Natural Gas Refinery construction site after an attack. Source: *Chung'ang ilbo,* July 15, 1988, reprinted with permission.

the project, establishing a trusted relationship with the Iranian government that would continue to bring in more lucrative contracts. Daelim also notes that the surviving workers tried even harder and completed the project earlier than scheduled thanks to "the determination to prove that their co-workers would not have died in vain."[16]

It is not uncommon to witness survivors of a catastrophe—such as the Daelim workers in Iran—expressing misguided loyalty to the very company responsible for the disaster they endured. This twisted *mentalité* of disaster capitalism manifested itself in an episode of tragicomedy during the rescue operation at Sampoong. The rescue team found a dutiful employee, having watched over a minor company asset amid the disaster that miraculously spared him, still refuse to leave his post despite the danger of further collapse: "There was a stairway right next to the main staircase pillars. We went down to the second-level basement floor and found a security guard there. He had been on the side of the building that didn't crumble, watching over a safe at the foods section. I asked, 'What are you doing here, Mister?' He said he had to keep an eye on the safe, holding a flashlight. You know, the safe for cash deposit. He said he had to safeguard it" (Ŏm Kyŏng'ŭi, a member of the volunteer rescue team at Sampoong).[17] In *Dreams of Gangnam*, the fictional Kim Chin rushes out of the department store at the last minute. An erroneous early news report accused the real-life Yi Chun of exiting the building fourteen minutes prior to the collapse without issuing any warning or evacuation order to the employees and customers. In fact, Yi Chun and his associates were holding an emergency meeting in the office building next to the department store at the time. Still, those who were responsible for the disaster managed to escape it unscathed while utterly failing to protect the people whose safety was entrusted to them. Criminal sentences for the company executives and a handful of colluding local officials were a far cry from justice. In the meantime, the workers were subjected to public scrutiny and judgment. Though many of their colleagues were among the casualties, surviving workers were haunted and stigmatized by their association with Sampoong. Significant revelations about the Korean-style disaster capitalism came from the worker response, including the wrongheaded dutifulness to safeguard the company's cash deposit in the rubble, voluntary mobilization to assist the rescue operation, or even the magnanimous defense of the maligned company executives:

> You may have frequently heard, "Sampoong executives and employees all fled, knowing that the building collapse was imminent; all the dead were

innocent customers." That's not true at all . . . Of the 502 deaths, a huge proportion was our fellow employees. Hundreds of them. We were so aggrieved . . . all surviving employees communicated with one another and gathered at the company-owned storage yard. And we talked about, "What can we do?" At the time we felt deeply sorry for even being alive. So we decided, "Let's do volunteer work for the rescue operation" to express condolences for our deceased colleagues. (Yu Sŭngju, a Sampoong Department Store employee)[18]

Too many people were taken out in stretchers, but I could walk . . . I didn't feel like going to hospital for a few stitches. Our uniform was made of very absorbent fabric, so even some small cuts splattered blood all over. I took a subway home in that bloodied uniform . . . The media was telling the story that Sampoong executives had known about the impending collapse, but gone ahead with normal operation. How would they have known that it would crumble like that? I think they forced the operation just because they were greedy for money, bigger sales revenue. Not that they intentionally let the disaster happen. (An anonymous Sampoong employee who survived the collapse)[19]

Fueled by the dangerous mixture of righteous indignation and erroneous information, the public eagerly demonized Sampoong, often making little to no distinction between the employer and the employees. This public vilification was deeply upsetting to Sampoong employees, who had also been victimized by the disaster they were all but powerless to prevent. Furthermore, the discourse of blame obscured the underlying logic of disaster capitalism, which is to push the boundaries of public and workplace safety for the sake of profit. The ultimately self-destructive decisions the disaster capitalist Yi Chun had made were likely out of reckless ignorance rather than malicious intent or cruel cynicism. Many surviving Sampoong workers were much more clear-eyed about this logic than the rest of society as they mourned their loss and suffered through symptoms of post-traumatic stress disorder (PTSD). Punitive justice was not the only remedy for disasters like Sampoong. What the victims, surviving families, and their close acquaintances desperately needed to heal the wound was solidarity—not just among themselves but from society at large (figure 4.3).

Figure 4.3. A bereaved family member at the Sampoong Disaster site, June 29, 1995. Source: Seoul Metropolitan Government, reprinted with permission.

Solidarity, Survival, and Redemption

> The coroner Yi Kyuwŏn drew a large circle on the blackboard and divided it up in two with straight lines at the 170-degree angle. He marked the larger portion of the circle with oblique lines and said, "The absolute majority of the Sampoong deaths were women. A good number of them were female employees of the department store. The rest were female customers, some of whom visited the store with their children."[20]

Twenty days after the Sampoong collapse, a national television evening news program broadcast a segment with the headline, "Is It a Crime to Be a Sampoong Employee?" It tells the story of how Sampoong employees and their families were being shunned by the public even though two-thirds of the dead were the employees. The story focuses on the bereaved family of Yi Yŏngch'ŏl, the chief of the Equipment and Facilities Department at Sampoong, whose body had been found late in the rescue-and-recovery operation. Until then, his widow and children were distraught by the malicious rumor that he had escaped the collapse and gone into hiding. Noting that many surviving Sampoong employees and their families were also unfairly maligned, the story concludes, "They are silently swallowing tears and looking out for their colleagues still buried under the rubble."[21] To be precise, forty-seven regular employees of Sampoong perished. The others, 258 out of 502 total deaths, were either dispatched or part-time workers who could not be held responsible for any part of the disaster.[22]

The disaster's disproportionate impact on the majority working-class and female department store staff was not fully appreciated until much later. Literary scholar Cho Yunjŏng admits that contemporary memories of Sampoong largely consisted of such media-driven narratives as "surprise and anxiety about the department store collapsing in [less than] just ten seconds, denunciation of those who stole expensive luxury items in the ruins, admiration for the rescued survivors who stayed alive under the rubble for more than 350 hours," without much contemplation on "what kind of people were there" to suffer the consequences of the disaster. "The luxurious image of the department store . . . the identification of victims as rich customers out to spend money—these images of Sampoong eliminated or curtailed the likelihood of expressing condolences to the victims." Simply put, the Sampoong collapse was derided as "Gangnam's disaster."[23] It took a decade for Chŏng Ihyŏn's novella "Sampoong Department Store" to breach the long silence on the working-class victims in the literary domain.

As mentioned in chapter 2, Chŏng is one of the trailblazers of twenty-first-century Gangnam literature, writing in the first-person voices of a college student ("Romantic Love and Society") and an adolescent ("Girl's Generation") to portray the perspectives of girls and young women navigating the dark corners of Gangnam. The Sampoong story is similarly told in a first-person voice, but unlike the previous works, it is autobiographical fiction adapted from the writer's own experience.[24] Just like the singer Kim Kwangsŏk's wife, the writer-narrator had been in the department store on the day of the disaster and narrowly escaped the fate of more than a thousand victims. The narrator recounts a casual conversation she overheard among department store employees: "Several people in saleswoman's uniform were chatting around the cashier's desk. *Have you heard? They say the ceiling of the fifth-floor cold noodle restaurant has just caved in. Really? Is this building gonna collapse today? No, not today, over my dead body—I'm sporting new pants today.* They were giggling loudly."[25] While such painful memories of the day's events and aftermath occur in sporadic fragments, these form the background to the central relationship between the narrator and her friend R, a female sales worker in the Sampoong women's apparel department. They were high school classmates who barely knew each other in school. R lived just outside the school in Gangbuk, while the narrator commuted across the Han River by school bus because she had fallen short of the residency requirement to attend the Eighth School District in Gangnam. The Han River class border was replicated in the social microcosm of a classroom. Upon graduating from high school, R entered the workforce directly, while the narrator went to a four-year college. Four years later, their unanticipated reunion takes place in the reverse direction: this time, it is R who commutes across the river to Sampoong, a stone's throw from the narrator's apartment. Ordinarily the class border between them would hinder any meaningful interaction beyond the exchange of pleasantries, but their chance encounter at the department store somehow blossoms into an intimate friendship.

This unlikely friendship is possible mostly because of the narrator's own precarious situation at the end of her college years. Her job search has yet to turn up any good results, and she finds herself either aimlessly passing time or assembling job applications in the public library near home. On her way back from the library, the narrator stops by Sampoong, gives R a call, and they strike up a friendship. They become close enough that R offers her abode—the same place near their old high school—for the narrator to occupy while R is at work. It is an enlightening experience for the narrator, an outsider to the working-class lifeworld R suddenly opens to her. When R's department is understaffed, she even asks the narrator to fill in for a few hours of part-time work. This results in an utterly humiliating incident when the narrator fails to carry out apparently simple tasks. As Barbara Ehrenreich notes in *Nickel and Dimed,* a book of undercover journalism on low-wage work, "no job is as easy as it looks to the uninitiated."[26] The narrator learns a hard lesson about the toil of retail work, which was invisible to her as a customer. Meanwhile, R takes the blame for her friend's incompetence:

> Getting an earful from the manager, R was just biting her lips. I was, I just wanted to run away from there. Once the manager went away, R told me, "Sorry, it's my fault." In retrospect, that's what I should've said. I barely opened my mouth and said, "Are you OK?" "Of course, it's nothing," R answered, with a twinkle of sadness in her eyes. She shook the dust off the shoulders of my work uniform and continued, "You've worked hard today. The rush hour is over and you can go now." I couldn't respond. She said, "I'll take care of today's paycheck for you later. So hurry, change your clothes." I asked, "Are you gonna be OK working all alone?" She said, "Yeah, doing it by myself is more convenient" ... Leaving R alone, I rushed out of Sampoong, as if being chased by the pink-colored department store building; I felt like I could hear its thumping footsteps behind me.[27]

Then the narrator adds only a passing reference regarding the impact of this incident on their friendship: "It is not rare to become distant from someone who you used to be close to; especially so if you're all grown up. A short while after the [humiliating] incident, I got a job."²⁸ She ceases contact with R and commences her new life as a white-collar employee. Several months go by, until one day she casually pays a visit to Sampoong. Unable to locate R, she leaves a voice message instead and walks home. Within a few minutes after arriving home, she hears a loud boom outside.

As an alter-ego of the author, the narrator calmly recounts the unfolding events, as though to contain the emotional turmoil brewing within. She numbs herself with spectacles of the disaster broadcast daily in the mass media. Eventually, though, her emotions find an outlet at the climax of the narrative arc:

> Several days later, a morning newspaper carried the list of the dead and missing persons. I didn't read it. Next to the list was a special column penned by a female celebrity. In it, she speculated that the disaster might have been God's warning to our country against extravagance and hedonism since Gangnam's Sampoong Department Store had been known for lavishness. I called the newspaper's customer service to protest. The newspaper refused to divulge the guest columnist's contact information. Feeling helpless, I yelled at the customer service rep. *Has she ever been to the store? Does she personally know anyone who was there?* I must've breathed out angrily. I felt sorry but couldn't help myself. I'm still grateful to the newspaper rep for holding the phone line until my crying stopped.²⁹

The denouement of Chŏng Ihyŏn's story fast-forwards to a decade after the disaster. The narrator still refuses to ascertain her friend's probable demise, holding out empty hopes for R's life after Sampoong. This act of make-believe is how she cherishes the memories of their brief friendship, which showed her, and the reader, a glimmer of solidarity across the class divide. And it is the solidarity that makes Chŏng Ihyŏn's "Sampoong Department Store" stand out from the rest of twenty-first-century Gangnam literature, including Chŏng Migyŏng's "My Son's Girlfriend," another story of cross-class solidarity discussed in chapter 2. While Chŏng Migyŏng's protagonist experiences an ineffectual, pitying empathy toward her son's girlfriend, the emotional connection between narrator and her missing friend R is an affective solidarity that catalyzes demands for social justice. The loss of her friend mobilizes the narrator to protest, defending the honor of not just her dear friend but also of the workers and other innocent victims of disaster capitalism. What feminist critique names as "affective solidarity" is at work as the narrator's political action is driven by "a broader range of affects— rage, frustration, and the desire for connection," and not necessarily rooted in "identity or other group characteristics."³⁰ Her cry for solidarity may have been ignored at the time, but the story she wrote ten years later found echoes in the literary domain and beyond.

Following *Dreams of Gangnam,* Hwang Sŏg'yŏng embarked on a project to compile a personally selected list of the "101 masterful short stories of South Korean literature," in which Chŏng's novella was ranked chronologically at 95. "Sampoong Department Store" therefore likely influenced Hwang's own storytelling. *Dreams of Gangnam* also features a female temporary worker named Im Chŏng'a, who is buried alive under the rubble and desperately awaiting rescue. In pitch darkness, she finds another survivor nearby, who happens to be the department store owner Kim Chin's longtime mistress and former madam of the Hotel Riverside nightclub in Sinsadong, Pak Sŏnnyŏ (see chapter 1). Although their interaction is severely limited under the circumstances, the author weaves both characters' backstories into a familiar narrative of twentieth-century Korean underclass life. Pak, who escaped rural poverty through the sex-industry route and made a fortune by attaching herself to the corrupt businessman, feels sympathy for Im, whose dirt-poor family has struggled to find their footing in a rapidly urbanizing country. Their tenuous solidarity in this dire situation cannot endure, but it underscores the relative proximity between the rich and the poor, between the middle strata and the working class, at the origin of Korean capitalism. For Hwang Sŏg'yŏng, though, cross-class solidarity is secondary to the main theme of working-class tenacity, illustrated by the dramatic rescue of Im Chŏng'a seventeen days after the collapse. Thus, the survival and redemption of the working-class heroine draws the curtain on Hwang's puppet theater of disaster capitalism.

The Politics of Memorialization: Trauma and Solidarity in the Wake of Sampoong

Mun Hongju's *Sampoong: A Night of Festivities* is the second literary work that took its title from the site of the disaster, eight years after Chŏng Ihyŏn's groundbreaking novella. In this fictional account based on a vast array of nonfictional sources, Mun takes a microscopic approach to the collapse and its sordid aftermath, exposing minute details of corruption, confusion, incompetence, rank opportunism, and cruel apathy that repeatedly traumatized the victims and their families. While it is a novel focused on Sampoong, one of the most damning indictments it lays against Korean society involves a subsequent disaster, the Taegu Subway fire that claimed 192 lives in 2003. This was an arson that quickly spiraled out of control, mainly due to the subway operators' botched emergency response. Local government-business collusion was also a factor, as the passenger cars were made of cheap, highly flammable material in violation of safety regulations. In the disaster's aftermath, accountability was again limited to a handful of people, including the arsonist, the train conductor, and some private suppliers. None of the high-ranking officials or managers were punished. In contrast, the victims and their families had to suffer unimaginable indignities for a long time:

> A Christian minister, who had lost his sixteen-year-old daughter in the fire and now represents the bereaved families, told [a reporter] on the eve of the nine-year anniversary of the disaster, "The wound is getting worse as time goes by. I'm afraid that tomorrow's memorial ceremony might be interrupted like last year."
>
> His worries came true, predictably. Like last year, local merchants came out in droves to interrupt the memorial ceremony.
>
> Dozens of raw eggs flew across the air. The memorial statue was pelted with eggs. They encircled the statue with barbed wire, and spilled salt on the ground. Someone deployed a fire extinguisher and tossed flour at the bereaved families.
>
> Protest banners were flying . . . with such slogans as "No dead bodies in the pristine P'algong Mountain," as if the victims' dead bodies were defiling the land. Hundreds of deaths must have meant little to them compared to their daily livelihoods, unless they were directly affected by the disaster.
>
> Just the same as Sampoong had been.[31]

The final chapter of Mun's novel is entitled "Citizens' Forest" ("Simin'ŭi sup"), referring to the public park where the Sampoong Memorial Tower is located—the Yangjae Citizens' Forest, more than six kilometers away from where Sampoong once stood. The two places had no apparent connection with each other beyond their location in the same administrative district of Sŏch'o. Families of the victims had requested a memorial at the disaster site, and the Seoul Metropolitan Government (SMG) and the Sŏch'o District Office initially committed to the build. Two years later, however, the SMG reneged on their promise and sold off the land, a parcel of prime real estate, to make up for the huge budgetary deficit created by disaster management and victim compensation costs. The SMG still insists that "the opposition from neighborhood residents" to the memorial was another major factor in reversing the decision, but that justification was hardly credible given the SMG's tendency to force through controversial urban planning measures over civic protests. Whatever the actual motivation, the SMG admits that the memorial site ended up in the remote public park because many elected representatives of this affluent district did not want to see the memorial built in their own backyards, which "hurt the victims' families."[32] In Mun's final chapter, a family member of one of the Sampoong casualties travels to the Sampoong Memorial. She voices her exasperation as she passes by what looks like a dumping ground for unrelated, unattended monuments, among them a cenotaph for South Korean guerilla fighters during the Korean War and a memorial for the bombing victims of the Korean Air Flight 588. She "couldn't understand why these memorials had been all erected here together. It was as if they were eyesores that didn't belong anywhere else but in the farthest corner of the park."[33]

The sustained onslaught of disaster capitalism has had a psychological impact contrary to affective solidarity with the victims. The shunning of disaster memorialization has since become a routine NIMBY (not in my back yard) practice for local merchants and property owners who insist that such memorials would drag down the value of their assets and businesses. Already noticeable from the Sŏngsu Bridge collapse (chapter 3), NIMBYism has dogged every high-profile disaster since Sampoong: the Taegu Subway fire, the Yongsan forced eviction fire of 2009, and the Sewŏl Ferry sinking. Public apathy toward recurring disasters has set in as well. On the day of the Sampoong collapse, the late singer Kim Kwangsŏk and his audience shared laughs over the news of the disaster, divulging a dispiriting loss of shock and outrage; Chŏng Ihyŏn and other witnesses recall that empathy or compassion was in short supply while bodies were still being recovered. In this context, Kim Kwangsŏk's despair in "My Dream" sounds almost prophetic:

> Buried among people who can't escape
> we, too, live our forgetful lives
> Unable to look up the skies
> everyone's tired, tired, tired, tired.

Sampoong established a pattern of public amnesia that would reemerge in the ensuing disasters. As one newspaper article puts it, "the pledge of 'never forget' lasts only for a moment, and soon everyone frantically strives to erase any 'trace of that day'" of disaster.[34] The erasure of Sampoong's trace was completed with the construction of luxury high-rise apartment towers in its place. These gigantic monuments to public amnesia happened to be built by none other than Daelim Industries, the construction company that had earned its disaster capitalist bona fides in the battlegrounds of the Iran-Iraq War.

The Sewŏl Ferry sinking, for all its extremely troubling consequences, did not fundamentally change the psychological dynamics established in the preceding disasters. During the early period of the Sewŏl disaster, public outpouring of grief and compassion was deep, wide, and far-reaching. Soon, however, it succumbed to a toxic political atmosphere of polarization as the bereaved families and activists demanded accountability from the incompetent state and its beleaguered head, President Park Geun-hye [Pak Kŭnhye]. Memorial vigils were coupled with demands for a thorough investigation, and these public gatherings solidified into a political protest movement. In response, Park's right-wing populist followers joined forces with the state to deploy disturbing tactics, such as online trolling, doxing, misinformation campaigns, and counterprotests openly mocking and belittling the victims and their families.[35] The venerated scholar and public intellectual Cho Haejoang bemoaned that the disaster "became stuck in the opposing logics of the two political parties . . . the left-wing opposition party tried to use the issue to expand its own power, [and] the right-wing government, tense at the possibility of being blamed for the disaster, tried to bury it altogether."[36] The politicization of disaster helped reinforce public apathy toward the plight of the bereaved families. The families insisted on public visibility: they occupied the Kwanghwamun Plaza, the most prominent public square in the entire country, and pitched tents to create a makeshift memorial space (figure 4.4).

Figure 4.4. The Sewŏl Memorial Space at the Kwanghwamun Plaza, April 1, 2018. Source: Garam at Wikimedia.

Their continued presence and visibility also exacerbated the prejudice against disaster memorials among certain segments of society. Within a few months, detractors lobbed complaints about "the Sewŏl fatigue" as though the public was suffering from compassion fatigue or burnout from the excessive demands and "sense of entitlement" of the victims' families.[37] Despite vicious personal attacks and the mounting pressure of public amnesia, the Sewŏl victims' families continued to struggle year after year. Still, what they desperately needed was not merely compassion but solidarity—just what the Sampoong victims' families had needed in their own struggle.

Feminist scholar Candace Johnson grants that affective solidarity "might generate empathy and compassion, but what is relevant is not simply the level of understanding or the appropriateness of the emotional reaction, but also the commitment to action."[38] Among many allies of the Sewŏl families who have helped sustain their movement, one figure stands out as an avatar of affective solidarity—a Sampoong survivor named Yi Sŏnmin, who has passionately defended the right of the Sewŏl victims to be remembered. Using the pseudonym Sanman ŏnni (distracted sister), Yi posted a short, powerful essay online, "A Sampoong Survivor Is Telling You, Who Feel Tired of Sewŏl."[39] She dismantles a typical right-wing attack line that the Sewŏl incident is no different from previous disasters, including Sampoong, and therefore the Sewŏl families do not deserve any special attention. Asserting a survivor's perspective, she contrasts Sampoong with Sewŏl in terms of the state's response. After Sampoong, according to Yi, the state took responsibility: the official investigation began immediately and ended conclusively; the president "spoke to the nation with a bitterly aggrieved face, bowing his head in apology"; the victim compensation fund was disbursed in a timely manner as promised; therefore, "while I wasn't entirely convinced or satisfied with what I had gone through at the time, I reached a certain degree of understanding." Then she points out that the Sewŏl disaster has been mired in controversy on all counts.[40] As a disaster survivor living with PTSD, Yi is keenly aware of the importance of "apology" and "understanding" in making sense of the trauma. The state's inadequate response to the Sewŏl disaster compelled her to continue speaking out about the ongoing struggle, which lets her old wound from Sampoong be healed as well.[41] She is not the only Sampoong survivor to express these sentiments. More than a hundred people involved in the Sampoong disaster—survivors, bereaved family members, rescuers, investigators, and prosecutors—agreed to be interviewed for the record during the first two years of the Sewŏl disaster and protests. The result of this oral history project finds a certain resonance between the two traumatic events decades apart from each other: "Watching the outpouring of records and civil solidarity after the Sewŏl disaster in 2014, I realized that 'individual memories' of Sampoong disaster experiences were never properly recorded. I also realized that we could shake off this feeling of helplessness by weaving those memories into a small layer of history. The trauma of the bereaved families hasn't been healed yet. Some of them wanted to meet with the Sewŏl families. I saw sympathy and compassion flowing between the two traumas" (Kim Chŏng'yŏng, oral historian).[42] The politics of memorialization has a long and complex history around the globe.[43] Korean disaster capitalism has pitted a movement of remembrance for victims and their families against the forces of public amnesia. The Sampoong collapse remains one of the largest, deadliest civilian disasters in modern history. More than a quarter century later, the stories of Sampoong are still being written. They are not just about the tragedy of human suffering or the injustice of disaster capitalism, but about empathy, redemption, and solidarity.

CHAPTER 5

Place Maketh Man
Gangnam as the Locus of Social Evil

In contemporary Korea, Gangnam is widely regarded as a breeding ground for "social evil" (*sahoeak*). This enduring reputation is periodically reinforced by scandalous events stemming from the unholy trinity of Gangnam's capitalism: speculative real estate and finance, an entertainment industry with alleged ties to sex trade and organized crime, and a private tutoring industry attached to a fiercely competitive college-prep education system.[1] Even so, the incident that captured headlines in early 2019 still managed to elicit shock, as it implicated the trendsetting K-pop industry—the new national pride—into one of the ugliest scandals involving sex, drugs, violence, and police corruption. The previous year, there had been a test score–fixing scandal involving an elite high school just across the street from Tower Palace and other super-gentrified high-rise complexes of Togoktong. Finally, in 2016, the Korean society was jolted by the misogynistic knife murder of a young woman in a public restroom near Gangnam Station.

While these events were egregious and sensational, one positive response to the murder case was a mass mobilization that transformed the area into a site of commemoration for the victim, and of sustained protest rallies against gender violence. It was an early awakening of militant feminist activism that eventually converged with the global #MeToo movement. Young women were outraged that the killer had passed up six male patrons coming in and out of the restroom before ambushing the victim. While the crime was particularly heinous, media coverage was focused on the killer's mental illness and provoked a sharp feminist rebuke of skirting the preponderant issue of misogyny and violence against women. Various male responses ranging from insensitivity to victim blaming to callousness, not to mention obvious trolling by right-wing hate groups, fanned the already-burning flame of gender animosity among Korean millennials. In a matter of days, Exit Number 10 of Gangnam Station was covered with thousands of sticky notes voicing condolences and outrage, the work of anonymous protestors and passersby (figure 5.1).

A total of 1,004 notes were collected and published as a booklet shortly thereafter.[2] Some of these missives included the proper noun "Gangnam," adding a

Figure 5.1. Sticky memorial: Gangnam Station Exit Number 10 canopy plastered with adhesive notes. Source: revi, CC-BY-2.0-KR.

sinister overtone to the tragic affair. They were also harshly critical of the media's initial focus on the female victim, not on the killer:

> *#160:* "Female victim of the restroom murder" is not right [about media labeling of the case]; "Gangnam killer male" is.
> *#197:* Why has the perpetrator disappeared, and why are there only the victims [in the media coverage]? #GangnamKillerMale.
> *#339:* Say a woman were justified to slash a complete stranger for disrespecting her. Then all Korean women would become serial killers, because they are suffering from all kinds of disrespect and harassment just because they are women. Stabbing, murder, crime cannot be justified. #GangnamKillerMale.
> *#504:* To Gangnam Station Killer: You know what? Your mom, who gave birth to you, is a woman, too. You'll burn in hell.

The hashtag #GangnamKillerMale (*kangnam sarinnam*) thus became a battle cry against the evils of gender discrimination and violence. Furthermore, there was one message that seemed to forecast another kind of scandal brewing: "Police colluding with illicit business; men harassing vulnerable women" (*#708*).

Two years later, a luxury hotel nightclub named the Burning Sun opened for business about a half mile north from Gangnam Station. It barely took a year for bombshell exposés to drop, accusing the club of sex crimes, prostitution, violence, drug trafficking, and bribing local police. The club was fronted and partially owned by Seungri (Yi Sŭnghyŏn) from the superstar boy band Big Bang, which was managed by the K-pop juggernaut YG Entertainment. The criminal investigation expanded to target YG's founder and top management for their involvement and other crimes. Women's protest demonstrations resumed in the Gangnam Station area in response to the facts of the case, which included sex crimes, drug trafficking, and illegal gambling allegedly committed by these K-pop moguls. The public was reminded yet again of the foul "sense of place" that persists around Gangnam.

Placing the Sense of Evil: From Human Geography to Cinematic Representational Space

As a key concept in human geography, "sense of place" is what distinguishes a place from a space as geometric abstraction.[3] "Sense" here indexes a range of human experiences in relation to a specific spatial arrangement and contained objects. This phenomenological notion references both significance (meaning) and affect (feeling). With evil and other negative dispositions, affect or feeling is a main phenomenological analytic. Persons subjected to evil might frame their experience in terms of fear, indignation, resentment, or helplessness. Perpetrators of evil may be motivated by greed, exhilaration, intoxication, and other feelings of repugnant pleasure. Gangnam is principally understood through an affective analysis of the evil sense of place. Despite the spectacle of accumulation and upward mobility, or the glamor and marketability of K-pop, people feel, and are affected by, its inherent vice.

However, the evil sense of place should not be confused with the critique "that place itself, the seeking after a sense of place has come to be seen . . . as necessarily reactionary."[4] Take, for example, the Nietzschean-Heideggerian notion of *Heimat* (home; homeland) as a prototypical sense of place, with all the baggage of romanticism, nostalgia, and Nazi appropriation.[5] It is considered reactionary precisely because *Heimat* evokes positive, good feelings—definitely not a sense of evil—among those who subscribe to variants of *Herrenvolk* ideology. The Marxist geographer Doreen Massey's question "Can't we rethink our sense of place? Is it not possible for a sense of place to be progressive; not self-closing and defensive, but outward-looking?" reflects her agreement across the ideological spectrum that a sense of place should be about something positive and good.[6]

This "see no evil" attitude is shared by the Right and the Left. However, it was none other than Karl Marx and Friedrich Engels who pointed out that progress and evil had not been far apart in recent human history. They observed industrial capital "dripping from head to foot, from every pore, with blood and dirt" and having "thoroughly revolutionized" places that "had known no progress for thousands of years."[7] For much of the past five centuries, the land across the river from the old fortress city of Seoul remained sparsely populated with sleepy farming villages. Now it is one of the most outward-looking urban areas driven by industrial and postindustrial capitalism of the last five decades. If such progress is integral to Gangnam, so are the greed, corruption, and bad morals that constitute its sense of place.

The story of Gangnam shows how progress is not equivalent to moral virtue and may in fact be antithetical to it, depending on context. Similarly, an evil sense of place may not be regressive or even reactionary. On the contrary, it could be just as progressive and proactive, especially when it is driven by capital accumulation. At the same time, however, the "progressive yet evil" sense of place should not be reduced to the abstract process of capital accumulation. Rather, it has to be enriched to the point of actually revealing how the abstract space, as defined by Henri Lefebvre, is being produced in a concrete manner: "Formal and quantitative, it erases distinctions, as much those which derive from nature and (historical) time as those which originate in the body (age, sex, ethnicity) . . . The dominant form of space, that of the centres of wealth and power, endeavours to mould the spaces it dominates (i.e. peripheral spaces), and it seeks, often by violent means, to reduce the obstacles and resistance it encounters there."[8] Therefore, as geographer Tim Creswell has noted, Lefebvre's theory of the production of social space actually takes space out of geometric abstraction and into something much closer to the heart of human geographers—place. If, as Lefebvre elaborates, a space is simultaneously represented, representational, and practiced, and transformed from the absolute (natural) to the historical (political) to the abstract (capitalist) space in its social production, then there is little difference between his notion of space and the human geographic notion of place.[9]

An evil sense of place has to be explored in practice and in representation. Cinema as moving image is a good, if not perfect, medium for such an exploration. It is even better if the film is an allegory of the larger social space, visually exploring the sources of evil in depth. There is a theoretical question lurking behind the various cinematic representations of Gangnam this chapter will go through: Is it human activity that creates the sense of the place, or does the place dictate the human sense of it? There seems to be a split within the critical geographic tradition over this question.[10] Lefebvre's theory may appear a little dated at this point, but it serves well the purpose of intervening in and analyzing the question while keeping a critical distance from these two polemical positions.

Gangnam's direct association with social evil has been a frequent topic in this book, to the point of considering a new literary and cinematic subgenre that could be called Gangnam noir. Cinematic portrayals are more immediate and visceral than other forms of cultural expression, making them more suitable for analysis of Gangnam's affective dimension. As mentioned in chapter 2, Yu Ha transitioned from poet to filmmaker to continue his attack on Gangnam's excesses. *Once upon a Time in High School* (*Malchukkŏri chanhoksa,* 2004) and *Gangnam Blues,* the last two films of his Gangnam trilogy—the first being the botched film adaptation of his bestselling book of poems, *On a Windy Day We Must Go to Apkujŏngdong* (1993)—focus on Gangnam's humbler origins, unearthing misdeeds at one of the top college-prep high schools and the real estate speculation infested with political corruption and gangster violence during the formative years of Gangnam development. Such a foul sense of place has inspired a series of cinematic villains associated with Gangnam. Thus, it is not a coincidence that some memorable villains of twenty-first-century cinema are located in Gangnam, such as the atrocious teacher-kidnapper Mr. Paek in Park Chan-wook's *Lady Vengeance* (*Ch'injŏrhan kŭmjassi,* 2005), the obnoxious male sex worker ("host") Chaehyŏn in Yoon Jong-bin's *Beastie Boys,* and, more recently, the enigmatic playboy Ben in Lee Chang-dong's *Burning.* While those villain characters are impressively sinister, it is Gangnam's sense of place beyond all personality traits that make their villainy compelling, connecting individual malfeasance to the larger social evil. Moreover, Gangnam often makes the evil contagious to other characters who collude in the villains' misdeeds or become enmeshed in corrupt social institutions.

Schoolyard as Graveyard: Violence of Class Hierarchy from Adolescent Memories

The metaphor of contagion is also an important feature of the cinematic representations of evil in Gangnam. A case in point is Yeon Sang-ho's feature-length directorial debut, *The King of Pigs.* It is not simply because this animated film begins with a gruesome scene of the knife murder of a woman, foreshadowing the Gangnam Station murder five years later. The film demonstrates the effectiveness of allegorizing children's lifeworlds to reflect societal dysfunction through open abuses of power, manipulative behavior, and class hierarchy. *The King of Pigs* joins a tradition of political allegories that includes William Golding's

Lord of the Flies (1954), tremendously popular in South Korea since he received the Nobel Prize in 1983, and the novelist Yi Mun'yŏl's *Our Twisted Hero* (1987), a story of bullying in a rural elementary school that allegorizes 1980s military dictatorship. Yi's novel was celebrated as a major literary achievement and followed by an acclaimed film adaptation (dir. Pak Chong'wŏn, 1992). Compared to these two renowned literary works, however, Yeon's narrative is more naturalistic than allegorical since it is largely based on the filmmaker's own experience. In media interviews, he acknowledges the autobiographical nature of the film:

> *Question:* Did you have similar experiences portrayed in the film?
> *Yeon:* A lot. Mostly it was during the middle school years . . . I went to a middle school in Gangnam, and then moved to Gangbuk for high school. There wasn't much of a class difference among the kids in Gangbuk and so it was relatively peaceful. It was much more intense in Gangnam. When it comes to Gangnam, class difference is so stark among the parents that the hierarchy among the kids is something hardly imaginable. It was almost like in the military.[11]

> Yeon: I went to Sin'gu Middle School in Apkujŏngdong. Many episodes in the film, such as poor Chongsŏk being ridiculed and having his pants ripped off because he was wearing his sister's brand-name jeans to school, and Ch'an'yŏng, who was doused with urine over his head for having sided with the weak, are all true stories . . . When I moved to Gangbuk, there was no feeling of incompatibility at all between rich and poor kids, between students with good grades and those with bad grades. In Gangnam, these two groups of students don't even talk to each other . . . I'm doing art, so I get to meet very rich and very poor people alike, and I keep finding both sides holding the same kind of prejudice against each other.[12]

Beyond Yeon's identification of the fictional middle school with the real one he attended, there are few references to Gangnam in the entire film. Still, bullies enabled by their superior social status—rich family background, good grades, delegated classroom authority as class presidents or hall monitors—are most prevalent in Gangnam, as Yeon noted. The brutally honest depictions of middle school bullying offer a powerful, if dispiriting, attestation to the micropolitics within the class-stratified Korean society. Typically, the schoolyard bully drama ends as kids leave school one way or another. In *The King of Pigs*, however, the main victim characters Chongsŏk and Kyŏngmin carry the trauma of their school years well into their adult lives. As the bottom-dwelling "pigs" preyed upon by the top "dogs" in the school hierarchy, they started latching onto the renegade character Ch'ŏl, a hardened street kid who openly challenges the "dogs" and the school authorities enabling them. Ch'ŏl uses violence and cruelty to subvert the existing power structure, though he is keenly aware of the evil in his actions. Ch'ŏl invites Chongsŏk and Kyŏngmin to his hideout in an abandoned boarded-up house to teach them a lesson about how to survive the dog-eat-pig world. Brandishing a knife before a stray cat he has tethered, Ch'ŏl gives a sort of initiation speech: "This knife distinguishes humans from animals . . . when the knife was invented, something unexpected was created, too. That was the evil. The knife is as sharp as that cat's paws and we don't want to let go of it, though it's not part of our body. That's what makes us human—the evil. What should we do to gain power? Living as a nice person? Heh, no way. We should become evil to gain power. Don't wanna continue to live like a wuss? Be a monster, got it?"

Finishing this pronouncement, Ch'ŏl assumes the likeness of an "evil monster" before his disciples' eyes by repeatedly stabbing the cat and urging them to do the same (figure 5.2). Stunned by the violence, Chongsŏk and Kyŏngmin are reluctant to join ranks with Ch'ŏl. They instead find a glimmer of hope in the newly transferred student Ch'an'yŏng, who stands up for himself against the dogs and questions the legitimacy of the hierarchy. Ch'an'yŏng's surrender to the dogs after an incident of utter humiliation, however, turns the pigs' weary eyes once again to their anointed king, Ch'ŏl, as a last stand against the institutionalized evil embodied by the dogs. Ch'ŏl's violent resistance is certainly gratifying as he metes out retribution to the dogs, but the viewer cannot help seeing its futility against the existing power structure that would readily crush any unruly pigs, including the fearless king among them. Ch'ŏl's fate aligns with Giorgio Agamben's concept of *homo sacer*: "*Sacer* designates the person or the thing that one cannot touch without dirtying oneself or without dirtying; hence the double meaning of 'sacred' or 'accursed' (approximately). A guilty person whom one consecrates to the gods of the underworld is sacred."[13] Ch'ŏl becomes the king of the oppressed, but he remains outside of institutional power and thus cannot effect any change. Expelled from the school system, he thus turns into a *homo sacer* condemned to "bare life," which refers to a "life that is lived beyond recourse to legal and political representation," like those of "ghost detainees" of the Guantánamo Bay or of Palestinians in refugee camps.[14] Ch'ŏl becomes the one who can be killed with impunity yet cannot be sacrificed, as borne out by the film's narrative arc. The surviving "pigs" Chongsŏk and Kyŏngmin carry the lifelong guilt of their secret knowledge that Ch'ŏl could not have been

Figure 5.2. Becoming evil: Ch'ŏl assaulting a stray cat with a knife. Source: screenshot from *The King of Pigs*.

truly sacrificed. When the secret finally unravels with another cruel event in the same schoolyard, the director's alter-ego character Chongsŏk is left alone, wailing helplessly. Then a phone call comes from his concerned girlfriend, asking him where he is. Somehow this prompts him to stop crying immediately and look up at the skies. The frame rapidly zooms to a full aerial view of Gangnam's nighttime glory, and Chongsŏk's voice delivers the film's final words in a chilling tone: "This is a place of cold asphalt, and even colder bodies are rolling on it." In the film's grim portrayal, Gangnam's schoolyard has transformed into a graveyard for "bare life"—those who could not or would not conform to the concentration camp-style class rule.

There are three overlapping layers of violence in *The King of Pigs*. The first layer is the structural violence of class hierarchy allegorized by school bullying. Here Yeon Sang-ho borrows from the famous zoological allegory of George Orwell's *Animal Farm* (1945), only to invert it, with pigs at the bottom rung of class hierarchy. Orwell's satire of totalitarian communism is also upended by Yeon's deadly serious account of the authoritarian capitalism that produced Gangnam. According to Yeon, the film's extreme violence and cruelty reflect the mood of Korea's Generation X. Having come of age during the 1990s' transition from military dictatorship to civilian democracy, they did not find society becoming any less cruel to the weak and vulnerable.[15] Cinematic representation acutely paralleled actual incidents: a high-profile case of school bullying coincided with the two-month theatrical run of *The King of Pigs*. The incident went public only after the victim's suicide. Although the real-life suicide following bullying took place in the city of Taegu, it involved second-year middle school students, just like those in the film. What is worse, the bullies tortured their victim physically as well as psychologically, rendering the cinematic violence almost tame by comparison.[16] This coincidence lends more credence to the film's thesis: at the roots of cruelty and predation against the weak lies the system of social inequality, which adolescent interactions reproduce in an unvarnished fashion. Recent studies on school bullying largely confirm Yeon's observations that adolescent bullies tend to come from middle- or upper-class families with higher socioeconomic status than their victims, and bullying is symptomatic of struggles for status in hierarchical peer culture.[17] The Orwellian animal metaphor of *The King of Pigs* highlights the political nature of structural violence still pervasive among the major institutions of postauthoritarian Korean society, such as the school, the military, and the workplace.

The second layer of violence is that of deviance, which constitutes violent resistance to the Foucauldian "discipline-penalty-delinquency" regime embedded in the school and other social institutions. Prior to his expulsion and turning into bare life, Ch'ŏl embodied such resistance against the regime of discipline.[18] Furthermore, by embracing evil to gain power, Ch'ŏl's actions reflect a Nietzschean inversion of values: "everything that elevates an individual above the herd and intimidates the neighbor is henceforth called evil; and the fair, modest, submissive, conforming mentality, the *mediocrity* of desires attains moral designations and honors."[19] Tragically, though, Ch'ŏl's pursuit of evil—a Nietzschean will to power—fails him and his disciples. What eventually breaks Ch'ŏl's will is not surveillance, discipline, or corporal punishment. It is the expulsion and ban that turn him into a monster, but not the powerful evil kind he wished to become. Rather, Ch'ŏl is what Agamben calls a werewolf, "a monstrous hybrid of human and animal" banned and thus condemned to social, if not physical, death by the community—in short, *homo sacer*.[20] Therein lies the limit of resistance to the structural violence, which the sovereign power can exercise to the maximum by banning and expelling those who dare to stand up against it.

The third layer is that of ritual violence. Primarily it refers to the ritual of "sacrifice" in René Girard's definition of the term: an act of "violence inflicted on the surrogate victim" who absorbs "all the internal tensions, feuds, and rivalries pent up within the community."[21] At first glance, Girard's notion of sacrifice appears discordant with school bullying, which is generally considered corrosive to social cohesion. But some recent studies characterize school bullying as a "self-serving and socially inclusive ritual" among the participants to normalize their in-group identity and brutal behavior against the singled-out victim.[22] Others point out that Korea's primary and secondary school settings, where students are assigned to the same classroom without movement throughout the school year and have exceedingly long school hours without much outdoor activity, can lead to antisocial behavior like bullying.[23] When it comes to Gangnam, as Yeon Sang-ho has noted, social tensions among peers are supercharged: a sharply polarized classroom based on students' socioeconomic status, combined with the high pressure of academic performance and competition, makes for an environment where scapegoating is likely. Through the bullying ritual, perpetrators form a group identity with a top-down hierarchy that is nevertheless servile to the school authorities. Their victims are like animal sacrifices, isolated and too intimidated to fight back. In this context, bullying constitutes ritual violence that reinforces social ranking and class hierarchy among school-age youth. Ritual violence is not limited to bullying, though. Ch'ŏl's initiation rite for his would-be disciples Chongsŏk and Kyŏngmin reenacts a bloody, quasi-satanic animal sacrifice. Such cruelty is not uncommon in gang rituals and clique hazing in the world of juvenile delinquency. Even though the film pits Ch'ŏl's violence squarely against the bullies, in reality juvenile delinquency and bullying are often closely linked. For this reason, Korean educational authorities and media commentators equate both as "school violence" (*hakkyo p'ongnyŏk*). In one form or another, ritual violence has plagued Korean schools before and since *The King of Pigs*.

If bullying is indeed a sacrificial act, what ultimately stands opposed to it is another ritual of violence—the victim's suicide. Inspired by Girard's theory of sacrifice, psychiatrist Vincent Riordan argues that "there are several parallels between the modern phenomenon of suicide and the archaic phenomenon of human sacrifice," one of which would be "a propensity, under certain circumstances, to acquiesce, if not to volunteer, to become sacrificial victims," especially if the "belief in the appropriateness of the sacrifice was shared unanimously by the entire community, and ideally, even by the victims themselves."[24] While it is an intriguing hypothesis to entertain for certain types—Émile Durkheim's "altruistic suicide" comes to mind—in modern society, it clearly fails to account for suicide due to bullying. Suicide is not a sign of acquiescence, let alone consent, on the part of the victims to be sacrificed for the community. On the contrary, it is the victims' last stand, indicting the entire community for scapegoating them without just cause. It is therefore not self-sacrifice but anti-sacrifice, the victim's refusal to bear the community's inner tensions and conflicts, and defiant exposure of these problems to the shame of the community. Sadly, each victim's final act of self-inflicted violence is ritualized as it is repeated by the next victim in an ongoing cycle of bullying and suicide.

In the final analysis, *The King of Pigs* leaves the viewer without the gratifications of poetic justice or catharsis. Ch'ŏl, the *homo sacer* of Gangnam's schoolyard, was neither truly sacrificed in the Girardian sense nor, as it turned out, committed to the ritual of anti-sacrifice.[25] The tensions and conflicts stemming from the class-divided society have only intensified since Chongsŏk and Kyŏngmin left school and entered their troubled adulthoods. They may not have been condemned and expelled like Ch'ŏl in the exercise of sovereign power, but the final outcomes are similar; the pigs have been bare life all along, and Chongsŏk only realizes it when he finds himself being returned to the same place—a graveyard of botched sacrifices.

From *Kisaeng* Tourism to Room Salon Empire: The Global-Polarization of Korea's Sex Industry

The King of Pigs also exposes the Gangnam underworld of sex work, which has expanded into commercial, residential, and even school zones. An important subplot that complicates the relationship between Ch'ŏl and Kyŏngmin is that Ch'ŏl's single mother works as an "assistant" (*toumi*)—a euphemism for a bottom-rung sex worker—at the Korean-style karaoke bar (*noraebang*) operated by Kyŏngmin's father and patronized by some teachers from their middle school. During the *noraebang* boom of 2005–2010, there were more than thirty-seven thousand establishments across the country. According to a study commissioned by the Ministry of Gender Equality and Family in 2010, as many as 20 percent of the *noraebang* establishments were involved in such illegal hiring, with an estimated total of twenty-six thousand *toumi* workers.[26] Typically, these *toumi* are middle-aged women working part-time for 25,000–30,000 won—about 20–25 USD—per hour. Kim Ryumi, an essayist who grew up self-identifying as a Gangnam underclass "loser," recalls her college days working part-time as a cashier at such a *noraebang*:

> Smallish neighborhood *noraebang* bars were optimized for those customers who expected booze and *toumi*. Middle-aged men [*ajŏssi*] needed ladies. No, even those younger than me wanted ladies, too . . . The *toumi* ladies were older than I thought. Their fashion style and appearance disabused me of my naïve, college-girl imagination. There was nothing special about them other than their heavy makeup and the revealing outfits

under their coats. It was perhaps better that way for their line of work . . . It was the ladies who looked shy at the sight of a young girl staffing the cash register.[27]

The low-end sex work of *toumi* is a conspicuous example of dispatched labor, like janitorial or package-delivery services, all of which have proliferated since the IMF Crisis. In addition to the general precarity of dispatched labor, *toumi*'s working conditions are exacerbated by two interrelated factors: the nominal illegality of sex work and the frequent exposure to physical, sometimes lethal, violence. Those *toumi* ladies who share their stories with journalists invariably mention the crushing burden of personal debt as their main reason for becoming *toumi* despite the stigma and well-publicized dangers.[28] Debt structures Korea's sex industry and its component hierarchies. At the bottom are *toumi* ladies working to pay off the debt they or their family have accrued elsewhere, while young female employees at some high-end "room salon" (*rumssarong*) hostess bars take out cash advances and short-term loans to maintain their top-tier status in the industry pecking order.

As noted in chapter 1 (the Sinsadong Circuit) and chapter 2 (Ch'oe Inho's "Savage"), Gangnam from its beginning has been the site of both the low and the high ends of the sex industry. But it is room salons that give Gangnam the dubious recognition as Korea's sex industry capital. Unlike *toumi*, whose work at *noraebang* is patently illegal, room salon hostesses are legally allowed for bars and clubs with a special entertainment liquor store (*yuhŭng chujŏm*) license. A recent count of such bars and clubs reached almost a thousand in the Gangnam District alone, more than double the number in the old downtown area, which has the nation's second-highest concentration of sex work establishments. No reliable estimate exists as to how many hostesses are employed, let alone how many of them are engaged in sex work. An educated guess based on available data puts the number of hostesses working in Gangnam at four–to–six thousand, and this is likely a vast undercount.[29] The room salon is entrenched in Korea's male-dominated business culture of hosting (*chŏptae*), offering private clients or public officials proverbial "wine, women, and song" to accompany formal business transactions.[30] The roots of hosting culture are found in the premodern *kisaeng* (courtesan-entertainer) class, but the immediate predecessor of the room salon is *yojŏng*, the Korean version of the Japanese *ryotei*, a highly selective traditional-cuisine restaurant where female entertainers—modern-day geisha/*kisaeng*—perform for rich and powerful male guests. The so-called *yojŏng* politics is one of the enduring postcolonial legacies that plagued both former metropole and colony alike, facilitating government-business collusion (*yuch'ak* in Korean, *yuchaku* in Japanese).³¹ The decline of *yojŏng* in the old downtown and the rise of room salons in Gangnam were contemporaneous with the political transition from Park Chung Hee's Yusin to Chun Doo Hwan's new military regime. The underlying business model remained the same, but it was "modernized" as the room salon business grew to meet the increasing demand for shady business deals generated by the rapidly industrializing economy.³² Literary scholar Jin-kyung Lee points out the link between the sex industry's modernization and the middle strata formation since the 1970s:

> As the accumulating capital began to trickle down, college-educated white-collar professional men, especially those who worked for large and prestigious companies, constituted the core of the newly emergent middle class that was forming as a result. Their demand for sexualized service labors, such as bar hostessing and others, was met by the supply of young women who migrated from rural areas to the big cities, especially to Seoul . . . during the [19]70s the idea of "hostess" and "hostess bar" conjured of modern and urban young women and middle-class white-collar male workers—often referred to as *saelŏrimaen* or "salary men"—in Westernized settings.³³

Through the 1970s and 1980s, lowbrow popular literature and cinema routinely valorized female sex workers. The so-called hostess genre tells salacious yet melodramatic stories about young female sex workers from poor, rural backgrounds. These heroines come to the city only to lose their innocence and chastity, fall in love with sympathetic but unhelpful men, and finally meet with a tragic end. The paradigmatic works of the hostess genre are Ch'oe Inho's novel *Heavenly Homecoming to Stars* (*P'yŏldŭrŭi kohyang*, 1973) and Cho Sŏnjak's novella *Yŏngja's Heyday* (*Yŏngjaŭi chŏnsŏngsidae*, 1973). Commercially successful film adaptations followed in consecutive years, with *Heavenly Homecoming to Stars* (dir. Lee Jang-ho [Yi Changho]) in 1974 and *Yŏngja's Heyday* (dir. Kim Hosŏn) in 1975. Hostess melodramas were built around the central theme of women's self-sacrifice for their loved ones—men, families, and the "nation" that exhorted sex workers to fulfill the patriotic duty of earning precious foreign currency. Jin-kyung Lee argues that Korea's "domestic" sex industry should be understood as a "national" segment of "a transnational phenomenon, that is, an intranational and intraethnic exploitation that actually takes place as part of the greater chain of compounded international and interracial, gendered and sexualized, and classed exploitation."³⁴ Indeed, sex work has always been international in its scope since liberation from Japanese colonial rule. First, it was

U.S. military prostitution that laid the foundation of Korean policy on sex work. Katharine Moon's book *Sex among Allies: Military Prostitution in U.S.-Korea Relations* (1997) implies that the Korean government's primary interest in the sex industry was to secure their military alliance with the United States. The state-regulated brothel complex was built around American military bases during the Park Chung Hee era, legal prohibition of prostitution notwithstanding. This led to a hypocritical and contradictory policy framework on sex work for both domestic and foreign clientele, which sociologist Jeong-Mi Park characterizes as the "toleration-regulation regime."[35] The same Park Chung Hee administration also imposed the deeply unpopular Normalization Treaty with Japan in 1965, opening the borders to a new "ally" or partner for the international sex trade. The new sexual alliance was economic rather than military: so-called *kisaeng* tourism catered to Japanese businessmen and "salarymen" (*sararīman*) white-collar workers, seeking rake-offs and crumbs from the growing bilateral relationship dominated by Japan's economic might. As Caroline Norma points out, "thorough methods of corporate entertaining, which were developed in Japan in the 1960s, became best practice business protocol in South Korea in the early 1970s."[36] Throughout the 1970s and well into the 1980s, *kisaeng* tourism flourished under the auspices of both countries' governments and major corporations, hosting Japanese businessmen and salarymen in old Gangbuk's familiar *yojŏng* settings or in new Gangnam's modern room salons.[37] It was no coincidence that the red-light districts along the vertical axis of Gangnam Boulevard took hold during this period. The major hubs of this sprawling network of sex and entertainment business were "tourist (*kwan'gwang*) hotels" with a special license the government issued to promote foreign—at that time, mainly Japanese—tourism. As we saw in chapter 1, the Hotel Riverside was arguably the most important hub in Gangnam's early nightlife scene, the beating heart of the Sinsadong Circuit.[38]

The global-polarization of the sex industry thus began quite early. By the mid-1970s, the genre of hostess literature included "confessional memoirs" (*kobaek sugi*) purportedly written by sex workers about their own lives. The memoirs recount various life trajectories for hostesses. Some women in the *kisaeng* tourism business became local mistresses (*hyŏnjich'ŏ*) of foreign clients, many of whom were Japanese businessmen on a long-term stay; others left for the U.S. on a sham marriage scheme; a few high earners managed to pay off their debt and work as freelancers, hosting "sex parties" for domestic and foreign clientele inside their private "mansion" apartments located in Gangnam or other fancy riverside residential areas.[39] A few others worked their way up the industry ladder, joining the ranks of "madams" in the booming room salon business. Although hostess cinema began to decline in the 1980s, such films as Song Yŏngsu's cult classic *I Can See the Chamsu Bridge outside the Window* (*Ch'angbakke chamsugyoga poinda,* 1985) and Kim Mun'ok's *The Flower of Gangnam* (*Kangnam kkossun'i,* 1989) occasionally reinforced the genre's allure, with Gangnam as the prime filming location. In the meantime, low-end sex workers toiled on as debt peons at local hostess bars, brothels, massage parlors, "ticket" teahouses, "love hotels," and other venues. Lee Jang-ho, whose *Heavenly Homecoming to Stars* had opened the floodgate of hostess films, turned toward social realism in *Children of Darkness* (*Ŏdum'ŭi chasiktŭl,* 1981) to criticize urban poverty and prostitution. Im Kwon-taek, a master auteur of Korean cinema, made *Ticket* (*T'ik'et,* 1986) to represent the plight of sex workers in the destitute countryside.

Democratization from the authoritarian military rule did not hinder the proliferation of room salons. If anything, economic liberalization under civilian democracy fostered a corporate-scale room salon empire rising from the underground economy, which was riddled with corruption, organized crime, and political scandals. The stereotypical image of sex workers also began to change in the 1990s, when the country-girl trope no longer described the new generation of hostesses, many of whom came from urban middle-strata families before stepping into Gangnam's flashy room salon empire. In a 1993 investigative news report, several high-paid sex workers detailed their various coping mechanisms, including profligate spending, recreational drug use, and "going to a host bar" to take their anger out on male sex workers by "doing the exactly same thing" their clients did to them. Even though their income level is comparable to or even higher than that of upper-middle-class professional women, they also need to invest much of it in "clothes and cosmetics" to carefully manage their appearances for the clientele.[40] With the corporatization of room salons, some major operators were emboldened to come out of the shadows and give a sanitized account of their business. Han Yŏnju, who calls herself "the grand madam" (*taemadam*) of a top-flight room salon in Gangnam, is proud of supporting "the livelihoods of numerous people in this country" through her establishment, where "millions of [dollars] were invested in the interior design, and hundreds of extraordinarily beautiful girls are working alongside a similar number of employees."[41] What she describes is the top-tier category in the room salon business known colloquially as *t'enp'ŭro*, literally "ten percent." Despite her insistence that *t'enp'ŭro* room salons are a clean, legitimate business and the hostesses are not engaged in prostitution, there is one common denominator for almost all women—and some men—working in the sex industry, from Gangnam's grand madam and her ace hostesses to *toumi* ladies in a neighborhood *noraebang*: personal debt.

It is noteworthy that Han, the grand madam, admits that she dove into the room salon business only because the failure of a previous venture, a *hag'wŏn* for piano lessons, had left her deeply in debt. Even though she categorically denies ever working as a hostess before becoming a madam—the typical path to attain such a position in the industry—her private life story in the memoir reads just like another hostess novel or film. In essence, it is a modern variation of the millennia-old story of women in poverty being sold or selling themselves as "debt slaves."[42] Still, what distinguishes Han's story from others is not the "original debt" that brought her to the room salon business, but the crucial role of debt in the industry she has both benefited and suffered from:

> It takes huge sums of advance pay to employ a team of A-rated girls. It is a risky business, like investing in a startup venture, to hand over money to those girls, who own no assets, in exchange for a simple identification document and an IOU . . . To hire a competent madam and A-rated girls, the owner needs to make an investment between millions and tens of millions [of dollars], an unimaginable amount for ordinary people . . . If a girl ran away without paying it off, it would fall on the madam's account . . . One by one, defaults on advance pay were added up to my growing liabilities.[43]

Eventually, her work exacted a penalty as Han served a ten-month sentence for fraud. In a failed bid to transition from one room salon to another, she was tangled in a complex web of debt surrounding her business, and jail was for her a de facto debtors' prison. This episode highlights the personal risks inherent to the sex industry, even for those high up in the business hierarchy.[44] If the grand madam can be exposed to such financial and legal liabilities, one must wonder how risky it is for her "A-rated girls," not to mention those working for much less scrupulous employers.[45]

Advance pay is a standard trap for debt peonage. The Korean word Han uses is *sŏnbulgŭm*, but in reality it is the Japanese loanword *maekin* (前金; *maikking* in a typical Korean pronunciation) that established itself as the business jargon, showing deep-rooted colonial and postcolonial associations with the Japanese sex industry. Once received, the money is quickly drained by servicing prior debt and paying for relocation, housing, clothes, grooming, and other work-related costs.[46] Soon the sex worker needs more money, which comes from more advance pay or predatory short-term loans arranged by the employer in partnership with loan sharks. Women's studies scholar Joohee Kim followed eleven sex workers' career trajectories, ranging from six months to over fifteen years. Among them, the case of a fifteen-year veteran sex worker known as "Jenny" is truly revelatory

132   Chapter 5

for the level of exploitation in sex work. Jenny received her first advance pay of three million won from a local hostess bar in 1996. The debt snowballed to twenty-five million won in just three years, at which point she was internationally trafficked to Macao, China. Expenses for the international travel and resettlement came out of another advance pay and were added to her debt. On her first stint in Macao, Jenny was promptly deported to Korea, which cost her even more. In 2003, the ballooning debt forced her to go to Macao again, pushing the total amount to a staggering hundred million won. With some luck, Jenny managed to escape from debt collectors and find work in a Gangnam massage parlor. From there she found opportunities to work in Australia and the U.S. on short-term visits.[47] Her case exemplifies two exploitative practices widespread in Korea's sex industry: debt peonage and international human trafficking.

Since the Seoul Olympic Games and the end of the Cold War, the sex industry has dutifully heeded the national government's call for globalization. As Korean women began to turn away from U.S. military prostitution, they were replaced by women trafficked from the Philippines, Russia, Uzbekistan, Kazakhstan, Peru, and Vietnam.[48] On the other side, Korean sex workers have been increasingly trafficked out of the country as Jenny's fifteen-year trajectory has illustrated. Foreign businessmen may no longer come in droves for *kisaeng* tourism, but the so-called tour girls (*wŏnjŏngnyŏ*) are going overseas—Japan being the top destination—for indentured sex work.[49] All the while, Gangnam's room salon empire has grown ever larger:

> To cite one example, the "Kim brothers" were arrested in 2012 for procuring sex workers and suspected of tax evasion. At the time, the brothers owned Asia's largest amusement and drinking establishment . . . The business had the front of a four-star hotel, but it had three basement levels with 180 individual "room salons" . . . Above ground, the hotel had nineteen floors with 169 rooms, used mainly by prostitutes and their clients. A client would have drinks in a basement room before taking the hostess who had served him up to a hotel room via a secret passageway for sex. This kind of operation is known as a "full salon," adapted from the "room salon" system but includes the "full course" of entertainment and prostitution in one building for a single price. The business employed five hundred hostesses and an additional thousand workers to manage the women and clients.[50]

The corporatization of Gangnam's room salon business shifted the sex industry's mainline from the vertical axis (Gangnam Boulevard) to the horizontal axis

(Teheran Road). Since the early 1980s, Gangnam's adult entertainment venues had become less dependent on the nighttime clientele coming from Gangbuk across the Hannam Bridge. Once Subway Line Number 2 was completed and tall skyscrapers built alongside Teheran Road, there were more than enough male office workers and managers in the area to fill their seats, order overpriced drinks, and ask for "girls."[51] Most of the office buildings at Teheran Road were at first occupied by financial institutions—banks, insurance companies, stock brokerage firms, and the like. In the aftermath of the IMF Crisis, many of these institutions were replaced with new information technology startups, which were flush with cash from government subsidies and venture capital investments. The strategic marriage of *haute finance* and high tech succeeded in jumpstarting the economy out of the crisis, creating the so-called Teheran Valley myth. This new economic partnership in turn spurred growth in the sex industry alongside the "Valley." In terms of its cultural atmosphere, Teheran Road was closer to Wall Street than the Silicon Valley it emulated. It was not just the large, upscale "full salons" that took advantage of the libertine business culture, but also a host of bit players in the industry: massage parlors, spas, love hotels, and, of course, *noraebang* bars. As shown in plate 4, they are distributed along the entire four-kilometer stretch of Teheran Road, on the eastern end of which sit the COEX Complex (Psy's Crystal Palace as described in chapter 1) and the Gangnam District Police Headquarters.

High tech was not the only industrial sector showered with public and private investments in the post-IMF economy. The national government designated the media entertainment industry as a "new growth engine," promoting and subsidizing what would become a global juggernaut known as the Korean Wave (*Hallyu*). In particular, new music-industry businesses representing the idol dance genre known as K-pop were established in Gangnam's opulent riverside neighborhoods, Apkujŏngdong and Ch'ŏngdamdong.[52] This area had already been well-known for celebrity-driven culture since the 1980s, but the arrival of the K-pop industry brought a new level of mass cultural prestige. By the early 2010s, the area was a favorite global tourist destination.[53] Gangnam's concentration of money, fame, and sex work occasionally erupted in huge public scandals. The Burning Sun incident mentioned earlier was especially disturbing because the Gangnam District Police not only had been involved in part of the celebrity perpetrators' lurid crime spree—sex trafficking, rape, spy camera recording (*molka*), drug trafficking, and assault and battery, among other allegations—but they also attempted a cover-up when those crimes were about to be exposed. K-pop's international reach turned the Burning Sun incident into a global scandal.[54] When it comes to the systematic corruption tying the entertainment and sex industries together, however, there was arguably an even more egregious case a decade prior to the Burning Sun scandal. A rising television starlet named Jang Ja-yeon (Chang Chayŏn) committed suicide in March 2009. In the note she left, Jang described having been forced by her manager to offer sexual services to at least thirty-one powerful male figures in the media entertainment industry, including scions of Korea's most influential news media conglomerate. According to the official investigation, it was Ch'ŏngdamdong where Jang attended two drinking parties with some of them, first at a karaoke bar and then at a room salon. Although a massive cover-up campaign effectively buried much of the allegations, the sordid details around Jang's tragic death revealed the age-old connection between show business and the sex trade.[55] With Gangnam as a nexus of institutionalized sex work and the ruthlessly competitive entertainment business, even aspiring media celebrities and performance artists were vulnerable to abuse and exploitation in the district's room salon empire.

Beastie Boys of Ch'ŏngdamdong: The Debt Trap and the Banality of Violence

> What is a debt, anyway? A debt is just the perversion of a promise. It is a promise corrupted by both math and violence.
> —David Graeber, *Debt: The First 5000 Years*

The films of Yoon Jong-bin are another portal into the effects of Gangnam's debtor economies, particularly on the construction of modern Korean masculinity. Yoon made an impressive debut feature film, *The Unforgiven* (*Yongsŏbatchi mot'han cha*, 2005), a grittily naturalistic portrayal of the lives of Korean military conscripts, young men in their late teens to early twenties under an oppressive hierarchical structure. The accolades received for *The Unforgiven* allowed Yoon to make two commercial films grappling with issues of gender and masculinity in Korean society, *Beastie Boys* (also known as *The Moonlight of Seoul*) and *Nameless Gangster: Rules of the Time* (*Pŏmjoewaŭi chŏnjaeng: Nappŭnnomdŭl chŏnsŏngsidae*, 2012). The latter was a blockbuster hit that solidified Yoon's stature in the film industry. Together, the three films are a veritable trilogy of toxic masculinity, with each focused on an unsavory male archetype: bad soldier, unscrupulous gigolo, ruthless gangster. Sandwiched between the two highly regarded parts of the trilogy, *Beastie Boys* did not receive much love from either viewers or critics. Calling it a sophomore slump would be unfair, though. The relative unpopularity of *Beastie Boys* was likely due to the discomfiting affects it produces in the viewer. While the entire trilogy deals with social injustices and moral degeneracy that are emotionally upsetting, *The Unforgiven* and *Nameless Gangster* skillfully weave them into dramatic narratives with compelling, relatable characters. By contrast, *Beastie Boys* is criticized for its lack of sympathetic characters and a relatively flat storyline. One review gives the film backhanded credit for its realistic depiction of Gangnam's sex industry by likening it to a wildlife documentary.[56] Yoon's apparent intention was to tell a story about unsympathetic characters doing the worst things to one another.

In several media interviews, Yoon repeated his intention to portray Gangnam's rapacious capitalism behind its glamorous veneer. The male sex workers or "hosts," who make a living off their female counterparts, formed the ideal subject material for such a story: "Right now, Gangnam is mainly about entertainment, the so-called *hwaryugye* [roughly translatable to "*kisaeng* circles"]. This subject material seemed like the best choice for making a convincing story about the desire for money in our capitalist system."[57] To that end, Yoon's film rewrites the conventions of the hostess genre. In a reversal of gender roles, the main characters are male sex workers, and women appear as their clients. In contrast to the valorized figure of the young woman from the countryside with a heart of gold, the men are portrayed as anything but heroes—indeed, they have few if any redeeming traits. In place of the lugubrious melodrama of women's self-sacrifice for their men, Yoon employs hard-boiled crime fiction with selfish men fleecing women of their money and vice versa. An advertisement of the film includes the title *Beastie Boys* over an image of two attractive young men wearing shirts halfway unbuttoned. The promotional copy on this poster reads, "Our night is more splendid than your day!," hinting at an erotic display of male sexuality. However, the film's sex scenes range from perfunctory to odious, devoid of the voyeuristic appeal of earlier hostess films. In short, *Beastie Boys* dismantles the generic conventions of romanticized sex work and sympathetic sex worker characters and introduces serious questions about the capitalist exploitation of their bodies.

Beastie Boys starts out innocuously like a buddy film. Chaehyŏn is the "leader" of a crew of hosts, the male counterpart of a "baby madam" in the room salon business hierarchy. As such, he plays the dual role of middle manager and sex worker. Chaehyŏn refers to himself as an "older brother" (*hyŏng*), which simply indicates his seniority and rank among the crew, as it does in any Korean young male group setting. But for the newcomer Sŭng'u, whom Chaehyŏn recruited as the fresh-faced ace of the crew, Chaehyŏn is more of a *hyŏng* as he lives with Sŭng'u's older sister. The two "boys" get along fine in a mutually beneficial relationship until Chaehyŏn's gambling addiction catches up with him. He is hounded by a loan shark, who at first threatens physical harm and later delivers on his threats. Chaehyŏn's desperate attempt to lure one of his clients to pay off his debt does not go smoothly since she is a hostess herself, more likely owing money than saving it. Chaehyŏn's business naturally suffers from this predicament, which in turn strains his relationship with Sŭng'u. Still, Chaehyŏn tries to be a good older brother to Sŭng'u by shrewdly cautioning Sŭng'u on how to handle clients as Sŭng'u is about to fall for one, a hostess named Chiwŏn. Sŭng'u believes that she works at a high-end *t'enp'ŭro* room salon, only serving clients at the table without engaging in prostitution afterward. Once he moves into her apartment, Chiwŏn casually asks Sŭng'u to loan her a significant sum to quit her hostess job and open a small business. Upon hearing about her request, Chaehyŏn warns Sŭng'u that this looks like the same trick Chaehyŏn plays on his own clients to get out of debt. Sŭng'u decides to offer Chiwŏn the loan in small installments, following Chaehyŏn's advice. Soon enough, the relationships between all characters deteriorate, and the tenuous brotherhood between the two men finally collapses, revealing the underlying chains of debt. As debt drives the "beastie boys" to extreme behavior, what started as a buddy film about two young, attractive men in the posh Ch'ŏngdamdong neighborhood ends up in a dead-end [*makchang*] drama of betrayals, broken dreams, and bloody retribution.

On its face, the film is about the evils of Gangnam's sex industry. At the same time, it is also a parable of the consumer debt crisis Korean society was facing in the 2000s, which at one point generated 3.6 million delinquent borrowers out of the 20 million economically active population. In the aftermath of the IMF Crisis, the government tried to stimulate the stagnant economy by expanding domestic consumption, but the population had little to spend in terms of disposable income or savings. Thus followed the policy of deregulation and public promotion of credit cards and other consumer loan products, which gave a free hand to the private finance industry. Consequently, credit cards were issued to just about anyone, even to minors in some cases, without an adequate consumer credit infrastructure or financial literacy education, resulting in the disastrous "card crisis" (*k'adŭ taeran*) of 2003.[58] A dialogue between Sŭng'u and Chiwŏn on their first date at a Japanese restaurant shows how readily the average Korean could be ensnared in a debt trap:

[Sŭng'u:]   Where did you spend all that money?

[Chiwŏn:]   Just bought whatever I wanted and traveled abroad, stuff like that. It was so fascinating—I could go on and on spending money I didn't have. So, I just kept on swiping [credit cards]. I don't know, I was just an immature kid back then.

[Sŭng'u:] So, have you made a lot of money since?
[Chiwŏn:] Not really. I've got barely enough to pay back my *maekin* [advance pay].

As discussed in the previous section, most people entering the sex industry are lured by advance pay, which compels them into debt bondage. Advance pay, usually referred to as *maekin*, takes the form of a no-interest loan from the employer in return for the worker's contractual service, which tends to be prolonged by various fees and penalties built into the contract. Even though none of the sex worker characters in the film has substantial savings, those who have good earning potential and little or no debt may command a large sum of advance pay. That is why Chiwŏn asks Sŭng'u to pitch in for her new business venture, and Chaehyŏn coaxes his hostess client into paying off his debt. Their romantic relationships are predicated on the ability to draw advance pay; *maekin* is the magic spell that binds them together. However, trouble begins when the magic of money dissipates or simply fails at the outset. What comes next is violence—not just from the loan shark but from the "beastie boys" themselves. The inexorable logic of debt collection prevails where there is no credible consumer protection measure: "Debt collection by [usurious] private lenders often goes beyond legal boundaries. In this regard, threats of violence, kidnapping and detention are not rare. As a desperate move to avoid this violence, debtors either commit crimes to make money or commit suicide as an exit option [escape]."[59]

There is no surprise about the loan shark tormenting Chaehyŏn. Having been repeatedly forewarned, he is still caught spending money in a gambling parlor. After receiving a severe punishment, Chaehyŏn tracks down the client he has been "working" on for the money and confronts her in a residential neighborhood of Gangnam. When she spurns his desperate plea, Chaehyŏn reacts violently; he knocks her down with a sudden, brutal body blow. As she lies on the ground writhing in pain, he unleashes a tirade of obscenities at her, mixed with an ironic utterance of "I love you." This violent outburst is all the more chilling because the scene is shot outdoors in broad daylight; there are even two schoolgirls in uniform passing by without remark. Presented without stylized filming techniques, the act of violence is not at all spectacular; rather, it feels immediate and raw. Yoon's portrayal removes the walls and closed doors behind which domestic violence against women usually takes place. Meanwhile, Sŭng'u grows suspicious of Chiwŏn's true intentions with the money he took out on *maekin* and gave her. He insists on accompanying her to a meeting with her business partner, who is her former client. Quite predictably, a confrontation ensues when the three of them meet on the sidewalk of Teheran Road. Chiwŏn tries to intervene before violence breaks out between the two men, only to be punched in the face by the irate Sŭng'u. She drops to her knees by the sidewalk, nose bloodied, while Sŭng'u walks away in disgust. Another act of misogynistic violence in broad daylight, this time taking place in the main business district of Gangnam, seems unremarkably quotidian. Nobody intervenes in the beastie boys' assault of the women.

These two scenes of physical abuse underscore the banality and ubiquity of violence against women, endemic in Korean society. In the first ever national survey on intimate partner violence (IPV) conducted in 1997—the year the IMF Crisis began—reported a 27.9 percent prevalence rate of physical violence against women. It climbed to 29.5 percent at the turn of the century, even though the embarrassed government hastily passed laws against domestic violence in the meantime. Korea's IPV rate at that time was not only the highest in the OECD, but also higher than nearly half of the fifty-three countries and areas surveyed by the United Nations. A decade of institutional and educational reform efforts managed to reduce the rate substantially, but it was still 13.5 percent in 2010. The spirited campaign against IPV was likely hampered by the prolonged debt crisis.[60] While the IPV rate showed some decline in the following decade, the increase in arrests for domestic violence, sexual assaults, dating violence, stalking, and other crimes against women indicates that IPV is an enduring problem. The rise in documented cases of violence against women coincides with the rise in Korea's total household debt, which exceeded its GDP in 2020.[61]

There is a nexus between debt and violence that creates its own twisted morality. The anthropologist David Graeber noted that "the very flexibility of the concept [of debt] is the basis of its power. If history shows anything, it is that there's no better way to justify relations founded on violence, to make such relations seem moral, than by reframing them in the language of debt."[62] As Graeber hypothesized, debt-induced violence is widespread to the point of banality, given its moral valence. The creditor/debt collector asserts a moral high ground and justifies violence against the debtor. Sŭng'u's physical abuse of Chiwŏn is such an exercise of creditor power. What about debtor's violence, as in Chaehyŏn's assault on his client? Graeber also theorized the debtor's subjectivity thus:

> We are not dealing with a psychology of cold, calculating greed, but of a much more complicated mix of shame and righteous indignation, and of the frantic urgency of debts that would only compound and accumulate . . . and outrage at the idea that, after all they had gone through, they should be held to owe anything to begin with.
>
> . . . Money always has the potential to become a moral imperative unto itself. Allow it to expand, and it can quickly become a morality so

imperative that all others seem frivolous in comparison. For the debtor, the world is reduced to a collection of potential dangers, potential tools, and potential merchandise.[63]

It is not that the creditor always wins in an immorality play of debt. Sŭng'u's obsession with Chiwŏn drags both into an abyss, whereas Chaehyŏn, upon successfully evading the loan shark, triumphantly reemerges in Japan's red-light district. In the end, the viewer is reassured that Chaehyŏn will resume the vicious cycle of debt and deception in a foreign land. He is therefore a worthy representative of Korea's globalizing sex industry of the twenty-first century.

Beastie Boys conducts a microsociology of the sex industry by depicting the lives and relationships of individual workers. The film relays a concrete sense of evil from the debt-violence nexus structuring their lives. To see how this banality of violence scales up to the level of social evil, one needs to take the entire area into account. There are tens of thousands of sex workers in Gangnam—thousands or more in the Teheran Valley alone. The old Sinsadong Circuit, including Apkujŏngdong and Ch'ŏngdamdong, became a sex-beauty-entertainment industrial complex, in which plastic surgery clinics, hair salons, cosmetics stores, fashion boutiques, and management agencies built a "business ecosystem" for high-end sex workers and media entertainers alike.[64] The industry's sheer scale, and the corporatization of room salons in particular, call for a macroscopic approach to the debt-violence nexus in order to fully appreciate the consequences of Gangnam's rapacious capitalism. The evil associated with this place can be apprehended through Lefebvre's concept of abstract space and Graeber's notion of debt. In a capitalist society, a loan presumes a formal, legal equality between two parties, achieved through the abstraction of mathematical quantity from human relations. It is "certainly the most ruthless and violent form of equality imaginable," but it is nonetheless equality "before the market."[65] Debt, in its monetary form, quantifies human relations by selectively using some natural and cultural distinctions originated from physical bodies, such as age, sex, ethnicity, appearance, and personality, while erasing other distinctions. The production of capitalist abstract space means that this process is massively scaled up to extract interests and profits. It may not be visible most of the time, but the whole operation is enforced and protected by the organized violence of the state, private security firms, or criminal syndicates. Violence is enacted whenever the accumulation of wealth and power in the abstract space of domination is met with "obstacles and resistance."[66]

Gangnam's sex industry has produced such an abstract space by luring tens of thousands of workers into de facto debt peonage, quantifying their physical and personal traits into monetary values written on their *maekin* IOUs. These IOUs are routinely bought, sold, and exchanged among various sex industry establishments as though they were legitimate promissory notes; nonperforming debts, held by those who cannot or will not render their contractual service of sex work, are liquidated to collection agencies, which viciously hunt down the delinquents. The production of abstract space reached its pinnacle when Korea's mutual savings banks joined the fray to repackage the sex worker IOUs into asset-backed securities, using the financial alchemy that had brought down the global economy in the 2007–2008 crisis. Ironically, the banks resorted to debt collateralization because they had been imperiled by the financial crisis. In the process, one of the oldest savings banks, which had duly kept a branch office open on Teheran Road, created a "specialized loan" product for businesses with entertainment liquor license—room salons and other legalized hostess/host bars and clubs—specifically located in Gangnam. The total amount of such specialized loans reached a titanic 133 million USD before the bank failed, exposing the depth of corruption in the finance industry. The specialized-loan customer list included much of the criminal underworld, including a gangster named Cho Yang'ŭn, arguably the most notorious organized crime boss of the late twentieth century.[67] Unsurprisingly, these bad actors altered or fabricated IOUs to inflate the values of collateral, leaving the sex workers under their employment liable for much bigger debts than the actual amounts paid out on *maekin*. Joohee Kim refers to the three-way collusion of money, sex work, and violence as "body-securitization" (*mom chŭngkwŏnhwa*) of the sex workers. The most advanced form of finance capitalism relied on "the traditional creditor-debtor relationship" sustained by "enslavement through threat and violence" and the twisted "morality of debt," assuming that terrorized sex workers were less likely to default on their IOUs en masse.[68] The financial engineers behind the body-securitization scheme did not make a bad bet on the low default risk of the sex workers. Rather, they vastly underestimated the creditors' recklessness, as room salon and host/hostess bar owners falsified the IOUs and bankers accepted them as collateral without question. The bankers were desperate to stay afloat in the credit crunch they themselves were facing, not unlike Chaehyŏn manipulating any and all relationships to escape his quandary. Such is the psychology of debt, a prominent source of Gangnam's evil sense of place.

Escaping the Community of Immorality: How to Change the Sense of Place

In *On the Genealogy of Morals*, Nietzsche wrote:

> The community, too, stands to its members in that same vital basic relation, that of the creditor and its debtors . . . The lawbreaker is a debtor

who has not merely failed to make good the advantages and advance payments bestowed upon him but has actually attacked his creditor: therefore he is not only deprived henceforth of all these advantages and benefits, as is fair—he is also reminded what these benefits are really worth. The wrath of the disappointed creditor, the community, throws him back again into the savage and outlaw state against which he has hitherto been protected.[69]

We have observed the fates of the two lawbreakers/debtors in the representational space of cinema. Ch'ŏl, the middle school outlaw in *The King of Pigs*, is consumed by the wrath of the school "community" according to Nietzsche's script, even though his supposed debt to the community is hardly discernible. The gigolo Chaehyŏn in *Beastie Boys*, by contrast, is guilty as charged almost to the letter as a delinquent on "advance payments" who "has actually attacked" and defrauded his creditors. The viewer may understandably be frustrated by Chaehyŏn escaping his due punishment. Still, it is questionable if he deserves to be thrown into the savage state as a *homo sacer*. Also questionable is the validity of Nietzsche's premise of the prehistoric community acting as both sovereign creditor and moral arbiter in the context of modern capitalism.[70] Nonetheless, a comparison between the two lawbreakers' relationship with their respective communities merits further discussion in order to address the question raised earlier: Does human activity determine the sense of place, or is it the other way around?

Ideally, a school community is governed by the principle of equality among peer students. Ch'ŏl's school, however, is beset by a class hierarchy that pervades the classroom, dividing dominant "dogs" from powerless "pigs." These divisions result from the representation of space—Lefebvre's concept referring to urban planning, policy, and administration—that originally conceived Gangnam as a middle-strata utopia but ended up producing a space of polarization. Like their parents, the adolescent students are affected by unequal distributions of wealth and power, yet the children are more reactive to these dynamics. The immorality of the students, manifest in such incivilities as bullying, creates a sense of evil in the place they inhabit. To continue with Lefebvre's terminology, spatial practice makes the sense of place (see table 1, page 14). The spatial practice of bullying is a distortion of the Nietzschean creditor-debtor relation, in which the "dogs" commit arbitrary violence as though they were creditors, whereas the "pigs" endure the fate of debtors without having owed anything. Ch'ŏl rebels against this perversion, paying back the "dogs" in kind. To best them at their own game of violence, Ch'ŏl wholeheartedly embraces the sense of evil embedded in the place. His rebellion is futile, however, as Ch'ŏl cannot change the fundamental spatial practice from physical violence and intimidation to something constructive and affirmative. The evil sense of place therefore remains intact, and the disappointed take revenge on the outlaw, who has lost the protection of the community.

The concept of community might seem incommensurable with the practices of the sex industry, although some hostess films present examples of sisterly solidarity among female sex workers.[71] The highly competitive business atmosphere of Gangnam's corporate room salon empire has little room for any communitarian morals to set. As we have seen, human qualities and relations are measured and traded in terms of loan contracts. Almost without fail, sex workers end up in debt peonage because of the exploitative nature of the industry. No legal protection is afforded to them since they are not considered "workers" under labor laws, not to mention the anti-prostitution laws that can hold them criminally liable. Consequently, sex workers are enmeshed in the modern savagery of capitalist society. Among the sex worker characters in *Beastie Boys*, Chaehyŏn is a singularly unscrupulous figure who exploits even those nearest to him. At the same time, however, he is most aware of the brutality of their circumstances and most determined to survive at any cost. His deceptions and immorality are a standard practice in the abstract space of the sex industry in Ch'ŏngdamdong and along the Teheran Valley. Not all sex workers behave like him, of course. Sŭng'u's naivete about the industry and affection for Chiwŏn lead to disaster. Even Sŭng'u's sister, herself a seasoned veteran of the sex industry, has a soft spot for her partner Chaehyŏn, who repays her generosity with another gut-wrenching betrayal. If there is a moral to the story, it is that this particular sense of evil is so deeply ingrained in the spatial practice of sex work that any attempt to veer away from the "psychology of the debtor" in favor of positive human emotions would be unwise.

The practice of social evil in relation to the sense of place invokes Marx's time-tested maxim: "Men make their own history, but they do not make it as they please; they do not make it under self-selected circumstances, but under circumstances existing already, given and transmitted from the past."[72] People create the sense of the place they inhabit or occupy but they also become subjected to that very sense of place—it is an interlocking process between spatial practice and "lived" experience of space to "make sense" of the place. By design, Gangnam's representation of space is conducive to social evil, whether it is exploitative sex work or class oppression. Still, the evil sense of place unfolds from specific spatial practices, as when rich schoolchildren torment their working-class peers or a male sex worker exploits his female counterpart in a host bar. Without changing spatial practices, the sense of evil will remain in place.

The challenge for would-be reformers, as *The King of Pigs* and *Beastie Boys* have shown in the representational space of cinema, is in overcoming existing, seemingly insurmountable circumstances to initiate new spatial practices. For all his rebelliousness, Ch'ŏl never renounces the logic of violence behind the cycle of bullying and victimization. Chaehyŏn's survival and Sŭng'u's downfall suggest that genuine human feelings like affection and trust are a terrible weakness—an implicit directive to foreclose any possibility of solidarity among the exploited.

Change is possible even in Gangnam, however. More often than not, changes in spatial practices come from without, taking the form of an intrusion or interference that disrupts an existing cycle of domination and exploitation in the abstract space. In the aftermath of the 2016 Gangnam Station knife murder, a small, anonymous message of condolences grew to thousands of notes and annual mass rallies around the memorial site. The symbolic meaning of Gangnam Station changed from a fashion and nightlife scene into a space of feminist organizing and consciousness raising. Communications scholar Jinsook Kim argues that the "sticky note activism" on the Gangnam Station murder case "contributed to affective counterpublics and mobilized and politicized affect and emotions such as grief, fear, guilt, and sympathy."[73] Up until that moment, the entire Gangnam area had never been known for radical political activism or mass mobilization. Since then, Gangnam Station has been a flashpoint of the feminist movement, followed by anti-feminist trolls and right-wing activists. The Burning Sun incident brought the feminist street demonstration back to Gangnam Station, and for the first time, the sex-entertainment industrial complex was held to account by a mass social movement. For many, Gangnam remains a locus of social evil, but its sense of place is malleable, even to a radical feminist turn. It does not turn away from "progress" and co-opts new practices, especially if they advance capitalist accumulation. The question remains as to what spatial practices can transform Gangnam's sense of place toward better dreams for its communities.

CHAPTER 6

Gentrification beyond the American Dream
The Transformation of Tree-Lined, In-Between Streets

Though gentrification as a concept has been in circulation for over a half century, it now explains spatial aspects of wealth inequality across a diverse worldwide geography. In mainstream media outlets, gentrification is deployed as a readily understood concept not requiring further explanation, rather than as a specialized vocabulary term. Gentrification is, or at least used to be, a "dirty word" in the West. Notwithstanding some attempts to positively reevaluate gentrification, its negative and critical connotations remain largely intact.[1] In contrast, the concept of gentrification has been relatively neutral in Korean discourse until fairly recently. The word still does not invoke as visceral a reaction as "urban redevelopment" (*tosi chaegaebal*) to Koreans, whether they are beneficiaries or victims of the redevelopment, which typically indicates the wholesale demolishment and reconstruction of a given area. In the absence of an appropriate vernacular equivalent, the English loanword *chent'ŭrip'ik'eisyŏn* denotes gentrification in Korean. It is only recently that the term has had currency in Korean academe and media. Then is this a relatively new phenomenon in Korea? How and to what extent does *chent'ŭrip'ik'eisyŏn* differ from the established processes of urban development? Does it constitute a new spatial practice that may initiate changes in the production of space?

Decontextualizing Gentrification from Western Metropolises

Typical issues associated with the concept of gentrification, such as class-based spatial segregation, working-class displacement, contradictory roles of "gentrifiers" and their ambiguous social-class status—new middle class, creative class, etc.—have long been discussed under the rubric of urban development in the Korean context, especially that of Seoul. The term "gentrification" in its classical sense is a bad fit for the crown jewel of Seoul's urban development, Gangnam. Gangnam development did not involve a renewal of the old inner-city neighborhoods; it was a massive expansion into sparsely populated rural areas surrounding the city. In this sense, Gangnam's creation may be described as "new-build" gentrification, but even this may not be a perfect fit, as nothing was there to be demolished and rebuilt anew. It was no "revanchist" gentrification as there were no previously lost urban areas to reclaim. Nor was Gangnam development "emancipatory," because formerly pristine farmlands were bulldozed and then subjected to a bonanza of opportunistic real estate speculation.

The concept of gentrification, in its classical formulation, is modeled after changes occurring from the 1960s onward in major cities at the core of the Global North, such as London, New York, and Paris. A defining feature of gentrification is the displacement of inner-city, working-class residents by middle-class newcomers who engage themselves in preservation, rehabilitation, or redevelopment of the neighborhood suffering from disinvestment and blight.[2] Thus, gentrification in the original sense does not involve new urban development. Neil Smith expanded this classical formulation somewhat by arguing that gentrification is driven by the reinvestment of capital in the old urban center; that gentrification takes place not only in residential but also commercial areas; that gentrification may include some new development, although it is still mainly concerned with already urbanized—and then deteriorated—areas. This Anglo-American model of classical gentrification presupposes three historical processes: (1) the creation and maintenance of the thriving urban core until the mid-twentieth century; (2) the suburbanization and flight of the upper and middle classes from the urban core, starting from the end of World War II; (3) the disinvestment and decline of the urban core.[3] Gangnam development, where farmland areas with low population densities were plowed over for large residential areas and commercial districts, does not fit the classical meaning of gentrification. An important difference is that Gangnam development did not entail spatial displacement or expulsion of the working class and urban poor on a significant scale.

The debate over the classical gentrification model has been ongoing. Critics argue that any form of urban development that causes displacement should be considered gentrification.[4] Another perspective counters that gentrification is being confused with urban development in general, yet the distinctions need to remain salient.[5] In urban studies, questions remain about the definitional precision for gentrification. However, there are some clear lessons about how to decontextualize the concept of gentrification from the West and apply it to urban development in the non-Western world, whether it is in East Asia or in the Global South. One way to do so is to allow for more diverse types, such as new-build gentrification and super-gentrification. Some gentrification scholars argue for a separate treatment of non-Western patterns of urban development at the risk of overly diluting the concept.[6] Moreover, practices consistent with the classical gentrification model are now evident in small pockets of Gangnam. What is more interesting about the gentrification in the Karosukil and the Saikil neighborhoods in Gangnam, I would argue, is the temporal displacement of the process, rather than any possible residential displacement that may have resulted. In other words, this kind of gentrification does not occur in uniform series of waves. There are figurative undertows and rip currents that defy any simple characterization. In this sense, case studies of the Gangnam neighborhoods enrich our understanding of the varieties of gentrification around the globe.

The term "gentrification" was born in a very specific historical context of 1960s' London. A classical pattern has emerged in many other cities across the Global North since then, prompting geographers and urban sociologists to identify the process in stages. The classical pattern was formulated in four stages, which I outline below:

1. Pioneer stage: led by "a small group of risk-oblivious pioneer individuals" who move into underserved working-class and lower-income residential areas and renovate spaces for personal use.[7]
2. Like-minded crowd stage: renovations become more widespread and attract people of the same or similar social-class background as the pioneers. This stage often involves name and boundary changes of the existing neighborhoods in the area. Real estate speculation and displacement begin, albeit on a relatively small scale.
3. Mass mediation stage: with an increase of mass media representations, large-scale developers come in and escalate rents and real estate values. Consequently, the established lower-income and working-class residents are increasingly displaced by newly arrived middle-class professionals. The neighborhood's visual aesthetic is transformed in line with mass-mediated, middle-class sensibilities.
4. Corporate expansion stage: widespread appeal among the middle class prompts further real estate investment and new building projects surrounding the gentrified neighborhood. Pioneers lose influence and interest in the area and move on, thus completing the cycle of displacement. The logic of the real estate market takes over.[8]

Decontextualization, or as Loretta Lees put it, "decolonization" of the gentrification concept implies a flattening of these distinctions, such that stages

1–2 are bypassed and any type of urban development involving mass displacement would fit in this analytic frame. While many researchers maintain the difference between gentrification and redevelopment, the globalization of urban development has forced many to reconfigure the concept of gentrification in a broader sense. Therefore, it now includes such processes as "new-build gentrification," which does not start from renovating old structures, and "super-gentrification," which displaces even the middle-class gentrifiers with super-rich "financifiers."[9] These conceptual "renovations" have broadened the scope of gentrification studies to accurately assess development in non-Western contexts and the Global South in particular.[10] The decontextualized process of gentrification is, however, often recontextualized into a broader political-economic history under gentrification "wave" theory. The first wave is the classical pattern as described above, featuring the first two stages in the post–World War II Global North up until the early 1970s. The second wave involves broader state policy interventions into local and national housing markets under the banner of urban renewal, which took place on the heels of the retrenchment of the Keynesian welfare state from the late 1970s through the early 1990s. In the third wave, a neoliberal capitalist dynamic overtakes the spread of gentrification into the Global South.[11] The problem is that Seoul's urban development is a unique instance. The city's development has been contemporaneous with waves of gentrification in the Global North since at least the early 1960s, if not earlier, and yet diverges from this scheme of temporal progress. To say that Seoul's gentrification began in the 1990s as a part of global third wave is not only ahistorical but also in effect recolonizing the concept of gentrification by portraying it as a "close, but not quite" mimicry of the Western trend. The temporal displacement of gentrification waves is key to understanding Gangnam development in Korea. As I will explain in the next section, it was the second wave that hit first, followed by the third, and then the classical pattern emerged as a sort of rip current in between these powerful breaking waves.

Gangnam Development: New-Build Gentrification or New Urban Sprawl?

One may think of Gangnam as a prototype of the Asian mega-gentrification that is currently underway in Mainland China. However, there are important differences. The development of Gangnam was more centrally planned and directed than the heterogeneous and multidirectional change witnessed in Chinese cities such as Yuexiu or Guangzhou.[12] On the contrary, the grand plan of Gangnam development was first envisioned at the very top of the national leadership and executed in a militaristic fashion to certain degrees. The main elements of the plan included key infrastructure for national economic development—including the Seoul-Busan Expressway, major bridges, traffic grids, new subway lines toward the southeast side of the Han River, massive housing sites and commercial lots from reclaimed floodplains and converted farmlands, and the relocation of key government ministries and public institutions to encourage migration and settlement of the new middle class. The state-led gentrification of Gangnam started in the late 1960s with the construction of the expressway and gained momentum through the next two decades. While the Gangnam project did not go exactly as planned, its success was apparent by the early 1980s, as emblematic high-rise apartment buildings filled the skyline. Although the government ministries largely stayed clear of Gangnam, the Supreme Court and the National Prosecution Service were relocated there. New middle-class families were drawn to Gangnam mainly by relocated elite public and private high schools, which provided a huge incentive for social mobility. For the new middle class, the ensuing real estate boom in Gangnam firmly established their means for increasing wealth.

In the context of contemporary gentrification research, Gangnam development conforms to the model of new-build gentrification in two respects. First, Gangnam was a direct result of large-scale urban planning—in other words, government policy intervention. Secondly, the process created new residential and commercial areas on the outskirts of the already-packed city, avoiding direct mass displacement. In these respects, the case of Gangnam development seems to prefigure the "third-wave" gentrification beginning in major Western cities in the early 1990s.[13] There are important differences with this model of third-wave, new-build gentrification, even beyond the absence of a comparable first- or second-wave of gentrification in Korean urban history. In urban studies, there is a general consensus that gentrification in any form implies displacement. Even new-build gentrification causes serious problems of indirect displacement.[14] During the initial phase of Gangnam development (1970s–1980s), residential trends more resembled the suburbanization around United States cities, long before Ruth Glass coined the term "gentrification." Gangnam development followed the pattern of American suburbanization in two significant ways. First, it precipitated the decline of the old city center of Gangbuk and the loss of its population. Second, as the newly developed districts had originally been floodplains and farmlands with low population density, they absorbed the upper- and middle-class population fleeing from the crowded Gangbuk, without any mass displacement of original residents. Accordingly, Gangnam development is better characterized as a Korean-style suburbanization and urban sprawl than new-build gentrification.

To be clear, there are considerable differences between American- and Korean-style urban sprawl. Korea's geographic limitation and high population density prevents the low-lying horizontal expansion typical of American suburbs. Koreans managed to solve this problem by going vertical; they built a forest of high-rise apartment complexes, each of which constitutes a relatively secluded residential community. In addition, Gangnam was never simply a suburban bed town. Rather, it was planned as a new city center with mixed-use capabilities, first referred to as a New Seoul (Saesŏul) or South Seoul (Namsŏul) in the early Park Chung Hee–era urban plans.[15] Even so, there is an undeniable parallel between American- and Korean-style sprawl in terms of its social function. If the low-rise suburban single-family homes with ample square footage were a spatial expression of middle-class affluence after World War II, high-rise apartments in Gangnam have had a similar meaning for the Korean middle strata who enjoyed the benefits of economic growth since the 1970s.[16] Suburbanization, broadly understood as a process of social-class mobility in spatial terms, is exactly what created Gangnam in the first place. However, Gangnam's success did not ease the chronic housing shortage in Seoul, and the housing policy inched toward the new-build gentrification model. From the mid-1980s onward, the government turned its attention to long-neglected outskirts of Seoul where lower-income and working-class dwellings were concentrated, including shantytowns (*p'anjach'on*) and moon villages (*taltongne*) for "redevelopment"—the process of forced eviction, demolition, and high-rise apartment construction. This approach brought the Korean housing policy much closer to the second-wave gentrification, with mass displacement and resistance. Previously low-income and working-class residential areas outside of Gangnam, such as Moktong, Sanggyedong, and Pongch'ŏndong, were demolished and redeveloped in favor of high-rise apartment complexes, and direct mass displacements and militant protests by the original residents became almost routine.[17]

Meanwhile, Gangnam-style urban sprawl continued with new bed town projects in Pundang and Ilsan, crushing desperate small-scale resistance along the way. As geographer Hyun Bang Shin points out, Seoul's gentrification since the 1980s—with the completion of the initial phase of Gangnam development—can be largely explained by the political economic approach Neil Smith laid out (discussed in the previous section). The main driving force appears to be the economic motives of homeowners and developers converging on the Joint Redevelopment (*haptong chaegaebal*) Program, with project finance as the main method of funding, which involves a high financial risk.[18] The spectacular collapse of Gangnam landmark constructions, the Sŏngsu Bridge and the Sampoong Department Store, followed by the economic collapse of the IMF Crisis, did not hinder enthusiasm for Gangnam's real estate development. On the contrary, this series of disasters further strengthened the drive to redevelop aging high-rise apartment housing stock in Gangnam and elsewhere. The redevelopment drive coincided with third-wave gentrification in Seoul, as global capital inflows helped fuel the "apartment reconstruction" (*ap'at'ŭ chaegŏnch'uk*) boom, which demolished twenty- to thirty-year-old "obsolete" apartment complexes wholesale and built even higher-rise complexes in their place. It was also during this time that Samsung Corporation finished construction on its seventy-story-tall Tower Palace, heralding the start of super-gentrification in Gangnam. The reconstruction boom continued through the 2000s, replicating development feats of the 1980s, until the 2008 global financial crisis caused an abrupt halt. As seen in chapter 3, Ŭnma and other apartment complexes that missed the golden opportunity of the early 2000s reconstruction boom had to suffer consequences of dilapidation.

The First Wave Arrives Last: Classical, Commercial Gentrification in Gangnam

From the perspective of the gentrification wave theory, Seoul's urban changes since the establishment of Gangnam would be seen as the third-wave gentrification writ large. Seoul, like many other metropolitan cities in the Global South or the Global East, skipped the first and second waves and began with the massive third wave, according to this view. But here comes an ironical twist: one of the emerging forces against the long-term dominance of high-rise development is promoting alternatives that often appear similar in many ways to classical gentrification. It is no longer strange to see those in the so-called creative occupations as Seoul's pioneering gentrifiers. This group includes artists, artisans, gourmet chefs, fashion designers, and architects, who bring their bohemian-inspired vision to old and declining neighborhoods. Their pioneering efforts began in Gangbuk around the college neighborhoods of Hongdae and Sinch'on, or the historic downtown neighborhoods of Insadong, Bukchon (Pukch'on), and Sŏch'on. Some of these urban pioneers have, somewhat incongruously, directed their attentions to Gangnam, the belly of the high-rise beast. As a matter of fact, there are still pockets of neighborhood space in Gangnam where the high tide of apartment construction has not yet receded. For those bored with the high-rise apartment lifestyle, an ideal alternative has presented itself in such places like Karosukil (Tree-Lined Street) in Sinsadong and Saikil (In-Between Street) in Pangbaedong, where they can find a charming European-style neighborhood. At last, first-wave gentrification has arrived in Gangnam as well.

Beyond their Gangnam location (see figure 1.3), these two neighborhoods share some distinct characteristics. First, both were built around a relatively short and narrow road, and their names were derived from their respective main roads, Karosukil and Saikil. Second, while these neighborhoods are a mixture of residential and commercial establishments, the biggest impact of gentrification has been on particular commercial facilities such as cafés, bakeries, galleries, workshops, and restaurants, rather than on residential communities. Third, the administrative units of Sinsadong and Pangbaedong, where these small neighborhoods are located, have had a prior history with other up-and-coming neighborhoods within them. Consequently, they are relatively well-equipped with the economic and cultural capital to promote the small-scale, culture-driven gentrification of the classical model. The second and third points of similarity mentioned above characterize Karosukil and Saikil as the areas of commercial gentrification. In other words, those who are at the threat of displacement are the gentrifiers themselves, who mainly run commercial facilities in these neighborhoods; the residents are less threatened by evictions, lease terminations, soaring rents, property tax hikes, and similar concerns, except when the expansion of the commercial area directly invades the residential area and begins to push out the residents. Under these circumstances, it is not easy for the pioneering gentrifiers and residents to develop any meaningful community ties. Even if the residents own their properties, the rising popularity of the neighborhood tends to aggravate the situation over their competing economic interests, often instigated by real estate brokers and developers.

Then does this belated classical gentrification have any significance as an alternative to the original "Gangnam Style" urban development? The following sections present a response based on a field research project. Between 2014 and 2015, I was a member of the research team that conducted in-depth interviews with twenty pioneering gentrifiers to examine policy and cultural changes of the neighborhood in the historical context of Gangnam development. This chapter will feature eleven of those interviews to reconstruct the narratives of gentrification in the two Gangnam neighborhoods (table 2).

Table 2. List of interviews with Karosukil and Saikil gentrifiers

Name initial	Gender and age	Occupation	Location	Interview date
C	Female, 30s	Manager, nonprofit	Saikil	1/6/2015
I1	Female, 30s	Architect	Karosukil	6/2/2015
I2	Female, 30s	Artisan, workshop	Saikil	1/16/2015
K	Female, 30s	Clothing store owner	Karosukil	6/2/2015
L1	Female, 50s	Café co-owner	Karosukil	6/2/2015
L2	Male, 40s	Architect	Karosukil	1/27/2015
L3	Female, 40s	Art gallery owner	Saikil	1/20/2015
L4	Female, 50s	Social entrepreneur	Saikil	1/6/2015
O	Male, 50s	Bar owner	Karosukil	1/6/2015
P	Male, 40s	Designer boutique owner	Karosukil	6/12/2015
Y	Male, 50s	Live café owner	Karosukil	1/6/2015

Karosukil, Sinsadong: The High-Speed Growth of the Gangnam Hinterlands

Sinsadong was the first major gateway to Gangnam as the traffic entered Gangnam Boulevard from the Hannam Bridge. In the early days of development, before Sinsa Station opened on Subway Line Number 3, the area emerged as a center of the adult entertainment industry. In the 1980s, nightclubs, cabarets, and double-feature movie theaters specializing in erotic films lined the Sinsadong section of Gangnam Boulevard. In the back alleys were motels, markets, bars, and restaurants clustered into a semi–red-light district. These alleyway businesses still exist today. The distance of about four hundred meters from the lively Sinsadong intersection shielded the Karosukil area from the associations with adult nightlife, depicted for example in Chu Hyŏnmi's "The Man from Sinsadong" or "Street of Love" by Mun Hŭiok (see chapter 1). As Gallery Ye (Ye hwarang) moved from Insadong early on in 1982, other galleries began entering the street, and it became known as Gallery Street in the 1990s. In addition, with the proliferation of businesses specializing in interior design, antique goods, and import furniture stores, the street, together with nearby Nonhyŏndong, was sometimes called Furniture Street—albeit not with the same level of household recognition as the current Karosukil.

Rather, the transition of Karosukil into its contemporary form occurred in tandem with the temporary decline of Gallery Street. As the economic recession hit the art world following the IMF Crisis, galleries either closed or moved away. It was the beginning of the 2000s when designer clothing stores, European-styled cafés, flower shops, bakeries, music cafés, and LP bars—bars playing vinyl records—began filling that gap. According to a newspaper article in 2001, which introduced the name "Karosukil," more than thirty designer boutiques were built near this street around 1995, and they hosted exclusive events such as the Street Fashion Show. Not only was Karosukil located near the high-end fashion markets of Apkujŏngdong and Ch'ŏngdamdong, the area's relationship with the fashion industry naturally settled when the Parisian fashion school Esmod opened their Seoul branch in Karosukil. As noted in the newspaper article mentioned above, the area already seemed to be recognized as a new center of fashion. In the 1990s, a few fashion designers opened small workshops that doubled as stores in the area. However, even at the time of an LP bar's opening in 2002, the owner O remembered it as a "quiet" place, with "a little café, a gallery, and a couple clothing stores," with a residential area on the other side of Karosukil that did not have any commercial activity. Interestingly, when traversing the residential areas around Karosukil, particularly the alleys on the eastern side, one finds small signs of home-sewing factories in operation. This suggests that the residential area surrounding the roadside streets has long functioned as the hinterland of the Sinsadong main road's adult entertainment industry as well as the fashion industry of Apkujŏngdong and Ch'ŏngdamdong. In other words, clothes that were designed and manufactured in such a quiet and inconspicuous neighborhood were bought by the women working in the nearby adult entertainment establishments and by merchants for retail in the neighboring department stores and boutiques.

The best example of the relationship between the adult entertainment industry and the fashion industry is a designer boutique that played a key role among the pioneering gentrifiers. This clothing store, Boutique N, was run by a fashion designer and her husband, an entrepreneur. When it opened in 1998, their main customers were mainly escort workers in the surrounding area of Sinsadong, especially the so-called local wives (*hyŏnjich'ŏ*), whose clientele included sojourning representatives of Japanese companies (see chapter 5). Boutique N gradually became famous, and at one point was able to enter the luxury department stores in the Apkujŏngdong-Ch'ŏngdamdong area. Although the boutique has been pushed to the surrounding area a few blocks away from Karosukil, the businessman owner P expressed pride in his role attracting and organizing designer shops and cafés operated by fellow gentrifiers, who shared a similar mindset in the early days before Karosukil gained widespread appeal. This couple also resided in the neighborhood. However, they identified more with their roles as fashion and industry pioneers for Karosukil than as its residents.

Sinsadong is also surrounded by high-rise apartment complexes, located in Chamwŏndong to the west and Apkujŏngdong to the north and east. As a result, the modest low-rise multifamily townhomes and single-family houses around Karosukil resemble a hinterland. The Korean real estate market tends to increase in price in high-rise apartment complexes. Around Karosukil, aside from a few high-rise residential areas, the relatively cheap rent in the area was an important condition that enabled the pioneering gentrifiers to pursue new and unique ventures without much capital. In addition, great traffic conditions that can attract floating populations, as well as a residential area with a "cultured" customer base nearby, were both instrumental to the commercial prosperity of Karosukil. Apkujŏngdong and Ch'ŏngdamdong, both representative hot spots of the northern Gangnam area in the late 1980s and early 1990s, were gradually losing popularity by the early 2000s, when Karosukil was up-and-coming. In the meantime, Sinsadong emerged as a new land of opportunity after having long been the hinterland to its popular neighbors.

Some of the business leaders of the early Karosukil were migrants from Ch'ŏngdamdong. Ch'ŏngdamdong had followed Apkujŏngdong to emerge as the center of Gangnam's fashion and food service industry since the late 1990s. These leaders formed their own personal network and led the second and third stage of gentrification. One such leader is Kim Young-hee (Kim Yŏnghŭi), widely known as the mother of Mr. "Gangnam Style," Psy. Kim married into a wealthy business family that had settled early on in Gangnam. As she began venturing into the restaurant industry, she achieved success in opening fusion Japanese and Korean restaurants in Ch'ŏngdamdong. She formed a partnership with an interior designer who had become famous for creating European-style atmospheres in some of the representative establishments of early Karosukil. They opened restaurants and bars in worn-out buildings and named them after their building numbers. These became a favorite spot for the pioneering gentrifiers and customers. In 2006, Kim Young-hee opened a Korean restaurant by renovating an old home. This restaurant lasted more than ten years at the center of Karosukil, where many other businesses had come and gone.

In 2004, a self-styled "flower and cake café" combined the two areas of floristry and desserts to open in the middle of Karosukil. The café, Bloom and Goûte, was started by two journalists who had built their knowledge working at a women's magazine before quitting to go to France and England to train in confectionary and floriculture (figure 6.1). Bloom and Goûte became famous as it led the

Figure 6.1. The flower café Bloom and Goûte in Karosukil. Source: *Han'guk ilbo*, May 1, 2008, reprinted with permission.

trend in outdoor café design and became part of the history of Karosukil. Café co-founder L1 found the keys to success in a combination of spatial structure, people, and lines of vision:

> The first thing we attempted was a seating arrangement where you were sitting facing the street, like in Paris, France, and in the summer, the folding doors would completely open so that the inside space would be completely visible from the outside, and people seated inside could also see outside. People liked that kind of culture . . . the final item in café interior design is the people. People like fashion designers, magazine writers, interior designers, and stylists would fill the last element of interior design and they would sit inside and look out to the people outside, creating an interaction. (L1 interview)

Karosukil's pioneering gentrifiers of galleries, boutiques, cafés, restaurants, artists, businessmen, and interior designers did not formally organize themselves but formed a loose network that shaped the neighborhood culture through the early 2000s.[19] This network was an important factor in shifting the Gangnam center of fashion from Apkujŏngdong to Ch'ŏngdamdong in the late 1990s, and then to Karosukil. This organically and spontaneously formed relationship was far from an organization with a driving policy or aesthetic view. Despite the efforts of "alley leader" (*kolmoktaejang*) Boutique N's owner P, the network did not develop into a merchant association (*sangjohoe*) to represent the commercial interests of the neighborhood.

> Question: Even if it were not an organization like a merchant association, did you ever have unofficial meetings and work together?
>
> L1: We did have something like that but it was unofficially done ... I think we were just personally good friends ... We're not as social as we may seem, so we don't socialize with people much.
>
> P: Because people weren't coming, we decided to attract the crowds ourselves. But we didn't have money and we didn't have the means to mobilize the leading magazines. So that's why we decided to get together and do the publicity ourselves. We met up a couple times. But we were all writers and journalists and we mixed like oil and water. There were those who wanted to pursue the idea, while there were others who wanted to quietly focus on their own work. We made a lot of attempts, but many of the projects didn't work. We did manage to do things like the Carless Street and flea markets by bringing in an editor from a major magazine.

Although the process was not smooth, the pioneering gentrifiers were able to attract personal and professional networks and resources, and they also ran relatively successful small-to-medium-sized events. As those in the creative industries started filling in the space opened by these pioneers, a kind of generation change commenced in 2005, marking the start of a third stage of gentrification. At this time, Sinsadong J Tower was built at the entrance to Karosukil from Dosan Boulevard (Tosandaero) and became a landmark building. As the site of the multinational advertising company TBWA, ranked third in the industry, there was an influx of advertising and movie industry into the surrounding Karosukil area. Some of TBWA's employees even went so far as to publish a book entitled *What's All the Fuss about Karosukil?* effectively creating a professional specialty out of publicity for the area.[20] Media representations of Karosukil increased, and land value and real estate prices also rose. Gallery Ye, which had left during the IMF Crisis, also had a flashy return with a new building. Their return helped Karosukil beat out Ch'ŏngdamdong to emerge as the hottest spot in Gangnam.

During this time, architectural design also flourished as one of the creative industries in Karosukil. Many of the architects who grew up in the vicinities of Karosukil returned to their neighborhoods after completing higher education and professional training. These architects contributed to the expansion of Karosukil by raising its prestige as a more luxurious cultural street. For example, an architect who designed the interior of a bakery in the Karosukil area states: "The facade of an elegant building, which seems to be copied and pasted from a town in Europe, and the newly paved rubber sidewalk, make the 2007 Karosukil more stylish. However, I think the street scenery could be more diversified if the places that retain Karosukil's history were to be kept with the new ones, as they have more stories to tell. I still wish the basement café, where I was afraid of being kicked out for wearing a high-school uniform fifteen years ago, was in business, with its small sign displaying 'SINCE 1992.'"[21] As relayed by this architect, many connect the scenery of Karosukil from the days where it was called Ginko Tree Street and Gallery Street to the early 2000s Karosukil. The area and its venues inspire humanistic and aesthetic interpretations. However, there also exists a negative perspective of the commercialism of the Karosukil. Architect L2, who opened an office for his residential housing business, stated the following:

L2: This [street] is solely for consumption. The culture is based on consumption, so I wouldn't necessarily call it a culture.

Question: Do you think there is a native Karosukil culture?

L2: No, it keeps changing.

Question: But there is a sense of lushness?

L2: Yes, it is like an extension of the change Apkujŏngdong and Ch'ŏngdamdong already went through.

Another Gangnam-native architect, I1, was not so charitable to Karosukil either: "[Karosukil] wasn't that cheap of a neighborhood, so it wasn't created by people who didn't have money." She further observed, "[People] were looking for a place that was undervalued for its location and atmosphere to start their businesses." She expressed skepticism about the fundamental difference between Karosukil and the underlying Gangnam areas.

Despite the negative views, Karosukil also went through many efforts to create a unique, independent local culture like the case of the Hongdae and Itaewon vicinities.[22] Among these initiatives was the webzine *Hello Garosugil*, an "infrequent project newspaper" that published eleven issues between the fall of 2008 and the winter of 2012. The webzine included interviews with people in Karosukil, such as the local workers and visitors. Along with the interviews, there were feature articles introducing the small designer studios and the hidden attraction spots, creating affinities among local readers. The webzine went a step further and also created a blog, a flea market, a block party, and a winter event where people built snow figures in the street. Despite these efforts, the webzine did not enjoy continuous success. After the film festival in 2012, all the publications and official projects were put on hold, and repeated interview requests with the webzine editor were politely declined.[23]

A live music café owner, Y, who was heavily exposed to the youth culture from his history of being a rock musician in the late 1970s, opened his café on Karosukil in 2007. At first, he was impressed by the young people who moved into the area around the same time with high hopes and dreams. However, as the rent hike began in 2010, Y sadly observed the newcomers having to leave the area. As it soon turned out, it was not only the newcomers who were priced out of the neighborhood; even the pioneering gentrifiers who seemed to have settled well by then were vulnerable to the pressure to relocate. The owner of the aforementioned LP bar, O, was not enthusiastic about the steep rise in both foot and car traffic, and moved his establishment to Apkujŏngdong, the washed-up glitzy neighborhood from two decades ago, in 2012. Even Bloom and Goûte, which stood as the emblem of Karosukil culture, was pushed to the back alley—colloquially known as Serosukil—the same year. These relocations were the early signs of corporate-driven gentrification on a massive scale.

In that same year, 2012, Cheil Indutries (Cheil mojik), a Samsung affiliate specializing in the fashion business, opened a flagship branch store of its SPA (specialty-store retailer of private-label apparel) brand Eight Seconds in Karosukil. Eight Seconds was actually a countermove to its U.S. competitor, Forever 21, which had opened a branch in the previous year. Similar multinational brands such as Zara and Giordano also entered the rapidly changing Karosukil neighborhood. The multinational corporations backing these chain brands could afford skyrocketing rents for maximum visibility. The corporations sometimes leased entire buildings or even purchased and renovated them to raise the height from one or two stories to six stories or even taller, altering the street scenery remarkably in a few short years. The fashion industry is the most powerful driving force of the corporate gentrification now dominating Karosukil. Even in this business, however, there are still some independent spirits that keep their places in the neighborhood. An independent clothing store owner, K1, used to frequent Karosukil during its early years, when she was a college student. After learning about international fashion trends abroad and gaining hands-on experience in Korean clothing distribution and retail, in the summer of 2009 she launched her own store at the heart of Karosukil, just across the street from where Bloom and Goûte once stood.

K1 seemed to share many of the aesthetic sensibilities of those idealistic urban pioneers who had arrived in the neighborhood in the early 2000s. But unlike the displaced, she also possessed a sharp business acumen, which made her a rare survivor of the corporate onslaught. In our interview, K1 calmly explained the steps she took to survive the fierce competition and pressure from the corporations. She cultivated a deferential rapport with the building owner, who was of her father's generation, making sure to give him holiday greetings and gifts every year. She also kept close relationships with the street parking attendants, who played an important role in attracting customers in a neighborhood like Karosukil, where the lack of parking space is a perennial issue for businesses. Though her business had endured, K1 was not optimistic about the future of independent business in Karosukil. Just like the live café owner Y, another survivor still standing, she was not hopeful about the prospects of organizing neighborhood business owners into merchant associations to protect their interests against landowners and corporations. Although there were a few cases where desperate storeowners battled forced eviction and won partial victories, the corporatized gentrification of Karosukil appeared to be a fait accompli at the time the field research was completed.[24]

Gentrification in Pangbaedong Café Street, Sŏrae Village, Saikil: Social Enterprise and Municipal Support

As we saw in chapter 1, Pangbaedong had the upscale Café Street as its main attraction for most of the 1980s. Once surpassed by Apkujŏngdong and Ch'ŏngdamdong in the 1990s, however, Café Street began a long decline to a run-of-the-mill commercial backstreet, not unlike the area in between the Sinsadong intersection and Karosukil. Gone were the posh restaurants and cafés, including the venerable Italian restaurant Forest of Roses, which finally shut its door in 2007 after a three-decade run. Their spots were taken over by barbeque restaurants, dive bars, and coffeehouse chains. It took some time for Pangbaedong to regain some of its prestige lost to rival districts to the east, but it always maintained the air of exclusive coolness, thanks largely to the presence of affluent, exotic residential communities. Sŏrae Village is such a community that triggered the next round of gentrification in Pangbaedong. When the school for French-speaking children, Lycée Français de Séoul, moved to the current location adjacent to Pangbaedong in 1985, it created a mixed French-Korean community called Sŏrae Village. Although the neighborhood was difficult to reach by any means of transportation, soon the exotic French street cafés, boulangeries, and restaurants began to attract many visitors from outside. The fact that Sŏrae Village is located next to one of the most exclusive gated communities in Seoul did help boost its public image as well. The so-called Pangbaedong Villa Town (*billach'on*) hosts a number of luxurious low-rise mansions owned by some of the richest people and largest corporations in Korea, such as the founders of the Lotte and Daewoo conglomerates (figure 6.2). The district government office has always been very supportive of this "multicultural" village of mostly white Westerners, and so have their Korean neighbors, many of whom volunteered to assist foreign residents settling in new environments. Thus, Sŏrae Village has

Figure 6.2. Stairway connecting the Pangbaedong Villa Town to the Saikil neighborhood, festooned with barbed wire. Source: author's collection.

solidified its image as a haven for European chic in Korea. Once a tiny neighborhood, Sŏrae Village has gradually expanded its reach along the main road Sŏraero, with increasing new businesses since the late 1990s.

The name Saikil refers to the road (*kil*) number 42 (*sai*—when two digits are pronounced separately in Korean), a narrow alleyway of about four hundred meters that passes through the low-lying, unassuming residential area just under the hills where the Villa Town and Sŏrae Village are located.[25] It is a tiny place indeed, even compared to the original Karosukil area. Apparently Saikil itself did not amount to much without the spillover effect from the better-known neighborhoods nearby: Café Street to the west and Sŏrae Village to the east. In terms of cultural trendiness, the shift from Café Street to Sŏrae Village is an analog to the larger transformations between Apkujŏngdong and Ch'ŏngdamdong in that era. As mentioned earlier, Karosukil was originally a hinterland of Apkujŏngdong and Ch'ŏngdamdong, but gained in prestige due to the ever-revolving trend cycle. Incidentally, Saikil is in a comparable position relative to Café Street and Sŏrae Village. In the current iteration of the trend cycle, this easily overlooked piece of Pangbaedong hinterland has gained attention out of proportion to its small area.

It was around 2012 that small galleries and other pioneering gentrifiers moved to Saikil. Previously, there were mostly community establishments such as a neighborhood bathhouse, hair salons, corner stores, and cram schools. Some of these newer venues were migrating from Ch'ŏngdamdong and Karosukil. Gallery owner L3 was pushed out of Ch'ŏngdamdong when the landlord of her gallery refused to renew the lease in order to demolish the building and construct a new one in its place. L3 had no plan to move to Karosukil, which she thought would be vulnerable to the same threat of displacement. She found out about Saikil while searching for a location that would make her gallery more accessible. The location needed to be less crowded, with an affordable rent, and easily approachable by local residents.

Unlike the Apkujŏngdong-Ch'ŏngdamdong-Karosukil area, which received little or no assistance from the Seoul Metropolitan Government or the municipal Gangnam District Office, both Sŏrae Village and the Saikil neighborhood have benefited a lot from policy interventions by the Sŏch'o District Office, which has continuously played an important role in shaping these neighborhoods. In the case of Sŏrae Village, the district office has been actively involved in mobilizing the volunteer support for foreign residents under the banner of promoting multiculturalism. By the time Saikil was up and coming, a group of new policy buzzwords were gaining momentum in the national and municipal administrative circles—corporate social responsibility, social enterprise, and social economy. The Sŏch'o District Office was quick to jump on this new trend, pursuing public-private partnerships with large corporations in order to revitalize the local economy. The Sŏch'o Creative Hub is the product of this partnership initiative, operated by a nonprofit foundation called Seed:s with financial support from Hyundai Motors.

The hub, which opened its door in 2011, has the objective of incubating social enterprises and providing a daily meeting venue for local residents and young social entrepreneurs.[26] It was conceived as a start-up support facility for local educational and cultural enterprises. A female social entrepreneur, L4, stepped foot in Saikil to put the ideal into action. L4 had previous experiences with "village-making" (*maul mandŭlgi*) social enterprise projects on Cheju Island and in Posŏng County, Southern Chŏlla Province, which made her new project a strong candidate for incubation support from the hub. A long-time Sŏch'o district resident hailing from nearby Old Panp'o, L4 possesses impressive credentials as a culture and arts educator. Her business proposal to the hub was a job creation program for highly educated women whose professional career was interrupted for various reasons, most commonly marriage and childbirth. For this program, she bought a building in the Saikil neighborhood and opened a café on the first floor, a gallery on the second, and a vocational art school for local housewives on the third. In her original plan, L4 attempted to create an employment placement service with cooperation from the Sŏch'o District Office. However, she also knew that many local housewives were not as invested in the program's stated goal: "The moms who are aware of this service are well-off, so they are not interested in being employed, but rather donating their talent through volunteering." Although "women experiencing career interruption" (*kyŏngnyŏk tanjŏl yŏsŏng*) are the intended beneficiaries of this program, the focus is on cultural self-achievement rather than individual financial need.

L4: [Women experiencing career interruption] are searching for their identity. If you don't do anything, it feels as if you are dead because you've lost yourself and your purpose.

Question: Are you saying there are psychological problems?

L4: Yes. Surprisingly, many of them suffer from depression. This neighborhood is not profligate, but most residents focus on self-development. They are devoted moms, but also send their children to study abroad. These moms have a structural problem in that they are negligent about finding themselves.

In fact, many gentrifiers in Saikil were themselves women who had experienced career interruptions. The gallery owner L3 opened her business ten years

Figure 6.3. European chic: artisanal workshop and café at Saikil. Source: author's collection.

after she quit her job at a design company and stopped working as a freelance illustrator. Her business partner, who helped transform the gallery into a restaurant/gallery, also quit her job after marriage. Through the business partner's experience living abroad in Europe and Canada for her child's education, she developed the skills and knowhow to help launch a restaurant (figure 6.3). Social enterprise projects for this demographic of highly educated homemaker women have had successes in the local community. C, the manager at the Sŏch'o Creative Hub, saw much potential in culture and arts education for youth and housewives, and predicted continuous investments in these projects by the Seed:s Foundation.

Can Community Building and Gentrification Be Made Compatible?

Unlike Karosukil, the Sŏch'o District Office and the Saikil gentrifiers are in careful coordination to plan future commercial development. They also make conscious efforts to keep close ties with the local residents. To avoid repeating the painful displacement from previous "hot spot" locations, social entrepreneur L4 partnered with several affluent gallery owners to purchase buildings.

This purchase eliminated worries over rising rents or obstinate landlords. The Pangbae Saikil Culture Street Association hosts a flea market twice a month and two festivals a year with the full support of the district office. Thanks to their concerted effort, the relationships between the local residents, gentrifying newcomers, and old-time local merchants are amicable overall. However, some conflicts and discomfort still persist.

I2, an artisanal workshop owner, has been an active participant in the Saikil Association. Through her participation, she realized that old-time establishments like corner stores, hair salons, hardware stores, and dry cleaners were being alienated from the festivals and flea markets dominated by new, gentrifying businesses. Moreover, the "clean and pretty" veneer of gentrification communicated a silent pressure of displacement for established businesses that catered to the local residents rather than visitors to the neighborhood. When the social entrepreneur L4 advocated for a more upscale 2013 street festival, several realtors and local merchants accused her of an ulterior motive to escalate neighborhood real estate prices, once it was known that she owned the building housing her business.

In Saikil, the pace of gentrification seems to be manageable, which is a rather positive sign for the local community. A loss of momentum, however, could lead to a decline of commercial viability of the neighborhood and eventual failure. Most of the gentrifiers interviewed for the research recognized this dilemma. The small size of the Saikil neighborhood compounds the gentrifiers' anxiety that the experiment may falter due to the lack of space for commercial expansion, among other drawbacks. To mitigate these risks, some of the leaders of the Saikil Association and the district office have worked to turn the area into a specialized "arts district" by designating Saikil as the Culture Street that connects two bigger and better-known hot spots: the French-Korean Sŏrae Village and the Pangbaedong Café Street. This ambitious plan was put forward by L4, and earned initial backing from the district mayor. The plan has yet to be implemented, due to complex regulatory issues as well as internal dissent within the association:

> Question: Haven't you thought about the possibility that the identity of Saikil might fade or disappear if it's merged with Sŏrae Village and the Café Street?
>
> I2: Some of us, especially last year's board members, are thinking that we need to create a cultural atmosphere so that people can come here and spend an entire day. In fact, we've had some dissenting voices among ourselves. At first, we had

some disputes over the geographic coverage of our association. Some argued that it should cover Saikil only, but others said we needed to expand it to the main road because the alley is too short . . . so it has been expanding ever since because that's how we can survive together as a commercial area. It may take time, but that's what the district office wants also. So when we suggested, without much thinking, a shuttle bus route connecting the three places [Sŏrae Village, Saikil, Café Street], the district mayor fell in love with the idea instantly. But she was very disappointed when the transportation department told her that city regulations and ordinances would make it difficult.

Administrative and regulatory hurdles are not the only problems with the expansion plans. Some residents, like the gallery owner L3, quoted below, are critical of the intervention of the district office and the commercial expansion itself, which may divide the local community:

Question: Is there anything you want from the government, politicians, journalists or academics who are interested in your area?

L3: To be blunt, I do not expect anything from them. Instead, I wish they would not take interest in us. I appreciate the interest from the government officials and politicians. But I don't welcome their attention because they're likely to exaggerate their modest contribution for their own purposes, and it raises the rent before we're even on the right track. If the media and academia make it a big deal and raise the expectations too high, people would be disappointed upon visiting here. This place is still in a nascent stage. Business interests and property owners' interests may affect it negatively. Even if everything goes well, it will take a long time for this place to develop its own color and flavor.

The Saikil experiment, which combines some elements of small-scale classical gentrification, social entrepreneurship, and public-private partnership initiatives, is still ongoing. At this point, as L3 has observed, it is still unclear whether a happy balance between new community building and commercial expansion is attainable. If so, it would be the first viable form of alternative urbanism countering Gangnam development and, paradoxically, emerging from Gangnam itself.

Gangnam's Rip-Current Gentrification

In late 2015, not long after the field research for this chapter was concluded, the flower café Bloom and Goûte completely withdrew from Sinsadong and relocated to the Panp'o area across Gangnam Boulevard. The exit of this legendary café that witnessed the vicissitudes of Karosukil over the years confirmed once again the breakneck speed of gentrification taking place in Gangnam. The co-owner of the café, L1, stated that they had learned a hard lesson from prior involuntary relocations, and purchased the building when Bloom and Goûte moved to the back alley of Karosukil. This latest relocation, then, was not caused by a tyrannical property owner. Whatever the reason for the relocation, the departure of Bloom and Goûte closed a brief window of opportunity for alternative urbanism in Karosukil. The area was finally overrun by the corporate tide of commercial gentrification.

I refer to the case of Karosukil during this period as "rip-current gentrification," but not because it defies the general current of wholesale urban (re)development typical of Gangnam. Rather, Karosukil exemplifies an epiphenomenon, subordinate to the massive tide of development while appearing here and there occasionally, on a small scale. Gangnam development would leave some pockets of relatively untouched hinterland, as it did in an old corner of Sinsadong. This process gave an opening for the urban pioneers armed with new, cosmopolitan cultural tastes to express their twenty-first-century urban aesthetics. On the surface, it may seem like a diametric opposite of twentieth-century Gangnam. In effect, however, the pioneers brought back a tide of development not so distinct from what had swept through twentieth-century Gangnam. What has happened to Karosukil may be characterized as either first- or third-wave gentrification, but that seems like only a minor point of distinction—after all, waves often change shapes and directions depending on winds and terrain—compared to the inexorable tide of Gangnam development.

It took Karosukil only fifteen or so years to cycle through all four stages of classical gentrification, demonstrating the enduring force of the real estate–driven capitalism behind Gangnam development. If the twentieth-century version of Gangnam development fits perfectly into the policy profile of the developmental state under the successive military-authoritarian regimes, the twenty-first-century version is governed by the dynamics of neoliberal capitalism, which allows for such rip-current gentrification to capture the cultural sensibilities and tastes of the new urban pioneers. These urban pioneers accumulate their cultural capital working in the mass media, fashion, advertisement, and entertainment industries. When they first gathered spontaneously in the Karosukil area and started their neighborhood beautification campaign, it appeared as though the neighborhood would turn into the "walkable blocks" and "livable streets" of New Urbanism.[27] However, Karosukil today shows all the signs of the commercial gentrification that plagued the nearby Apkujŏngdong Rodeo Street two decades ago. By comparison, the Saikil neighborhood in Pangbaedong sustains hopes for an alternative urbanism with a small-scale, organic, community-based approach. Many urban pioneers in this neighborhood participate in public policy discourses on "social enterprise" or "social economy." With municipal government support, their organized efforts to improve upon the neighborhood have made some significant progress. It remains to be seen whether the Saikil pioneers can resist the rip-current gentrification that overwhelmed Karosukil. In particular, the pioneers, the municipality, and the residents continue negotiations with one another, given the contradiction between the economic logic of commercial expansion and the social ethics of protecting local neighbors. In addition to this collaborative effort by the stakeholders, there are other deterrents to corporate-driven development, such as the small size and relatively poor access to mass transportation. However, these deterrents could sabotage their entrepreneurial efforts if the small neighborhood does not attract enough attention and foot traffic to sustain its commercial viability.

Gangnam's rip-current gentrification is essentially commercial in nature: urban pioneers move in for business, not residential, purposes. Further, displacement is a concern of the small, neighborhood merchants and shop owners, including urban pioneers themselves, rather than the resident population. The Karosukil neighborhood has already undergone many rounds of displacement with respect to its commercial establishments, but the surrounding residential area has not seen much change in terms of property value (still relatively low compared to nearby upscale places) and land use (there is still a stable ratio of commercial to residential use). Rents for residential housing might have risen over the years, but probably not by a lot, since the housing market in Gangnam is much more dependent on the availability of good schools than access to commercial amenities. The same is largely true of the Saikil neighborhood, which is even smaller than Karosukil in size, and therefore its impact on the nearby residential area, including the luxury villas on the hilltop, would be minimal. At the regional level, therefore, the rip-current gentrification in Karosukil and Saikil is of minimal significance to the residential pattern of Gangnam. For this reason, rip-current gentrification is more of an epiphenomenon in the new phase of Gangnam development dominated by new-build gentrification and super-gentrification. As such, it does not have much of an impact on socio-spatial mobility and class relations over the urban space.

Nonetheless, rip-current gentrification provides two opportunities for reconsidering Gangnam development. First, its retrospective style—emulating classical, first-wave gentrification—contributes to decontextualizing gentrification theory, as a viable alternative to the three-wave model of gentrification. As noted earlier, Gangnam development in the 1970s–1980s is more accurately understood as a vertical mode of suburbanization/urban sprawl than as second-wave, new-build gentrification. Second, and more importantly as we look ahead, rip-current gentrification highlights new cultural sensibilities and alternative urban discourses and practices. Gangnam has long been reviled for its uniform, standardized urban aesthetics of high-rise apartment complex in some corners of Korean society; the critique is especially pointed among highbrow elite or countercultural circles. Thus there has been little surprise at a classical pattern of gentrification emerging from such an old downtown neighborhood as the Bukchon Hanok Village since the early 2000s.[28] The evidence of a similar pattern within Gangnam, though, has a different meaning altogether; it suggests that even supposedly complacent upper-middle-class Gangnam residents are imagining different urban landscapes than what they have been used to for decades. The question is, then, whether these nascent signals indicate changes that can withstand the might of Korea's speculative urbanism on its very home turf, Gangnam.

Conclusion
Burning Down the House or Reaching across the River

> America is the strongest nation; it ostentatiously displays its power over the weak nations. This will be the future of Gangnam, which has become full of itself. The more America wields its power, the higher anti-Americanism surges among other nations. Likewise, anti-Gangnam sentiments rise proportionally to the increase in Gangnam's housing prices.
>
> —Hong Yŏng'ae, Cho Ŭnju, and Yu Sujŏng, "Is Gangnam Another America?"
>
> *The Rich in Gangnam*

In Lee Chang-dong's 2018 film *Burning*, the character Ben, surname unknown, is an avatar for twenty-first-century Gangnam. Despite his English name, Ben also speaks "perfect" Korean. The Korean American actor Steven Yeun (Yŏn Sang'yŏp), who plays the role of Ben, ironically finessed his language skills to master such Koreanized English pronunciations as the word "potluck" (*p'allŏk*) and the American novelist's name Faulkner (P'ok'ŭnŏ).[1] Everything else about Ben, however, alludes to lengthy sojourns in North America or other Anglophone regions. Just like K and Chaeyŏng, the two "Chamsil friends" from Kim Sagwa's novel *In Heaven*, many children of Gangnam's elite and upper-middle-strata families receive immersive English education as a formative aspect of their upbringing.[2] Ben is a self-professed member of the group Thorstein Veblen theorizes as the "leisure class," as evidenced by his demeanor: when Jong-su (Chongsu), the down-on-his-luck protagonist of *Burning*, asks Ben what he does for a living, he responds with a condescending smirk, "To put it simply, I play."[3] Never informed throughout the film of what Ben does, the viewer learns about Ben only by watching him "play" with other people, including Jong-su's (ex-)girlfriend Hae-mi. In that sense, the viewer might sympathize with Jong-su's lament, "mysterious people who are young and rich, but you don't know what they really do. There are so many Gatsbys in Korea." Ben is indeed one of South Korea's innumerable Gatsbys. While there are no exact equivalents of Daisy and Tom Buchanan or Nick Caraway, there is a scintillating, Roaring Twenties–style tension among the trio of main characters in *Burning*. In this ill-fated love triangle, each vertex points to a specific place where social class dynamics have played out historically:

> Jong-su is in Paju [P'aju], the rural northwest. The male antagonist Ben is in Gangnam, the hyper-urban southeast. At the dead center [of Seoul] is the mysterious girl Hae-mi, who lives in Huamdong, located on the western edge of the old Haebangch'on *wŏllammin* [early North Korean refugee] neighborhood. Not everyone would recognize the historical connection, but it might not be a pure coincidence that Hae-mi and Jong-su are portrayed as a sort of internal refugees within their own country: powerless, broke, alienated, yet still dreamy youths of "Hell Joseon [Chosŏn]" South Korea.[4]

Jong-su, an aspiring novelist, struggles to maintain the farmland his father left behind to serve a prison sentence for assaulting a government officer. Hae-mi, a gig worker who trades on her good looks to manage accelerating credit card debt, dreams of a cosmopolitan jet setter lifestyle. On a whim, one day she departs to Africa and returns with Ben, whom she has met at an airport. Jong-su, Hae-mi, and Ben spend time together at Jong-su's P'aju farmhouse and attend lavish Gangnam parties at Ben's mansion and upscale venues. Over time, Jong-su feels that he is losing Hae-mi to Ben. Though Jong-su and Hae-mi share the common experience of economic precarity and virtually unachievable artistic and literary ambitions, the glamourous promise of Gangnam proves too much for Hae-mi. Gradually she is estranged from Jong-su and his humble means, and drawn into the orbit of Ben's wealth and privilege. Then Hae-mi disappears without a trace, which leads to a confrontation between Jong-su and Ben. Using these slightly overstated characters, the film stages a traditional puppet theater (*kkoktugaksi norŭm*) to narrate the circumstances of modern youth in globalpolarization. As discussed in chapters 4 and 5, Hwang Sog'yŏng applied this puppetry method to *Dreams of Gangnam*, but many of his literary "puppets" were flat caricatures of such real-life villains as Yi Chun, the Sampoong disaster capitalist, and Cho Yang'ŭn, the room salon gangster boss. Instead of saturating the narrative with historical realism, Lee Chang-dong effects verisimilitude by deftly mixing dreams and dreamlike sequences with tense personal relationships between purely fictional characters. As a result, *Burning* renders a screen projection of the polarizing dreams Korean youth are subjected to.

In those polarizing dreams, Gangnam makes frequent appearances as the theater of capitalist phantasmagoria. In the acerbic poetry of Kwak Chaegu,

Hwang Chiu, and Yu Ha, the consumerist utopia is recast as American Murŭng, a commodity fetishist landscape infested with Coca-Cola and McDonald's logos. At the height of Korean commodity fetishism is Gangnam's prototypical highrise apartment, which Mun Ch'ŏnghŭi describes as a "massive weapon" in the guise of a rainbow. In Ch'oe Sŭngja's 1984 poem, Kirin's young family lived in a modest, affordable Togoktong apartment, no pricier than a comparable apartment across the river in Gangbuk. Since 1990, Gangnam's average apartment price has risen twentyfold, compared to a ninefold increase elsewhere in Seoul. A two-bedroom apartment in Gangnam today would cost forty-six years' worth of the average entry-level salary.[5] Korea's bloated real estate market, and the astronomical housing prices in Gangnam in particular, cannot be accounted for solely by economic logic. Property value inflation is driven by a veritable mass fetish for what Karl Polanyi referred to as a "fictitious commodity"—land.[6] In the case of high-rise apartments, this commodity is even more speculative, since the extra vertical space converts to a mere speck of land on the earth's surface, as Hwang Chiu's poem laments: "Out of thin air people create a space, make it a private property, and put the sacrosanct price on it." The prospect of acquiring this fictitious commodity and achieving the dream of social mobility, according to sociologist Myungji Yang, has turned "from miracle to mirage" in about three decades, "the short heyday" of the middle strata.[7] The brilliance of Psy's "Gangnam Style" is to condense the phantasmagoric roller-coaster ride of capitalist development into a four-minute music video.

It remains to be seen whether this development constitutes historical "progress," and if so, what the progress means. On the one hand, the political clout of the middle strata enabled the democratic transition during the tumultuous 1980s and early 1990s. It is true that during this period Gangnam did send a few liberal opposition politicians to the National Assembly instead of authoritarian loyalists. However, once the working-class militancy alarmed the middle strata shortly after the 1987 democratic uprising, Gangnam politics have trended consistently toward conservatism. Early Gangnam literature by Ch'oe Inho, Pak Wansŏ, and, most conspicuously, Cho Sehŭi, already foresaw the schism within the community, the breakdown of neighborly love between those who imagined their fortunes to be rising and those who did not. *The Dwarf* series Cho had written over a decade closed with the nightmarish image of a seemingly deranged fugitive shouting "What we want is progress!" at the "malicious diseases"—reminiscent of the global pandemic at the time of this writing—that pursued him (see the introduction). That final piece of *The Dwarf* saga was published in 1983, still a few years before the opening fanfare of the 1988 Olympic Games in the Chamsil Stadium that heralded the triumphal era of Korean industrial capitalism. Progress had finally arrived, or so it seemed, until disaster followed.

Korea's disaster capitalism originates in the "shock doctrine" of the Vietnam War, in which more than 346,000 South Korean troops fought in alliance with the U.S. military from 1964 until 1973. During the so-called Vietnam [War] boom (*pet'ŭnam t'ŭksu*), nearly two hundred million USD of soldiers' remittances was used to fund the Park Chung Hee administration's economic plans and urbanization projects, including the Seoul-Busan Expressway and Gangnam development. It also meant that future construction *chaebŏl* were given a head start to build facilities for the U.S. military in war-torn Southeast Asia before moving on to another conflict zone in the Middle East. When Samir Amin foresaw "global polarization" at the end of the Cold War, Korean construction companies had already made a significant contribution to such a "world in chaos."[8] The pattern of exploiting disaster overseas culminated in devastating consequences after companies returned home to Korea: first the structural failures of Sŏngsu and Sampoong and the loss of more than five hundred lives, and then a series of bankruptcies that triggered a national economic collapse with the IMF Crisis.

Some disasters bring people together to help, commiserate, and recover. Others do the opposite, rending the social fabric, dividing winners from losers, and sowing resentment among them. It was the latter variety of disasters that struck Korea in the 1990s, while the country was swept into a globalization campaign. Thus began Korea's global-polarization. Some middle-strata families have fallen apart and drifted away like grains of sand. Others endure in precarious living conditions, like the Kim family in Bong Joon-ho's *Parasite*. Of course, in the same movie, the Paks, a gullible, naïve, but fabulously wealthy family, stands in contrast. For younger generations that have come of age since the IMF Crisis, global-polarization takes place in multiple layers of cultural identity and social division, as seen in the film *Burning* and the novel *In Heaven*. One thing is clear: it is increasingly difficult to build some sort of affective solidarity that cuts across those layers and divisions. Romance, friendship, and genuine empathy becomes a rarity between people of different class backgrounds who were not that different from one another a mere generation or two prior. In the later Gangnam literature of Chŏng Migyŏng, Chŏng Ihyŏn, Yi Hong, Kim Yun'yŏng, and Kim Sagwa, there is a frequent lament for the fragility of middle-strata camaraderie, which easily disintegrates into a competition of climbing the social ladder.

Some might argue that twenty-first-century Gangnam represents genuine progress, given the Korean economy's quick recovery and growth due to the global rise of high tech and media culture industries concentrated in the area.

Having received a crucial stimulus from public and private capital investments after the crisis, the technology sector indeed flourished in Teheran Valley. For the media entertainment sector, especially the music industry, the trajectory is more complex. As discussed in chapter 1, the music and adult entertainment businesses found their opportunities in the early years of Gangnam development. By the late 1980s, the Sinsadong Circuit and the Pangbaedong Corridor emerged as new trendsetters of popular music culture, the former known for its trot and dance music and the latter for ballads. Entertainment culture developed in tandem with the sex industry, which flourished due to government policies promoting *kisaeng* tourism in Gangnam. The proliferation of room salons resulted from the prevailing business culture of Korean capitalism, also driven by government policy. The sex-beauty-entertainment industrial complex was established in the Sinsadong Circuit, expanding along the horizontal axis of Teheran Road by the 2000s. The dangerous liaison between the sex and the entertainment industries has engendered public scandals, including the Burning Sun incident, which incriminated one of the largest K-pop entertainment companies—incidentally, the producer of Psy's "Gangnam Style."

Perhaps it is not surprising that the best-known visual media narratives of the Korean Wave (*Hallyu*) in recent years are also critiques of Korean "progress." Following Bong Joon-ho's *Parasite*, a string of Netflix dramas including *Squid Game, Hellbound* (*Chiok*, 2021), *All of Us Are Dead* (*Chigŭm uri hakkyonŭn*, dir. Yi Chaegyu, 2022), and *The Glory* (*Tŏ Kŭllori*, dir. An Kirho, 2023) feature apocalyptic portrayals of contemporary Korean society. The range of social evils represented in these dramas includes impoverishment, personal debt, cutthroat competition, school violence, and suicide. Yeon Sang-ho, the director of *Hellbound,* incorporated these themes into earlier works, such as *The King of Pigs*. Another forerunner text exploring Gangnam's social evil is Yoon Jong-bin's *Beastie Boys,* which focuses on the sex industry. Here, Gangnam's evil sense of place cuts in both ways: it is obviously destructive to the good morals of the community, while providing ample material for the media entertainment industry to export captivating visual narratives for a global audience. Unlike many other pessimistic depictions of Korea's societal ills in the wake of Psy's "Gangnam Style," *Burning* is exceptional in forging a sensational portrayal of global-polarization and its attendant miseries. Its polarizing dreams do not evoke a zombie apocalypse, a reality TV horror show, or a kitschy satire of wealth and power; rather, the film conveys the real fear and dread many Koreans harbor in their daily lives, if only unconsciously.

Lee Chang-dong's film is loosely based on Haruki Murakami's short story "Barn Burning" ("Naya o yaku," 1983), which was in turn inspired by William

Faulkner's story with the same title. The Korean film took only half of the original English title without translation—an elision that makes sense as the story unfolds. In Murakami's version, there is indeed a barn burner, or rather a character confessing to his habit of traversing the countryside and setting fire to other people's barns. Lee transposes a strange dialogue between the barn burner and the narrator in Murakami's story onto the conversation between Ben and Jong-su:

[Ben:] Sometimes I burn down greenhouses.

[Jong-su:] Excuse me?

[Ben:] I said sometimes I burn down greenhouses. I have a hobby of burning greenhouses. I choose an abandoned greenhouse and set it on fire. Once every two months? I think that's the best pace for me.

[Jong-su:] Pace? So you burn down other people's greenhouses?

[Ben:] Of course. It's a crime so to speak . . . it's very simple though. You spray kerosene then throw a lit match. That's it. It takes less than four minutes for it to burn down. You can make it disappear as if it never existed.

[Jong-su:] What if you get caught?

[Ben:] I won't get caught. Ever. The Korean police don't care about those sorts of things.

The only significant difference between Murakami's and Lee's versions up to this point is that Lee uses "greenhouse" in place of "barn"—hence the single-word film title, *Burning*. Before returning to Murakami's script, the dialogue takes an ominous turn as Ben goes on about greenhouses: "In Korea, there are tons of greenhouses. Useless, filthy, unpleasant-looking greenhouses. It's like they're all waiting for me to burn them down. And as I watch them burn to the ground, I feel great joy." The viewer is left to wonder what would account for this Gangnam Gatsby's antipathy toward the shabby, vinyl-clad greenhouses, nearly ubiquitous in rural areas and suburbs.[9]

Barns and greenhouses are both widely used in Korea. In one scene, Jong-su is shown working in the barn on his father's farm and later selling off the last little cow who lived there. Thus, the greenhouse motif and the character Ben's fixation on greenhouse arson are likely for allusive effect. One of Lee's earlier works, the temporally retrograde film *Peppermint Candy* (*Pakhasat'ang*, 1999), begins with a protagonist who was financially ruined in the IMF Crisis and took shelter in a greenhouse. Lee's use of greenhouses has a particular meaning in a global-polarized Korea: they are new sorts of shanties, or "non-house dwellings" (*pijut'aek chugŏ*) in which more than ten thousand destitute families or individuals reside. Over half of such dwellings are located within the Seoul Capital Area, forming plastic shantytowns of the twenty-first century. One such place, named Guryong Village (Kuryong maŭl), exists less than a mile away from Tower Palace, the totem pole of Gangnam's wealth and power.[10] Numerous journalists have used the iconic image of super-gentrified apartments towering over the plastic shanties of Guryong Village as an indictment of increasing inequality and social polarization. In this context, Ben's disdainful remarks on "useless, filthy" greenhouses and his expressed desire to burn them all down are unambiguously terrifying threats to the underclass who dare to occupy space near the high and mighty. The day after the conversation with Ben, Jong-su awakens from a dream of a burning greenhouse and his younger self standing transfixed before the flames. A conflagration of class animosity, built up for decades since Ch'oe Inho noticed the madness of land development in "Savage," may be only a lit match away from bringing down the entire social structure. Jong-su's dream reveals the instability and potential chaos that are consequences of global-polarization.

Not all dreams of Gangnam, however, reach the same infernal conclusion. Hwang Sŏg'yŏng reminds the reader of working-class perseverance by ending his book with the miraculous survival and rescue of the female Sampoong employee Chŏng'a. R, another Sampoong employee in Chŏng Ihyŏn's story remains an emblem of cross-class solidarity in the author's enduring memory. Overcoming their decades-old trauma, some courageous Sampoong survivors have come forward to memorialize their pain and reach out to the suffering families of the Sewŏl victims. The actual disaster, not a potential one looming over the horizon, has made people hope for and dream of a better future. Gangnam development, after all, was premised on the dream of social mobility, the last century's "mass utopian dream" of rising from the ashes of the catastrophic war. Even though that utopia turned out to be a pavilion on the sand, people still yearn for and strive toward different dreams.

Among those dreamers are new urban activists. Often seen as gentrifiers, they are bohemian segments of the Gangnam bourgeoisie, disenchanted with high-rise concrete aesthetics. The new urban activists have introduced small-scale, European urban styles and artistic sensibilities to their surroundings. Two such urban projects considered in this book, Karosukil and Saikil, demonstrate both the perils and potentials of new spatial practices. Karosukil has gone through the stages of classical gentrification to be hollowed out and absorbed into corporate chain stores. Saikil, on the other hand, has thus far managed to avoid the rampant commercialization that threatens to displace the local population, thanks to cooperative efforts among the urban activists, the resident community, and the municipal government. These small-scale experiments are unlikely to transform Gangnam as a whole, but they demonstrate the potential of local activists to affect the representation of space through new spatial practice, sparking new ideas for urban design, planning, and administration. It may be an idle dream at this point, but there is transformative potential for Gangnam. The evil sense of place can change from within if similar local initiatives emerge and gain collective momentum. Or the pervasive sense of social evil can be disrupted from without, by externally organized spatial practices. The "sticky-note activism" and mass rallies at Gangnam Station brought an incandescent protest movement against gender discrimination and violence against women to the area occupied by the sex-beauty-entertainment industrial complex. In 2019, a former employee of Samsung climbed an eighty-two-foot-tall traffic-camera tower standing at the Gangnam Station intersection. From that tiny perch across from the Samsung Corporate Headquarters, the twice-dismissed worker named Kim Yonghŭi launched a daring solo "high-altitude protest" accusing Samsung of its notorious anti-labor union policy. He did not come down to the ground for an astonishing 355 days, until the humiliated company agreed to apologize for firing him.[11] These acts of contention created unprecedented political spectacles at Gangnam's center of gravity, shifting public perception of the place from passive self-indulgence to active self-expression, if only temporarily.

Han Yŏng'ae, a mainstay of Korea's blues-folk music scene since the 1970s, released the song "Utter Nonsense" ("Maldo andwae") in her 1992 solo album. Han's lyrics were a cynical comment on the country's rudderless state of affairs and lack of meaningful communication among the people: "Where have we thrown away our standard of value / I don't know, you don't know, just follow blindly / it's a plastic world, blown up like a balloon." The song gained widespread popularity during the early 1990s political folk song boom, when Nochatsa, Kim Kwangsŏk, and like-minded singer-songwriters were also warmly embraced by the public. Like the repertory of Kim Kwangsŏk discussed in chapter 4, "Utter Nonsense" drips with irony and weariness, as if haunted by a premonition of the disasters to come. And just like Kim Kwangsŏk cheering himself out of depression in his swan song "Rise," Han's "Utter Nonsense" shares a hopeful note in the chorus: "Still, hope lies in human being [*saram*], you and I hand in hand / Hope remains shared by people, us human beings." Surveying Gangnam's representational space in this book, we may have already encountered such a figure of hope. Eun-hee is a middle school student in *The House of Hummingbird*. Through her emotional journeys in mid-1990s Gangnam, Eun-hee overcomes adversities large and small: betrayed friendship, spurned romance, social-class discrimination, traumatic loss due to disaster, and gendered domestic violence. Through it all, Eun-hee gradually matures as a human being, undaunted by the harsh challenges thrown at her. If there is anyone with the clarity of mind to see through the polarizing dreams of contemporary Gangnam, it would be the fictional, grown-up Eun-hee. Though she must have long departed her hummingbird house, Eun-hee would not want to see it burned down, even in the figurative sense. Hope may reside with characters like Eun-hee, who can extend a hand of solidarity across the river, across the border, and across rigid, arcane class divides.

Notes

Introduction: Gangnam, the Phantasmagoria of Korean Capitalism

1. Henceforth, South Korea and its people will be referred to simply as "Korea" and "Koreans" unless a distinction between North Korea and South Korea is necessary.
2. For the global impact of America's suburban dream, see Beauregard, *When America Became Suburban*, 164–167.
3. See Gelézeau, *Republic of Apartments*; Gelézeau, "Korean Modernism," 173–179. For a critique of Le Corbusier's "high modernism," to which we can add Gangnam as another example, see Scott, *Seeing like a State*, chap. 4.
4. Benjamin, *Arcades Project*, 460.
5. Cho S., *Sigan yŏhaeng*, 99.
6. Berman, *All That Is Solid*, 15.
7. Buck-Morss, "City as Dreamworld and Catastrophe," 9. Mike Davis was actually a few years ahead of Buck-Morss in his ever-so-clairvoyant book on Los Angeles, presenting dialectical images of the city and attributing the idea to Benjamin's friend and mentor Bertolt Brecht: "Los Angeles in this instance is, of course, a stand-in for capitalism in general. The ultimate world-historical significance—and oddity—of Los Angeles is that it has come to play the double role of utopia *and* dystopia, for advanced capitalism. The same place, as Brecht noted, symbolized both heaven and hell" (Davis, *City of Quartz*, 18).
8. J. I. Kim, "Birth of Urban Modernity in Gangnam," 371–372.
9. See Beauregard, *When America Became Suburban*, 147–156.
10. See Yun C., "Pet'ŭnam chŏnjaeng ch'amj'ŏn'ŭi an'gwa pak."
11. For the sordid details of political corruption over Gangnam's land speculation, see Son C., *Sŏul tosi kyehoek iyagi*, 1:96–150.
12. See SMH, *Kangnam sasimnyŏn*, 43.
13. Ibid., 8–9; Son C., *Sŏul tosi kyehoek iyagi*, vol. 1.
14. Nelson, *Measured Excess*, 44. See also Lett, *In Pursuit of Status*, 59.
15. Amin, "Future of Global Polarization," 75.
16. Amin also wrote, "The international polarization inherent in this [capitalist] expansion brings internal polarization: growing inequality in income, widespread unemployment, and marginalization" (*Empire of Chaos*, 89).
17. Yang, *From Miracle to Mirage*, 17, 137.
18. Koo, *Privilege and Anxiety*, 12.
19. See Yi C., "T'ugiwa kŏp'um"; Pak and Hong, "Chugŏrŭl t'onghan sahoejŏk kwasiŭi han'gukchŏk t'ŭksusŏng."

20. Harvey, *Brief History of Neoliberalism*, 157. See also Smith, "New Globalism, New Urbanism."

21. See Davis, *City of Quartz*, 128–134; and Park and Kim, "Contested Nexus of Los Angeles Koreatown."

22. See Smith, *New Urban Frontier*; and Lees, Shin, and López-Morales, *Planetary Gentrification*, among others.

23. Koo, *Privilege and Anxiety*, 48–52.

24. In fact, the 75–85 percent of total household assets in real estate has been the norm across the income/wealth spectrum since the early 1990s. The "Survey of Household Finances and Living Conditions" ("Kagye kŭm'yung pokchi chosa") results from 2010 until the present are available on the Statistics Korea website (https://kostat.go.kr/portal/eng/index.action). For the earlier data, refer to Yu K., "Urinara kakyeŭi kŭm'yung kyŏlchŏng'yoin punsŏk," 8.

25. P. H. Kim, "Branding the Sense of Place," 267. See also Oh, *Pop City*.

26. Yu Ha, *Parambunŭn narimyŏn apkujŏngdong'e kayahanda*, 61.

27. See Butler and Lees, "Super-Gentrification in Barnsbury, London."

28. Davis, *City of Quartz*, 34.

29. See Buck-Morss, *Dialectics of Seeing*; Dillon, "Montage/Critique."

30. Benjamin, *One-Way Street*, 352. For a detailed discussion, see Caygill, "Walter Benjamin's Concept of Cultural History."

31. Cho S., *Sigan yŏhaeng*, 249.

32. Benjamin, *Arcades Project*, 460.

33. Merrifield, *Henri Lefebvre*, 109.

34. Bourdieu, *Distinction*. See also Koo, *Privilege and Anxiety*, 14–15.

35. Bourdieu, *Distinction*, 124 (emphasis in original).

36. Ibid., 572.

Chapter 1: Boomtown Songs on the South of the River: The Origins of "Gangnam Style"

1. See Namgung, "Ssaiŭi 'kangnam sŭt'ail' myujikpidio kiho punsŏk," and O S., "Ssaiŭi kangnamsŭt'aire taehan chigak yŏngu," among others.

2. The list of academic literature on "Gangnam Style" is quite long. For Korean-language literature, see, among others, Kim and Kang, "K'eip'ab'esŏŭi t'ŭraensŭmidiŏ chŏllyag'e taehan koch'al"; Kwon, "Insig'ŭi mobilit'iŭi iron'gwa silche"; Yi Hyŏnsŏk, "Ssaiŭi yŏngsang myujikpidio kangnam sŭt'aire tŭrŏnan k'ich'iwa mim'e taehan yŏn'gu"; Yun I., "Homonaraensŭ." For English-language literature, see, among others, J. Choi, "Right to the City"; Lee and Kuwahara, "'Gangnam Style' as a Format"; Lie, "Why Didn't 'Gangnam Style' Go Viral in Japan?"; Tan, "K-Contagion."

3. "Ai Weiwei Does Gangnam Style," YouTube video, October 25, 2012, https://www.youtube.com/watch?v=n281GWfT1E8; "MIT Gangnam Style," YouTube video, October 27, 2012, https://www.youtube.com/watch?v=IJtHNEDnrnY.

4. Bakhtin, *Problems of Dostoevsky's Poetics*, 122. See also J. Choi, "Right to the City."

5. Tan, "K-Contagion," 87.

6. There is no single official name for Psy's dance move in "Gangnam Style." I use "horse-trot" mainly because the term "trot," which originated from the Western dance foxtrot, has a rich history with Korean popular music. I will discuss this later in the chapter.

7. Max Fisher, "Gangnam Style, Dissected: The Subversive Message within South Korea's Music Video Sensation," *The Atlantic*, August 23, 2012.

8. Jea Kim, "Korean Music: PSY's 'Gangnam Style' and 'Gangnam Oppa' in 'Architecture 101,'" *My Dear Korea: Eat Korean, Talk Korean, Surf the Korean Wave* (blog), August 9, 2012, https://web.archive.org/web/20121005044813/http://mydearkorea.blogspot.com/2012/08/korean-music-psys-gangnam-style-and.html (the original blog has been removed, but the post is still accessible via Internet Archive).

9. See Yi Tong'yŏn, "Everything I Know about Psy."

10. Bakhtin, *Problems of Dostoevsky's Poetics*, 142.

11. See Chapman, "Fyodor Dostoyevsky," 35.

12. Ryu S., *Sŏul akeidŭ p'rojekt'ŭ*, 236.

13. Most of the indoor filming took place in Incheon, especially the new town of Songdo. See Kim Yŏnghwan, "The Popularity of Psy's 'Gangnam Style' Music Video Also Lifts Its Filming Location, Incheon," *Han'gyŏre sinmun*, August 23, 2012, http://www.hani.co.kr/arti/society/area/548377.html.

14. Bakhtin, *Problems of Dostoevsky's Poetics*, 124.

15. See Hwang, *Kangnammong*, chap. 4. See also Porteux, "Police, Paramilitaries, Nationalists and Gangsters," 47–68.

16. Bakhtin, *Problems of Dostoevsky's Poetics*, 128.

17. See Kang, *Kangnam*, 73–74; SMH, *Kangnam sasimnyŏn*, 147.

18. See Son C., *Sŏul tosi kyehoek iyagi*, 1:168–171; SMH, *Kangnam sasimnyŏn*, 44.

19. For English-language academic literature on trot, see, among others, Y. Chang, "Trot and Ballad"; G. L. Pak, "On the Mimetic Faculty"; M. J. Son, "Politics of the Traditional Korean Popular Song Style T'ŭrot'ŭ." Recent "trot revival" among the younger generation audiences and in Korean mainstream media brought back academic interests in this controversial old-school genre.

20. Unlike Namsŏul or Yŏngdong, Gangnam has some cultural prestige attached to it since the name originated from China's Jiangnan (江南), the region south of the Yangtze renowned for its affluence, natural beauty, and refined culture since the ancient period.

21. See Korea Music Copyright Association, https://www.komca.or.kr/srch2/srch_01.jsp.

22. See SMH, *Kangnam sasimnyŏn*, 44. Chapter 5 will discuss the development of Gangnam's sex industry in further detail.

23. Ch'oe Sŭnghyŏn, "Nan wae namgwa tarŭlkka" [Why am I different from others], *Chosŏn ilbo*, April 7, 2006, https://www.chosun.com/site/data/html_dir/2006/04/07/2006040770493.html.

24. Sin, Yi, and Ch'oe, *Han'guk p'ab'ŭi kogohak ilguch'ilgong*, 243. See Kim and Shin, "Birth of 'Rok,'" for Shin Joong Hyun's status in Korean rock music history.

25. See Kang, *Kangnam*, 133–134, and SMH, *Kangnam sasimnyŏn*, 149.

26. Im Chinmo, "Param'ŭi adŭl kasu Yun Suil" [A son of the wind: Singer Yoon Soo Il], *Wŏlgan chosŏn*, June 2006, http://monthly.chosun.com/client/news/viw.asp?nNewsNumb=200606100041.

27. Nam Kug'in and An Ch'ihaeng interviews with author, May 10, 2012.

28. Ch'oe Pongho was a dominant impresario in the 1970–1980s. His story was adapted to the MBC television drama series *Light and Shadow* (*Pitkwa kŭrimja*, 2011–2012).

29. Spiked markers represent performance venues, record companies, and studios that formed the original Sinsadong Circuit in the 1980s; small dots represent contemporary music industry establishments registered with the Ministry of Culture, Sports, and Tourism since 2015 (http://data.seoul.go.kr/dataList/OA-17214/S/1/datasetView.do).

Notes to Pages 34–47

30. Ŏm Yongsŏp interview with author, May 24, 2012.

31. Yi Hosŭng, "Pangbaedong kkap'e changmiŭi sup" [Pangbaedong café, "Forest of Roses"], *Kyŏnghyang sinmun*, March 13, 2002, https://www.khan.co.kr/article/200203131707211.

32. Kim Suwan, "Sŏurŭi kkap'e munhwa kaesŏngsidaerŭl yŏnda" [Seoul, café culture opens an era of individuality], *Kyŏnghyang sinmun*, September 7, 1987.

33. Ch'oe Hosŏp interview with author, August 22, 2012.

34. The list includes the singer-songwriter Kim Hyŏnch'ol, the ballad–hip-hop duo Panic (Yi Chŏk and Kim Chinp'yo), and the rapper Verbal Jint (Kim Chint'ae), among others.

35. Yi Chin interview with author, May 29, 2012.

36. For a primer on the PSM, see A. Park, "Modern Folksong and People's Song," P. H. Kim, "Songs of the Multitude," and Jung-min Mina Lee, "Minjung Kayo."

37. See Harvey, *Condition of Postmodernity*.

38. See E.-Y. Jung, "Articulating Korean Youth Culture," and Maliangkay, "Popularity of Individualism."

39. The slogan came from a Korean book by the cultural activist group Mimesis (Mimesisŭ) entitled *New Generation: Do Whatever You Want*.

40. For the orange tribe, see Nelson, *Measured Excess*, 152.

Chapter 2: Paradise across the River: Gangnam in Literature

1. For the *minjung* movement and literature, see Barraclough, *Factory Girl Literature*; Namhee Lee, *Making of Minjung*; S. Park, *Revisiting Minjung*; Wells, *South Korea's Minjung Movement*.

2. Kwak, *Chŏnjangp'o arirang*, 22–23.

3. Kim Chesŏp was credited for this song adaptation. He was a prominent activist in the People's Song Movement as a member of Meari (Echo) at Seoul National University and later of Nochatsa. An Ch'ihwan, another Song Movement veteran who launched a successful career as a pop musician afterward, recorded "Coca-Cola" for his album *Beyond Nostalgia* (2016).

4. See Nelson, *Measured Excess*, 45–47.

5. For the concept of hyperurbanity, see Detweiler, "Hyperurbanity."

6. Ch'oe, "Migaein," 265.

7. The community was named Ettinger Village after Harry Bill Ettinger, a lawyer and board member of the American-Korean Foundation, whose personal donation contributed to the establishment of the village by the American-Korean Foundation. The incident took place at Taewang Elementary School in 1969, when parents of the students protested against the admission of five children from Ettinger Village, staging a rally in front of the Ministry of Education and refusing to send their children to school. See Matt VanVolkenburg, "Fighting Segregation in Seoul's Schools in 1969," *Korea Times*, September 24, 2019, https://www.koreatimes.co.kr/www/nation/2024/02/113_276063.html, and the Korea Democracy Foundation Open Archive, https://archives.kdemo.or.kr/photo-archives/view/00755939.

8. Ch'oe, "Migaein," 254. For a more in-depth analysis of "Savage," see Song Ŭ., *Sŏul t'ansaenggi*, 370–377.

9. For more about the "apartment fiction" (*ap'at'ŭ sosŏl*) subgenre and Pak's contribution to it, see Chŏng M., "Pak wansŏ sosŏlgwa," and H. S. Kim, "'My' Sweet Home."

10. Pak W., "Nakt'oŭi aidŭl," 305.

11. Ibid., 309. Note Pak's clever use of the homonym (*p'anŭn saram*) for tiller/seller.

12. For further analysis of "Kids in Paradise," see Song Ŭ., *Sŏul t'ansaenggi*, 387–392.

13. See Pihl, "The Nation, the People, and a Small Ball," and Y. Ryu, *Writers of the Winter Republic*, for the singular status of *The Dwarf* in modern Korean literature.

14. Cho S., *Dwarf*, 81.

15. Cho S., *Sigan yŏhaeng*, 164.

16. Hyundai received the approval for construction on the condition that it would set aside 952 of the 1,512 units for its employees who did not own a house. As it turned out, more than six hundred of those units were illicitly sold to others, including "high-ranking government officials, national assemblymen, prosecutors, and intelligence agents" ("Ap'aat'ŭ t'ŭkhyebun'yang modu yukpaengmyŏng" [A total of six hundred involved in the apartment parcel-out scandal], *Tong'a ilbo*, July 4, 1978).

17. Cho S., *Sigan yŏhaeng*, 164, 262.

18. Y. Ryu, *Writers of the Winter Republic*, 103.

19. Deleuze, *The Fold*, 125.

20. Cho S., *Dwarf*, 91.

21. In English-language literature, Charles R. Kim's *Youth for Nation* stands out as a comprehensive treatment of the April Revolution. See chapter 5 in particular for the critical distinction between "authorized protests" led by students and "unauthorized" protests by the underclass. Also see P. H. Kim, "Songs of the Multitude."

22. Cumings, *Korea's Place*, 393.

23. Inspired by the young worker Chŏn T'aeil's self-immolation in 1970, a number of student activists carefully cultivated a "labor-student alliance" (*nohak tongmaeng*) by dedicating themselves to labor organizing and worker education. In *The Dwarf*, the character named Han Chisŏp embodies the spirit of the labor-student alliance. For more on the students' role in the labor movement, see Hagen Koo, *Korean Workers*, chap. 5, and Namhee Lee, *Making of Minjung*, chap. 7, among others.

24. O Yun's *Marketing* series has two installments with the identical subtitle *Painting of Hell*, and Coca-Cola makes an appearance on both (I and V).

25. Buck-Morss, *Dialectics of Seeing*, 81. See Gunning, "Phantasmagoria and the Manufacturing of Illusions," for the uses of phantasmagoria by Marx, Benjamin, and Adorno.

26. For Coca-Cola and the American Dream, see Wagnleitner, "Propagating the American Dream"; Madsen, *China and the American Dream*, 219–220, 225; Samuel, *American Dream*, 84.

27. Y. Ryu, *Writers of the Winter Republic*, 101.

28. Yu Ha, *Parambunŭn narimyŏn apkujŏngdong'e kayahanda*, 63–64.

29. The car model was the Hyundai Pony, translated as the Ford Pinto. The Pony was billed as Korea's "first mass-produced car" in 1975 (*Korea Times*, February 21, 1975). The Pony became a proud symbol of Korea's industrial prowess.

30. S. Choi, "Merry Diary," in *Portrait of a Suburbanite*, 87.

31. See H. S. Kim, "*My Car* Modernity," and H. S. Kim, "'My' Sweet Home." Cho Sehŭi also addresses this in a short story published in *Roots of Silence*: "Han Yŏngsik finally got to ride an air-conditioned sedan after working exactly eleven years and eight months for the Ŭn'gang Group. Riding an air-conditioned company car at Ŭn'gang meant that he survived numerous fiery battles, standing tall; it also meant that as a member of the board of directors he would take an office space with a painting hanging on the wall within the corporate headquarters, participate in policy decision meetings, get a significant salary bump from the middle-manager years, and get job trainings in a hotel where afternoon lessons include golf

on a green field. On the company dime they could eat beefsteak and drink wine in a clean-cut restaurant where servers wear a suit and tie and operate without noise" (Cho S., *Ch'immug'ŭi ppuri,* 77).

32. S. Choi, "Merry Diary," 89. My reading of this stanza is somewhat different from Eunju Kim's translation cited here. In any case, see the extensive footnotes accompanying Kim's translation for obscure references and colloquial expressions in the original.

33. See Yang, *From Miracle to Mirage,* 18–19, and Koo, *Privilege and Anxiety,* 20–23. For a historical overview of the middle-strata debate and the "rediscovery" of Marxian class analysis in South Korea, see Sin K., *Han'gug'ŭi kyegŭpkwa pulp'yŏngdŭng,* chap. 3.

34. See Bae and Joo, "Making of Gangnam," 738–740.

35. See Wright, *Classes,* 56–57, and Sin K., *Han'gug'ŭi kyegŭpkwa pulp'yŏngdŭng.*

36. See the translator's "Introduction," in S. Choi, *Portrait of a Suburbanite,* vii–xvii. See also D. M. Choi, "Overview of Contemporary Korean Women's Poetry," and Williams, "'Female Poet' as Revolutionary Grotesque," for interpretations of Ch'oe's poetry from feminist perspectives.

37. For Yŏŭido development and its relationship with Gangnam, see Nelson, *Measured Excess,* 41–45, and Y. Oh, *Pop City.*

38. S. Choi, "Yeoui Island Rhapsody," in *Portrait of a Suburbanite,* 101, 103.

39. Kang and Kim, "Hwang chiuŭi ch'ŏn'gubaekp'alsimnyŏndae," 70.

40. See Pak C., *Ap'at'ŭ,* for Old Panp'o's significance in Gangnam development.

41. Hwang C., "Cheil han'ganggyo'e naradŭn kalmaegi," in *Saedŭldo sesang'ŭl ttŭnŭn'guna,* 97–98.

42. Hwang C., "Kubanp'o sanggarŭl kŏrŏganŭn nakt'a," *Kubanp'o sanggarŭl kŏrŏganŭn nakt'a,* 104–114.

43. See National Archives of Korea, "Korean residents in the U.S.A.," http://theme.archives.go.kr/next/immigration/ImmigrationLaw.do.

44. Once again, Ch'oe Inho shrewdly kept his finger on the pulse of Korean dreams about U.S. immigration as he wrote the novella *Deep Blue Night* (*Kipko p'urŭn pam,* 1982) and later adapted it into the eponymous film (1984), which achieved both box office success and critical acclaim.

45. On postcolonial mimicry, see Bhabha, "Of Mimicry and Man."

46. Yu Ha, "Parambunŭn narimyŏn apkujŏngdong'e kayahanda 1," *Parambunŭn narimyŏn apkujŏngdong'e kayahanda,* 60.

47. Yu Ha, "Parambunŭn narimyŏn apkujŏngdong'e kayahanda 3," ibid., 66. Sim Hyejin is an actress whose popularity peaked in the late 1980s and the early 1990s. Sŏ Chŏng'yun's book *Standing Alone* (*Hollosŏgi,* 1987), which Yu Ha apparently regards as a collection of potboiler poetry, sold three million copies.

48. See "'Kyŏrhon'ŭn mich'in chisida' ro toraon yuha kamdok, siwa yŏnghwaŭi nanaldŭl" [Director Yu Ha returns with *Marriage Is a Crazy Thing*: Days of poems and movies], *Cine21,* April 24, 2002, http://www.cine21.com/news/view/?mag_id=9735.

49. Buck-Morss, "City as Dreamworld and Catastrophe," 9.

50. See Son Minho, "Saeroun han'guksosŏl kangnam riŏllijŭm" [New Korean fiction, "Gangnam Realism,"] *Chung'ang ilbo,* November 20, 2006, https://www.joongang.co.kr/article/2513340, and Pak Haehyŏn, "Munhaksok kangnam'enŭn kangbujaman salji annŭnda" [Not all Gangnam residents are wealthy landlords in literary depictions of Gangnam], *Chosŏn ilbo,* March 3, 2008, http://news.chosun.com/site/data/html_dir/2008/03/03/2008030300019.html.

51. Mun C., "Apkujŏng'ŭl ttŏnamyŏ," in *Nanŭn mun'ida*, 158–159.
52. The upper middle class was 18 percent in Gangnam compared to 11.5 percent citywide, and Gangnam's working-class proportion (37 percent) is only slightly lower compared to the 40 percent citywide. While the regional income gap between Gangnam and the rest of Seoul was not as wide as one might have thought, the wealth disparity based on real estate value was substantial: the average Gangnam real estate asset was worth about 140 percent of the citywide average. See Sin K., *Han'gug'ŭi kyegŭpkwa pulp'yŏngdŭng*, 196–204.
53. Kim Miyŏng, "Welk'ŏm t'u kangnam," 214.
54. Yi Hong, *Sŏngt'an p'ik'ŭnik*, 82.
55. Chŏng I., "Nangmanjŏk saranggwa sahoe," in *Nangmanjŏk saranggwa sahoe*, 13.
56. Nowhere in the text is there any specific indication as to where the narrator lives, but everyone, including the literary critic who wrote an introductory review inside Jung's book, assume that it is Gangnam.
57. See Bourdieu, *Distinction*, 53–55, 120–121.
58. M. Jung, *My Son's Girlfriend*, 110–111.
59. Ibid., 108.
60. Ibid., 109.
61. Mun C., "Sŏurŭi mujigaedŭl," in *Nanŭn mun'ida*, 160–161.
62. Kim Y., "Ch'ŏlgabang ch'ujŏk chakchŏn," 121–122.
63. Kim Sagwa, "SF," 252.
64. See Lees, Shin, and López-Morales, *Planetary Gentrification*.
65. Kim Sagwa, *Ch'ŏn'gug'esŏ*, 121–122.
66. Ibid., 125–126.
67. Ibid., 126–127.
68. A classic example is the friendship between the dwarf family and Sin'ae in *The Dwarf*. Another example can be found in Yu Ha's *Gangnam Blues*, in which two childhood buddies are separately recruited by rival gangs and turn into bitter enemies over the lucrative territories of real estate speculation and adult entertainment during the early years of Gangnam development.
69. Yi Hong, *Sŏngt'an p'ik'ŭnik*, 191–192.
70. Pak W., "Nakt'oŭi aidŭl," 317–318.

Chapter 3: Two Lakes in Chamsil: Ecology, Class, Disaster

1. Cho S., *Sigan yŏhaeng*, 99.
2. Ibid., 104.
3. In particular, "The Fault Lies with God as Well" describes in gruesome detail the human casualties and environmental toll of the Park Chung Hee–era heavy and chemical industrialization. The title notwithstanding, Cho lays blame squarely on the upper echelons of Korean society: "Educated people made us suffer. They sat at their desks thinking only of ways to make machines operate at low cost. These people would mix sand with our food if they needed to. These were people who drilled holes in the bottom of the wastewater holding tank and let the sludge run into the ocean instead of passing through the filtration plant" (Cho S., *Dwarf*, 147). For further discussion on ecocriticism in *The Dwarf*, see Ch'a, "Chosehŭi sosŏrŭi saengt'aehakchŏk sangsangnyŏk yŏn'gu," and Ch'a, "Han'guk hyŏndaesosŏrŭi saengt'aejŏk kanŭngsŏng." See also Yi Soyŏn, "Kongsaeng'ŭi pŏp, sarang'ŭi saengt'aehak."

4. See Naess and Sessions, "Basic Principles," for the basic philosophical principles of deep ecology laid out by two of its founders. For an overview of deep ecology and its critique of anthropocentrism, refer to Keller, "Deep Ecology."

5. Cho S., *Sigan yŏhaeng*, 104–106.

6. See Ch'a, "Han'guk hyŏndaesosŏrŭi saengt'aejŏk kanŭngsŏng," for a chronological account of environmentalism in Korean literature.

7. Cho S., *Ch'immug'ŭi ppuri*, 90.

8. Cho's deepening ecological perspective is evident in this description of Ŭlsukto: "Even though many life-forms were settled in the ecosystem of the Naktong River Delta area, some people thought of migratory birds as the only living creatures in it. There were all kinds of fish, plankton, shellfish, animals, and even a few birds of prey. Furthermore—anyone would be careful writing about this—none other than 'humans,' more than five thousand of them, were living there. I understood this island as a 'school' . . . an excellent school that teaches what we must know all year long without school levies" (*Ch'immug'ŭi ppuri*, 87).

9. Cho S., *Sigan yŏhaeng*, 103.

10. Ibid., 144–145. See Y. Ryu, *Writers of the Winter Republic*, 21, for a characterization of Cho's work as literature of witness.

11. The Korea Federation for Environmental Movements (KFEM) lamented that the water quality of the Han and its tributaries in 1989 was not adequate even for industrial use, a far cry from the pristine river people had been drinking water from and swimming in until 1962. See KEFM, "The Pollution Situation of the Han River," http://kfem.or.kr/?p=37117.

12. See Kim Chunsu, "Han'gang'ŭi saengsan," 114.

13. The Royal Court records show a total of 176 floods of the Han during the 450 years of the Chosŏn era. Since the twentieth century, there have been six notable flood disasters in Seoul, and the biggest one hit in 1984, when the Han River development project was still under way. Despite the project's completion, occasional floods still plagued the Han until the late 1990s. See *Encyclopedia of Korean Culture*, s.v. "Floods," http://encykorea.aks.ac.kr/Contents/Item/E0064193.

14. Cho S., *Sigan yŏhaeng*, 145.

15. For *Godzilla*, see Noriega, "Godzilla and the Japanese Nightmare." Radical political interpretations of Bong's films are nothing new. See, among others, Lee and Manicastri, "Not All Are Aboard"; Gullander-Drolet, "Bong Joon-Ho's Eternal Engine"; Nam Lee, *Films of Bong Joon-Ho*.

16. Carson, *Silent Spring*, 177.

17. See Nam Chong'yŏng, "P'algusimnŏndae mulkogi ttejug'ŭm akch'wi, ŏllon 'sujungbot'at han'gang oyŏm wŏn'in'" [Mass die-off and stench in the 1980-90s "due to the underwater barrages polluting the Han," media reported], *Han'gyŏre sinmun*, October 4, 2011, http://www.hani.co.kr/arti/society/environment/499285.html.

18. Cited in Kim Chunsu, "Han'gang'ŭi saengsan," 113.

19. Hong Sŏng'yong, "Yŏnghwasok kŏnch'uk iyagi," 141. Only two out of the eleven parks are directly connected to a subway station. The first such station in Yŏŭido went into service in 1996—a full decade after the opening of the parks—and the second in Ttuksŏm followed four years later. In 2009, the Seoul Metropolitan Government (SMG) opened public bus stops at the observatory cafés it had built on some of the Han River bridges. These observatory cafés provide a direct entry to the riverside parks underneath.

20. Seoul Research Date Service, http://data.si.re.kr/node/389.

21. See the SMG report published in April 2017: http://opengov.seoul.go.kr/research/13214758.

22. Some Sevit was built under the banner of the Han River Renaissance Project, which was a major policy initiative for the then mayor of Seoul, Oh Se Hoon (O Sehun). Oh had been a national assemblyman from this area, Gangnam District Number Two, before becoming mayor. See J. Yun, "A Copy Is (Not a Simple) Copy."

23. For past drinking-water crises, see Kim Chunsu, "Han'gang'ŭi saengsan," 125–129, and Kang Ch'ansu, "Samsimnyŏnjŏn p'enol sudonmul p'adong . . . kŭ ch'unggyŏg'edo kyohun mot ŏdŏt'a" [The phenol-contaminated drinking water crisis thirty years ago . . . we still haven't learned the lesson from that shock], *Chung'ang ilbo*, June 22, 2019, https://www.joongang.co.kr/article/23503719.

24. Wenner, *Lennon Remembers*, 94.

25. See Ju-Hyun Park, "Reading Colonialism in *Parasite*," *Tropics of Meta*, February 17, 2020, https://tropicsofmeta.com/2020/02/17/reading-colonialism-in-parasite/, and Criss Moon and Julie Moon, "*Parasite* and the Plurality of Empire," *Public Books*, June 23, 2020, https://www.publicbooks.org/parasite-and-the-plurality-of-empire/.

26. See Ehrenreich, *Fear of Falling*, for the archetypal middle-class nightmares in the U.S. dating back to the 1970s. On the impact of the IMF Crisis on Korean society, see Jesook Song, *South Koreans in the Debt Crisis*.

27. The film's surprising resonance in Europe and North America can be attributed to global-polarization in the sense that even the so-called Western advanced countries are not immune to increasing inequality and polarization.

28. Pak W., "Nakt'oŭi aidŭl," 317.

29. Song Ŭ., *Sŏul t'ansaenggi*, 409.

30. Yi Y., *Chojohan tosi*, 187.

31. Ibid., 210.

32. For the "apartment game," see Pak H., *Ap'at'ŭ keim*.

33. Collusion (*yuchaku* in Japanese), formally referred to as "government-business collusion" (*chŏnggyŏng yuch'ak*), is an innate feature of the East Asian developmental state model Korea imported from Japan. See Chalmers Johnson, *Japan, Who Governs?*, chap. 11, and McCormack, *Emptiness of Japanese Affluence*, 34, for Japanese *yuchaku* especially rampant in the construction sector.

34. Kang-Yu, "Ŏttŏn sagyoyuk k'idŭŭi saeng'ae," 152.

35. Ibid., 153–154.

36. Ibid., 156.

37. Director Kim Bora recounts her memories of intense intra-community class hierarchy in a newspaper interview: "In my middle school, high- and low-performing students were assigned to separate classrooms. Test scores determined social class . . . Between friends, we knew everything about one another, which apartment building they lived in, what their fathers did for a living, and the like. Strange, isn't it? To judge others based on all these inessential things—we learned it all from adults. Society is still barbaric." See Kwŏn Nam'yŏng, "'Pŏlsae' kimbora kamdok, tebwijagŭro isib'ogwan'wang, 'ajik kalkil mŏrŏyo'" [*House of Hummingbird* director Kim Bora says "still a long way to go" after receiving 25 awards for her debut feature], *Kungmin ilbo*, August 20, 2019, http://news.kmib.co.kr/article/view.asp?arcid=0013621797.

38. The legendary PSM (Peole's Song Movement) artist Kim Hoch'ŏl wrote the song, with the lyrics adapted from "Finger Tomb" ("Son mudŏm," 1984) by the revolutionary worker poet

Pak Nohae. The English translation here is mine and may differ from the film's official English subtitles.

39. The reason is not clearly stated, but presumably it is either because she didn't score high enough on the nationally standardized high school entrance test or because her parents did not move to Gangnam in time. The eligibility criteria at that time included a minimum of three years of residency in Gangnam.

40. The average life cycle of apartments in Korea is about thirty years, far shorter than a theoretical hundred-year cycle of ferroconcrete structure. This shortened life cycle is due to the real estate market incentivizing wholesale demolition and reconstruction for property owners as well as the construction business. This practice in turn has largely disincentivized building durable structures for housing. See Kim Minjung, "Han'guk ap'at'ŭ p'alsipsari ch'oegoryŏng" [The oldest apartment in Korea is 80 years old], *Chung'ang ilbo*, July 28, 2019, https://www.joongang.co.kr/article/23537666.

41. Pak Wansŏ's "Identical Apartments" remains one of the best depictions of an identity crisis in Korean-style apartment living (see chapter 2). Chŏng Ihyŏn recounts the same childhood experience of misidentifying her own apartment in a tribute to Pak and the story. Chŏng Ihyŏn, "Talmun pang, talmun saram—pak wansŏwa ap'at'ŭ" [Similar rooms, similar people: Pak Wansŏ and apartments], *Munjang Webzine*, May 1, 2017, https://webzine.munjang.or.kr/archives/140015. Some of the most memorable shots of identical apartment corridors appear in Bong Joon-ho's directorial debut feature, *Barking Dogs Never Bite* (*P'ŭllandasŭŭi kae*, 2000).

42. Kim In'gu, "Ŭnma ap'at'ŭsŏ handalgan ch'waryŏng . . . chikchohadŭt ch'ŏn'gubaekkusipsanyŏn chaehyŏn" [Shooting in the Ŭnma apartments for a month . . . weaving the representation of year 1994], *Munhwa ilbo*, August 28, 2019, http://www.munhwa.com/news/view.html?no=2019082801032739179001. See also interviews with the producer and the cinematographer in Kim Hyŏnsu, "'Pŏlsae' ŭi ch'ŏn'gubaekkusipsanyŏn'ŭn ŏttŏkke t'ansaenghaenna" [How they recreated 1994 in *House of Hummingbird*], *Cine 21*, September 9, 2019, http://cine21.com/news/view/?mag_id=93871.

43. MBC Television had aired a special investigative news series on the safety of Han River bridges prior to the Sŏngsu Bridge collapse. The newscaster on MBC made opening remarks on the day of disaster: "Despite so many concerns, finally it happened today. The Sŏngsu Bridge collapse was a man-made disaster that had been all but predicted." MBC Time Machine, "Kusipsanyŏn sunsikkan'e munŏjin sŏngsudaegyo punggoe hyŏnjang" [1994, the site of the sudden Sŏngsu Bridge collapse], YouTube video, April 27, 2015, https://www.youtube.com/watch?v=hsywUHUGHxk.

Chapter 4: Solidarity amid Disaster Capitalism: The Sampoong Collapse

1. See P. H. Kim, "Songs of the Multitude," 74–76, and A. Park, "Modern Folksong and People's Song," 88–89.

2. The first verse of "Mung Bean Flower": "Living in the sunlight grasped by two empty hands / Living in a red twilight upon walls and iron bars / Burning, like a fire, in the soul late at night / Living in the deep, deep wounds by harsh blows / Day after day, living in the wide-open, bloodshot eyes of resistance / Sound of rattling keys fades into the endless night."

3. As an unfortunate consequence, his death has been mired in conspiracy theories and family feuds over the control of his estate. See Ock Hyun-ju, "Police Probes Mysterious Death

of Folk Singer's Daughter," *Korea Herald*, September 27, 2017, http://www.koreaherald.com/view.php?ud=20170927000761.
  4. Klein, *Shock Doctrine*, 6.
  5. Ibid., 17.
  6. Alexander Cockburn, "On Naomi Klein's *The Shock Doctrine*," *Counterpunch*, September 22, 2007, https://www.counterpunch.org/2007/09/22/on-naomi-klein-s-quot-the-shock-doctrine-quot/.
  7. Hong, An, and Pak, *Anjŏnsahoero toyakhanŭn kil*, 46.
  8. See Kee et al., "Systemic Analysis of South Korea Sewol Ferry Accident"; Suh, "Failure of the South Korean National Security State"; Suh and Kim, *Challenges of Modernization and Governance in South Korea*; Zhang and Wang, "Analysis of South Korea Sewol Sunken Ferry Accident."
  9. SCF, *Ch'ŏn'gubaekkusib'onyŏn sŏul, samp'ung*, 99.
  10. Hwang, *Kangnammong*, 376–377.
  11. Ibid., 173.
  12. Chŏn T'aeil, a twenty-two-year-old tailor at the Peace Market, whose self-immolation would give a jolt to the Korean labor movement, was instrumental in publicizing the disastrous working conditions of the garment industry. He and his fellow workers managed to get the major findings of their own labor survey published by a national newspaper: thirteen-year-old girls working sixteen hours a day in rooms only four-and-a-half-foot tall without a window or ventilation; and nearly every one of more than twenty-thousand workers suffering from various occupational diseases. See "Kolbangsŏ haru yŏlyŏsŏt sigan nodong" [16-hours-a-day labor in a back room], *Kyŏnghyang sinmun*, October 7, 1970.
  13. See Chang K., "Pokhap wihŏmsahoeŭi anjŏnmunje"; Han S., "Wae wihŏmsahoein'ga?"; Chŏng T., "Peg'ŭi chaegujijŏk hyŏndaehwa iron'gwa kaeinhwaŭi tillema," 269.
  14. Beck, *Risk Society*, 260. For example, the U.S. Interstate 40 bridge collapse in Oklahoma killed fourteen and injured eleven in 2002. Five years later, the U.S. Interstate 35W bridge collapsed in Minneapolis, killing 13 and injuring 145. The Morandi Bridge in Genoa, Italy, collapsed and killed forty-three in 2018. In 2021, a twelve-story beachfront condominium tower collapsed in Surfside, Florida, killing ninety-eight residents.
  15. During the two decades, Korean construction companies received more than 1,900 orders in the Middle East for about 170 billion in current USD, accounting for 90 percent of total overseas construction sales. See Chang Sŏnghyo, "Chungdong kŏnsŏlsijang'ŭn kyerŭg'inga: Iran, irak'ŭeman sach'ŏnp'albaeg'osib'yŏmyŏng chag'ŏpchung" [Is the Middle East construction market no longer worthwhile? More than 4,850 construction workers in Iran and Iraq alone], *Chung'ang ilbo*, July 1, 1988, https://www.joongang.co.kr/article/2255128.
  16. Sŏ Misuk, "Han-iran pansegi—p'okkyŏk, kyŏngjejejae sok ssaŭn silloega ch'oegoŭi chasan" [A half century of South Korea–Iran relations: The best asset is trust built in the midst of bombings and economic sanctions], *Yonhap News*, May 10, 2016, https://www.yna.co.kr/view/AKR20160509051300003.
  17. SCF, *Ch'ŏn'gubaekkusib'onyŏn sŏul, samp'ung*, 21.
  18. Ibid., 63–64.
  19. Ibid., 146, 150.
  20. Mun C., *Nanŭn mun'ida*, 183.
  21. Cho Chaeik, "Samp'ungbaekhwajŏm chig'wŏndoen'ge choein'gayo" [Is it a crime to be a Sampoong employee?], *KBS News*, July 19, 1995, https://news.kbs.co.kr/news

/view.do?ncd=3753028. Ironically, the facilities manager's death in the collapse helped the Sampoong owner Yi Chun's defense that nobody, including the manager, who presumably knew the building safety conditions better than anyone, recognized the imminent danger.
 22. Hong Sŏngt'ae, *Taehanmin'guk wihŏmsahoe*, 148.
 23. Cho Y., "Paekhwajŏm punggoeŭi kiŏkkwa chaenan chabonjuŭi," 112, 116.
 24. Yi Chaeŭn, "Modŏngŏri kkumkkunŭn nangmanjŏk saranggwa sahoe" [A modern girl dreams about romantic love and society], *Wŏlgan chosŏn*, January 10, 2014, http://monthly.chosun.com/client/news/viw.asp?ctcd=I&nNewsNumb=201401100055.
 25. Chŏng I., *Nangmanjŏk saranggwa sahoe*, 55.
 26. Ehrenreich, *Nickel and Dimed*, 155.
 27. Chŏng I., *Nangmanjŏk saranggwa sahoe*, 61–62.
 28. Ibid., 62–63.
 29. Ibid., 65.
 30. Hemmings, "Affective Solidarity," 148.
 31. Mun H., *Samp'ung*, 371.
 32. Kim Chin'hŭng, "Samp'ungbaekhwajŏm wiryŏngt'ab'ŭn wae yangjae simin'ŭi sup'e sewŏjyŏnna" [Why was the Sampoong Memorial Tower erected in the Yangjae Citizens' Forest?], *Naeson'an'e sŏul*, June 30, 2021, https://mediahub.seoul.go.kr/archives/2002100.
 33. Mun H., *Samp'ung*, 335.
 34. Pak Chiyun, "Subaek myŏng moksum as'agan chari … 'chipkap' ap'e ch'umonŭn hyŏm'oga toeŏtta" [The site of hundreds of deaths . . . condolences turned into hatred because of "house prices"], *Han'guk ilbo*, April 29, 2021, https://www.hankookilbo.com/News/Read/A2021042718030003719.
 35. Shin and Jin, "Politics of Forgetting," 435–436, 438–439.
 36. Haejoang Cho, "National Subjects, Citizens and Refugees," 183.
 37. See Yi Ch'ungjae, "Sewŏrho p'iro kadangch'ant'a" [The Sewŏl fatigue, what a nonsense], *Han'guk ilbo*, August 25, 2014. See also Cho H., "National Subjects, Citizens and Refugees," 173–174.
 38. Candace Johnson, "Responsibility, Affective Solidarity," 188.
 39. She later revealed her identity in media interviews. See Pak Chŏnghun, "Samp'ung saengjŏnjaŭi ilgal, 'Sewŏrho hyŏm'oga ton toenŭn sesang'" [A roar from a survivor of the Sampoong Disaster: Hate on the Sewŏl Incident makes money], *Ohmynews*, June 29, 2020, http://www.ohmynews.com/NWS_Web/View/at_pg.aspx?CNTN_CD=A0002654266.
 40. Sanman ŏnni, "Sewŏrhoga chigyŏptanŭn tangsin'ege samp'ung saengjonjaga marhanda" [A Sampoong survivor is telling you, who feel tired of Sewŏl, *Ttanji ilbo*, April 19, 2018, https://www.ddanzi.com/ddanziNews/509310045.
 41. See Yi Sŏnmin, *Chŏnŭn samp'ung saengjonjaimnida*. Also, Yun Taenyŏng's short story "Between Seoul and North America" ("Sŏul-pungmigan," 2015) fictionalized this affective solidarity between victims of the two disasters.
 42. SCF, *Ch'ŏn'gubaekkusib'onyŏn sŏul, samp'ung*, 277.
 43. Much of the academic discourse on the politics of memorialization still revolves around war, nationalism, political terrorism, and other aspects of state power (see Viggiani, *Talking Stones*; Shin and Jin, "Politics of Forgetting"). Recently, however, a more expansive approach to this topic has been developed in regards to "spontaneous memorialization" (see Margry and Sánchez-Carretero, *Grassroots Memorials*).

Chapter 5: Place Maketh Man: Gangnam as the Locus of Social Evil

1. The Gangnam kidnapping murder case and the Taech'idong *hag'wŏn* (cram school) district blackmail incident, both in the spring of 2023, are the latest headline-grabbing scandals at the time of this writing.
2. Kyŏnghyang sinmun, *Kangnam'yŏk sippŏn ch'ulgu*.
3. See Relph, *Place and Placelessness*; Tuan, *Space and Place*; Creswell, *Place*.
4. Massey, "Global Sense of Place," 24.
5. Blickle, *Heimat*, 6–9.
6. Massey, "Global Sense of Place," 24.
7. Marx and Engels, *Capital*, 834; Engels, *Principles of Communism*, 13. It should also be noted that in the original text, Engels singling out India and China for their supposed backwardness reveals the deeply rooted Eurocentrism and Orientalism of early political economy, regardless of ideological stripes.
8. Lefebvre, *Production of Space*, 49.
9. Perhaps the best way to put it is to take liberties with the American jazz great Sun Ra's film/album title *Space Is the Place* (1974), which happened to be released in the same year Lefebvre's *The Production of Space* was originally published in French.
10. The old-school human geography of Edward Relph and Yi-fu Tuan as well as such Marxists as Doreen Massey and David Harvey lean toward the former, whereas the recent nonrepresentational theory advocates for the latter. See Thrift, *Non-representational Theory*.
11. Pak Sŏnghun, "Twaejiŭi wang, yŏnsangho kamdog'ŭl mannada" [Meet Yeon Sang-ho, the director of *The King of Pigs*], *Sangsang palchŏnso*, November 23, 2011, https://koreancontent.kr/411.
12. Sŏ Hwasuk, "Pusan'gukcheyŏnghwaje aenimeisyŏn ch'oech'o samgwanwang 'twaejiŭi wang' mandŭn yŏnsangho kamdok" [Yeon Sang-ho, the director of *The King of Pigs*, which won three awards at the Busan International Film Festival for the first time ever], *Han'guk ilbo*, October 23, 2011, https://www.hankookilbo.com/News/Read/201110231268277014.
13. Agamben, *Homo Sacer*, 79.
14. Downey, "Zones of Indistinction," 124, 131.
15. Pak Sŏnghun, "Twaejiŭi wang, yŏnsangho kamdog'ŭl mannada."
16. It was this case of bullying followed by a suicide that galvanized public attention to a series of similar incidents that would follow, forcing the government to declare school bullying as one of "four social evils" to be combated. See Bax, "Contemporary History of Bullying," 93, 97.
17. For an overview of various social scientific approaches to school bullying, see Hong et al., "Integrating Multi-Disciplinary Social Science Theories."
18. Although Ch'ŏl is not openly defiant toward adult authorities, his attitude and demeanor represent "indiscipline" comparable to another thirteen-year-old boy in late nineteenth-century France who "reinscribed indiscipline among the fundamental [human] rights" in front of the judge penalizing him for vagrancy (Foucault, *Discipline and Punish*, 290–291).
19. Nietzsche, *Beyond Good and Evil*, 114.
20. Agamben, *Homo Sacer*, 105–106.
21. Girard, *Violence and the Sacred*, 7.
22. See Horton, "School Bullying," and Thornberg, "School Bullying as a Collective Action."
23. See Bax, "Contemporary History of Bullying"; Chung, Sun, and Kim, "What Makes Bullies"; Koo, Kwak, and Smith, "Victimization in Korean Schools."

24. Riordan, "Suicide and Human Sacrifice," 2, 4.

25. Contradicting interpretations of *sacer* in relation to sacrifice between Girard and Agamben—especially on the issue of whether the sacred can be sacrificed or not—are discussed in depth by Antonello, "Sacrificing 'Homo Sacer,'" and Depoortere "Reading Giorgio Agamben's *Homo Sacer*," among others.

26. The study's final report was classified, but some findings were leaked to the press. See Ha Ŏ., "Kangnam sŏngmaemae t'ŭkkurŭl kada," 53.

27. Kim R., *Ŭn'gŭn riŏl pŏraiŏt'i kangnam sonyŏ*, 118.

28. For more on *toumi* and violence, see Yi Yŏngp'yo et al., "Siptaebut'ŏ ajummakkaji seksŭsan'ŏb'ŭro" [From teenagers to middle-aged ladies, all headed toward the sex industry], *Seoul sinmun*, February 10, 2003, https://www.seoul.co.kr/news/newsView.php?id=20030210026001; and Kang Soyŏng, "P'ihaeja'e sajoehan kang'yunsŏng, wae noraebang toumiman sarhaehaenna" [Kang Yunsŏng asks victims for forgiveness—why did he target *noraebang toumi* for murder?], *Segye ilbo*, September 7, 2021, https://m.segye.com/view/20210907508161.

29. For detailed statistics, see Yi Chuyŏn, Yi Chihye, and Yi Chŏnghwan, "Yuhŭng'ŏpso t'ap ssŭri kangnam, yŏngdŭnp'o, chunggu . . . p'andoraŭi sangja yŏllina" [Top three entertainment districts, Gangnam, Yŏngdŭnp'o, Chung . . . will the Pandora's box open?], *Ohmynews*, April 10, 2020, http://www.ohmynews.com/NWS_Web/View/at_pg.aspx?CNTN_CD=A0002631615. The tenuous assumption that on average a Gangnam salon would hire four to six hostesses comes from the Seoul Metropolitan Government data and the leaked Ministry of Gender Equality and Family report cited previously.

30. Havocscope, a research firm specializing in the global black market economy, estimated the total revenue of Korea's sex industry at 12 billion USD in 2015, which ranks it at the sixth place in the global ranking, just behind the U.S. with 14.6 billion (https://havocscope.com/prostitution-revenue-by-country/). The Korean Institute of Criminology and Justice, a government think tank, published an estimate three times higher than that, about 36 billion USD. This was approximately 2.5 percent of Korea's GDP in 2015. See Kwon Chiyun, "Segye yug'ŭi sŏngmaemae sijang . . . 'han'guk namsŏng chŏlban sŏngmaemae kyŏnghŏm yu" [World's sixth largest sex trade market . . . half of the Korean male population have engaged in sex trade," *SBS News*, March 31, 2018, https://news.sbs.co.kr/news/endPage.do?news_id=N1004676372.

31. For *yojŏng* politics, see Kang, *Rumssarong konghwaguk*, and Yu Yŏngho, "Yojŏngjŏngch'i taewŏn'gak, paeksŏkkwa ŏlk'yŏ kilsangsaro iŏjin sayŏn" [Taewŏn'gak's *yojŏng* politics was associated with Paek Sŏk and continued to Kilsangsa Temple], *T'ong'il News*, November 13, 2014, https://www.tongilnews.com/news/articleView.html?idxno=109729.

32. For a micro-level analysis of the room salon business model, see Heisoo Shin, "Industrial Prostitution."

33. J. Lee, *Service Economies*, 99.

34. Ibid., 80.

35. J.-M. Park, "Paradoxes of Gendering Strategy," 76–79.

36. Norma, "Demand from Abroad," 407.

37. "In 1973, South Korea's earnings from tourism reached 269 million dollars, which was 8.4 percent of total export earnings that year. Kisaeng prostitution contributed roughly 40 percent of this tourism income" (ibid., 410). See also Kim Sŏngmin, "Sŏurŭi chaegujohwawa ilbon'in kwan'gwang," for how Gangnam development changed Japanese tourists' perception of Korea.

38. For the importance of tourist hotels in Gangnam during the 1980s, see Kim M., "Hot'erŭi tosi inp'ŭra kinŭng yŏn'gu," 90–92.

39. The best-known hostess memoirs are *Miss O's Apartment* (*Oyang'ŭi ap'at'ŭ*, 1976) and *Local Wife* (*Hyŏnjich'ŏ*, 1977) by the pseudonymous authors O Miyŏng and Kang Yŏng'a, respectively. Their accounts provide insights into the national scale of sex work in the Park Chung Hee era. Both stories were adapted to film by director Pyŏn Changho in 1978, but much of the sensitive detail—in particular, state-regulated *kisaeng* tourism and other kinds of sex work catering to foreigners—was omitted for fear of censorship. See No, "Ch'ŏn'gubaekch'ilsimnyŏndae sŏngnodongja"; Pak Soyŏng, "Ch'ŏn'gubaekch'ilsimnyŏndae host'isŭ sugiŭi yŏnghwahwa yŏn'gu"; H. S. Kim, "'My' Sweet Home," 125–127.

40. Ha Ŭ., "Kangnam'ŭi kogŭp maech'un yŏsŏngdŭl," 46.

41. Han Y., *Nanŭn ch'wihaji annŭnda*, 4.

42. See Lerner, *Creation of Patriarchy*, 133–134; Graeber, *Debt*, 181–182.

43. Han Y., *Nanŭn ch'wihaji annŭnda*, 139–141.

44. Heisoo Shin's research corroborates Madam Han's own risk assessment: "Because of the absence of structural restraints and the symbiotic relationship with the madam, hostesses move frequently within the same kind of entertainment establishment as well as between different kinds . . . Madams also move frequently, primarily due to the short contract period . . . Although a madam's work (attracting customers and controlling hostesses) is the most important aspect of the room-salon business, her position is extremely vulnerable. She is responsible for any financial loss caused by her patrons, and she has no fringe benefits or job protection. At the same time, her ability to move to other establishments is controlled by men in the industry" (Heisoo Shin, "Industrial Prostitution," 124).

45. There were two fires in red-light districts of the provincial city of Kunsan. They resulted in the deaths of nineteen sex workers, all victims of human trafficking and confinement. Five died in the 2000 fire, and the 2002 fire caused fourteen casualties. Public ire at these gruesome incidents prompted the government to enact the Special Law on Sex Trade in 2004. The anti-prostitution law, however, has been mired in controversy, including organized protests by the sex workers, whom the law is supposed to protect. See Kim and Kim, *Korean Women's Movement*, chap. 3.

46. The cost is considerable, especially for those high-end sex workers who feel constant pressure to "beautify" themselves. See Ha Ŏ., "Kangnam sŏngmaemae t'ŭkkurŭl kada," 46–47; Kim Joohee, "Instant Mobility," 65–73.

47. Kim Joohee, "Han'guk sŏngmaemae," 225–230.

48. See Seol, "International Sex Trafficking"; J. Lee, *Service Economies*, 125–126; Choo, "Selling Fantasies"; Sin Chihong, "Kijich'on insin, sŏngmaemae t'oronhoe" [Roundtable on human trafficking and sex trade in camptowns], *Han'guk kyŏngje*, April 2, 2006, https://www.hankyung.com/society/article/2002082985528.

49. There is no official data or even a reliable estimate for the number of Korean sex workers trafficked overseas, although some have alleged—without concrete evidence—that over fifty thousand Korean women were working for Japan's sex industry in the early 2000s (K. H. Shin, "Theoretical View," 88; Norma, "Demand from Abroad," 420). Occasional news reports confirm the existence of overseas sex trafficking networks. See Kim Sŭng'uk, "'Handal samch'ŏnmanwŏn' yuhog'e irwŏnjŏng sŏngmaemae" [Overseas prostitution to Japan, lured by "thirty million won a month"], *Yŏnhap News*, October 6, 2011, https://www.yna.co.kr/view/AKR20111006081351004.

50. Kim Joohee, "Instant Mobility," 56.

51. The subway line was not enough to attract businesses to Teheran Road. It took another big push by the government in preparation for the 1986 Asian Games and the 1988 Olympics to develop it into a major business district. See Kim P., "Olimp'ig'ŭn kangnam kaebare ŏttŏn."

52. Two of the so-called Big Three K-pop management agencies, SM Entertainment and JYP Entertainment, had their corporate headquarters, recording studios, and other facilities in the two neighborhoods. BTS's management company, Big Hit Entertainment (which recently changed its name to HYBE), started its business near Sinsa Station in 2005. The K-pop industry took over the old Sinsadong Circuit.

53. See Oh, *Pop City*, 144–146. A talent manager explains the industry logic of show business behind the rise of Ch'ŏngdamdong: "It takes many people to groom a talent for the entertainment business, and Gangnam has ideal conditions overall for such efforts . . . An entertainment celebrity's regular activities have to be organically connected with fashion and cosmetics industries, and high-level fashion coordinators and make-up artists are all concentrated in the Ch'ŏngdamdong area. Thus, the entertainment agencies have naturally settled around here" (Kim Sanghŏn, *Taehanmin'guk kangnam t'ŭkpyŏlsi*, 185).

54. For example, see two in-depth international news coverages: Laura Bicker, "Gangnam: The Scandal Rocking the Playground of K-pop," *BBC News*, June 25, 2019, https://www.bbc.com/news/world-asia-48702763; Matthew Campbell and Sohee Kim, "The Dark Side of K-pop: Assault, Prostitution, Suicide, and Spycams," *Bloomberg Businesweek*, November 6, 2019, https://www.bloomberg.com/news/features/2019-11-06/K-pop-s-dark-side-assault-prostitution-suicide-and-spycams.

55. See Sonia Kil, "Korean Prosecutors to Reopen Actress Suicide Case," *Variety*, April 2, 2018, https://variety.com/2018/tv/asia/korea-prosecutors-to-reopen-actress-jang-ja-yeon-suicide-case-1202742137/.

56. DJUNA, "Pisŭt'i poijŭ igonggongp'al" [Beastie Boys (2008)], *Tyunaŭi yŏnghwa naksŏp'an*, April 21, 2008, http://www.djuna.kr/movies/the_moonlight_of_seoul.html.

57. Mun Sŏk, "'Yongsŏbatchi mottan ja' yunjongbin kamdog'ŭi sinjak 'pisŭt'i poijŭ'" [The Unforgiven director Yoon Jong-bin's new film, Beastie Boys], *Cine21*, January 9, 2007, http://www.cine21.com/news/view/?mag_id=43839. See also Ch'oe Kwanghŭi, "'Pisŭt'i poijŭ' yunjongbin kamdog'ŭi hangbyŏn" [The Beastie Boys director Yoon Jong-bin's plea], *3M Hŭngŏp*, May 12, 2008, https://mmnm.tistory.com/387.

58. The biggest culprit of the crisis was the credit card company owned by the LG Conglomerate, which became insolvent and had to be bailed out by the government. See Kang and Ma, "Credit Card Lending Distress."

59. Hyun-Seok Yu, "Economic Threat to Human Security," 78. Although the Fair Debt Collection Law was enacted in 2011, intimidating tactics by loan sharks and debt collectors persist. See Kim Joohee, "Yŏsŏng momjŭngkwŏnhwarŭl t'onghan han'guk," 159–162.

60. For the national survey results on IPV, see Kim, Oh, and Nam, "Prevalence and Trends," 1555, 1561. And for international comparison during this period, see UN DESA, *The World's Women 2010*, 131–132. For a nuanced approach to the association between the debt crisis and violence against women, see Jesook Song, "Family Breakdown," 52–53.

61. The latest World Health Organization estimate on IPV shows that Korea's rate decreased to about 8 percent (WHO, *Violence against Women*, 72). However, another recent study reports that dating violence in Korea has increased steadily, reaching 19.9 percent in 2017 (Min, Lee, and Kim, "Integrative Literature Review," 261). The Ministry

of Gender Equality and Family reports that the number of domestic violence arrests increased sevenfold between 2011 and 2019 (http://www.mogef.go.kr/kor/skin/doc.html?fn=9ec69606ba10454aa763e6d3c37a975e.hwp&rs=/rsfiles/202202/).

62. Graeber, *Debt*, 5.
63. Ibid., 318–320.
64. See Ha Ŏ, "Kangnam sŏngmaemae t'ŭkkurŭl kada," 46–48; Kim Sanghŏn, *Taehanmin'guk kangnam t'ŭkpyŏlsi*; Oh, *Pop City*, 143. Sŏ and Pyŏn ("Kangnam munhwagyŏngjeŭi sahoehak") advance a systematic approach to the entertainment-beauty industry connection, but somehow overlook the sex industry, which is the largest among the three sectors. The entertainment-sex industry connection has become a frequent topic in the mainstream news media since the Jang Ja-yeon scandal. See Hong Chiyŏng, "'Hwaryŏhan yŏnyegye saenghwal yujiharyŏ' . . . sŏngmaemae yuhog'e swipke pajyŏ" [Lure of sex trade "to maintain flamboyant entertainment business lifestyle], *SBS News*, March 7, 2016, https://n.news.naver.com/mnews/article/055/0000385083?sid=102.
65. Graeber, *Debt*, 191.
66. Lefebvre, *Production of Space*, 49.
67. See Son Hyoju, "Hwangdanghan cheiljŏch'ug'ŭn . . . 'yŏjong'ŏb'wŏn tambo' yuhŭng'ŏpso'e ch'ŏn'obaeksasimnyug'ok taech'ul" [Preposterous Cheil Savings Bank . . . with female employees as collateral, made a 154.6 billion won loan to entertainment venues], *Tong'a ilbo*, October 1, 2011, https://www.donga.com/news/Society/article/all/20111001/40751507/1. Cho reportedly made ill-gotten gains of twenty-six million USD from the two room salons he had opened with the loan. The early story of Cho Yang'ŭn and his rival gangsters is fictionalized by Hwang Sŏg'yŏng in chapter 3 of *Dreams of Gangnam*.
68. Kim Joohee, "Yŏsŏng momjŭngkwŏnhwarŭl t'onghan han'guk," 153.
69. Nietzsche, *Genealogy of Morals*, 71.
70. In prefacing the quoted text, Nietzsche made it clear that he referred to "the criteria of prehistory (this prehistory is in any case present in all ages or may always reappear)" (ibid.). Graeber argued that Nietzsche's discussion of prehistoric societies is an illuminating "thought experiment" devoid of scientific evidence (*Debt*, 77).
71. For example, see Im Kwon-taek's *Ticket* (1986) and *Downfall* (*Ch'ang*, 1997), and Yu Chinsŏn's *Prostitution* (*Maech'un*, 1988). In real life, female sex worker organizations vocally protested the 2004 anti-prostitution laws and subsequent demolition of some of the well-known red-light districts around the country, as chronicled in Caroline Key's documentary *Grace Period* (2015).
72. Karl Marx, "The Eighteenth Brumaire of Louis Bonaparte," chap. 1, December 1851, *Marx/Engels Internet Archive*, https://www.marxists.org/archive/marx/works/1852/18th-brumaire/ch01.htm.
73. Jinsook Kim, "Sticky Activism," 58–59. See also Chŏng and Yi, "P'ost'ŭ kangnam'yŏk."

Chapter 6: Gentrification beyond the American Dream: The Transformation of Tree-Lined, In-Between Streets

1. See Slater, "Gentrification of the City." For an example of positive reevaluation of gentrification, see Cameron, "Gentrification, Housing Redifferentiation," 2373.
2. See Glass, "Introduction."
3. See Smith, "Gentrification and Uneven Development"; Smith, "New Globalism, New Urbanism."

4. For example, see Lees, "Geography of Gentrification."
5. See Lambert and Boddy, "Transforming the City"; Ley and Teo, "Gentrification in Hong Kong?"; Smith, *New Urban Frontier.*
6. See Davidson and Lees, "New-Build 'Gentrification'"; Lees, "Gentrification and Social Mixing"; Slater, "Gentrification of the City."
7. Mendes, "Gentrification and the New Urban Social Movements," 210.
8. This four-stage model is based on Pattison, "Process of Neighborhood Upgrading." See also Kerstein, "Stage Models of Gentrification."
9. For new-build gentrification, see Davidson and Lees, "New-Build 'Gentrification'"; Davidson and Lees, "New-Build Gentrification: Its Histories." For super-gentrification, see Butler and Lees, "Super-Gentrification in Barnsbury."
10. See He, "New-Build Gentrification," and Slater, "Gentrification of the City."
11. For the wave theory in general, see Smith, *New Urban Frontier,* and Bounds and Morris, "Second Wave Gentrification." The wave theory is applied to Korean urban history by Kyoung and Kim, "State-Facilitated Gentrification."
12. See Zhang et al., "Inner-City Urban Redevelopment."
13. See Hackworth and Smith, "Changing State of Gentrification."
14. See Davidson and Lees, "New-Build Gentrification: Its Histories," 398.
15. See SMH, *Kangnam sasimnyŏn,* 18–20; Son C., *Sŏul tosi kyehoek iyagi,* 167–240.
16. For American suburbanization, see Beauregard, *When America Became Suburban,* 14. About Korea's high-rise apartments serving a similar social function, see Kang, *Kangnam;* Gelézeau, *Republic of Apartments;* Pak H., *Ap'at'ŭ keim.* An important source of American influence on Gangnam's urban planning is Clarence Perry's concept of "neighborhood unit," which provided the theoretical basis for the ubiquitous "apartment complex" (*ap'at'ŭ tanji*) design. See Son C., *Sŏul tosi kyehoek iyagi,* 206–208; Gelézeau, "Korean Modernism," 173–179.
17. See Porteux, "Police, Paramilitaries, Nationalists and Gangsters"; Porteux and Kim, "Public Ordering of Private Coercion."
18. Hyun Bang Shin, "Property-Based Redevelopment and Gentrification," 907–908. Project finance is defined as "a funding scheme in which project debt is paid back with the future cash flow generated by the project hence it is neither based on the debtor's credit nor security but rather on profitability of the project" (Choo, Lee, and Park, "Impact of Leverage and Overinvestment," 723).
19. See Kim Minkyŏng, "Kŭgos'en munhwaga itta!" [There is a culture there!], *Chugan Tong'a,* January 18, 2006, https://weekly.donga.com/3/search/11/78198/1.
20. TBWA Korea, *Karosukiri mwŏnde nalliya.*
21. O Y., *Kŭraedo nanŭn sŏuri chotta,* 14–15.
22. Among others, see M. Cho, *Entrepreneurial Seoulite,* for Hongdae; and Ji Youn Kim, "Cultural Entrepreneurs," for Itaewon.
23. The webzine is still accessible as of this writing: http://www.hellostreet.net/.
24. For a relatively successful movement organization against commercial gentrification, see Y. A. Lee, "Reframing Gentrification." After the pandemic-induced recession, Karosukil seems to have lost its vibrancy altogether. See Yu Sŏnhŭi et al., "'Happ'ŭl ilbŏnji' esŏ 'pulkŏjin pamkŏri' ro" [From the "hot place number one" to a "lights-off night street"], *Kyŏnghyang sinmun,* August 4, 2021, https://m.khan.co.kr/national/national-general/article/202108041508001.

25. The official address of Saikil bears the name of its main street: Pangbaero sasib'ikil.
26. It has been relocated to old downtown Seoul since 2016.
27. See Congress for New Urbanism, "What Is New Urbanism," https://my.vanderbilt.edu/greencities/files/2014/08/What-is-New-Urbanism_-_-CNU.pdf.
28. For the gentrification of the old urban core in Gangbuk, and Bukchon (Pukch'on) in particular, see J. Yun, *Globalizing Seoul*.

Conclusion: Burning Down the House or Reaching across the River

1. See Calvin McMillin, "Watching the World Burn: On Lee Chang-dong's *Burning* (2018)," *Bright Wall/Dark Room* 82 (April 2020), https://www.brightwalldarkroom.com/2020/04/24/watching-the-world-burn/.
2. The pop star Psy is also in that category, although his study-abroad years were comparatively later, as a college student. Subsequent generations of Gangnam children (born after 1990) typically go to study abroad at or before early adolescence. See M. W. Lee, "'Gangnam Style' English Ideologies," and Juyoung Song, "English Just Is Not Enough!," 85–87.
3. All English translations of *Burning* come from the DVD subtitles. Ben's follow-up to this exchange is even more condescending and revelatory of modern bourgeois "leisure class" attitudes toward work and play. Facing Jong-su's incredulous reaction, "You play?," Ben continues, "Nowadays, there is no distinction between working and playing." For a theoretical insight into the relationship between work and play, see Benjamin, *Arcades Project*, 360–362.
4. P. H. Kim, "In Liberation Village," 149. For the "Hell Joseon" discourse among disaffected Korean youth, see Epstein, Kim, and Chang, "Because I Hate Korea"; Se-woong Koo, "Korea, Thy Name Is Hell Joseon," *Korea Exposé*, September 22, 2015, https://www.koreaexpose.com/korea-thy-name-is-hell-joseon/.
5. See Cho Haesu, Yu Chiman, and An Sŏngmo, "Imgŭm samsimnyungnyŏn moaya kangnam ap'at'ŭ sanda" [A Gangnam apartment would cost forty-six years' worth of salaries], *Sisa chŏnŏl*, October 28, 2019, https://www.sisajournal.com/news/articleView.html?idxno=192046. See also Yang, *From Miracle to Mirage*, 76–83.
6. See Polanyi, *Great Transformation*, 75–77. Although Polanyi differentiates between his fictitious commodities and Marxian commodity fetishism, these two concepts overlap in defining physical space as a commodity. The price differential between apartments in Gangnam and Gangbuk, for example, is a fetishized form of class divide between their respective owners/residents.
7. Yang, *From Miracle to Mirage*, 98–102.
8. Amin, *Empire of Chaos*, 7.
9. In Korean, *pinirhausŭ* (vinyl house) refers to a temporary greenhouse structure made of polyvinyl sheets and metal frames. Meanwhile, Murakami's barn burner has a very different attitude toward his targets: "The world's full of barns, that are, almost waiting for me to burn them down. A barn all by itself beside the ocean, a barn in the middle of a rice paddy . . . Anyhow, all kinds of barns" (Murakami, "Barn Burning," 87).
10. For Guryong Village, see Sunwoo, "Aging Population and Slum Resettlement"; Kim and Uršič, "Besieged Citizenship." For broader non-house dwelling issues, see S. Ha, "New Shantytowns"; National Human Rights Commission of Korea, "Pijut'aek chugŏsilt'ae p'aak mit chedogaesŏn pang'an" [Current status of non-house dwellings and

policy reform suggestions], November 2018, https://www.humanrights.go.kr/download/BASIC_ATTACH?storageNo=1068196.

11. See Sang-hun Choe, "South Korean Ends Yearlong Tower Protest after Samsung Apologizes," *New York Times,* May 29, 2020, https://www.nytimes.com/2020/05/29/world/asia/south-korea-protest-tower-samsung.html. For the significance of such a high-wire act in Korea's political culture of contention, see J. H. J. Han, "High-Altitude Protests."

Bibliography

Agamben, Giorgio. *Homo Sacer: Sovereign Power and Bare Life*. Translated by Daniel Heller-Roazen. Stanford, CA: Stanford University Press, 1998 [1995].
Amin, Samir. *Empire of Chaos*. New York: Monthly Review Press, 1992.
———. "The Future of Global Polarization." *Africa Today* 40, no. 4 (1993): 75–86.
Antonello, Pierpaolo. "Sacrificing 'Homo Sacer': Rene Girard Reads Giorgio Agamben." *Forum Philosophicum* 24, no. 1 (2019): 145–182.
Bae, Yooil, and Yu-Min Joo. "The Making of Gangnam: Social Construction and Identity of Urban Place in South Korea." *Urban Affairs Review* 56, no. 3 (2020): 726–757.
Bakhtin, Mikhail Mikhailovich. *Problems of Dostoevsky's Poetics*. Translated by Caryl Emerson. Minneapolis: University of Minnesota Press, 1984 [1963].
Barraclough, Ruth. *Factory Girl Literature: Sexuality, Violence, and Representation in Industrializing Korea*. Berkeley: University of California Press, 2012.
Bax, Trent M. "A Contemporary History of Bullying and Violence in South Korean Schools." *Asian Culture and History* 8, no. 2 (2016): 91–101.
Beauregard, Robert A. *When America Became Suburban*. Minneapolis: University of Minnesota Press, 2006.
Beck, Ulrich. *Risk Society: Towards a New Modernity*. Translated by Mark Ritter. London: Sage Publications, 1992.
Benjamin, Walter. *The Arcades Project*. Translated by Howard Eiland and Kevin McLaughlin. Cambridge, MA: Harvard University Press, 1999.
———. *One-Way Street and Other Writings*. Translated by Edmund Jephcott and Kingsley Shorter. London: NLB, 1979.
Berman, Marshall. *All That Is Solid Melts into Air: The Experience of Modernity*. New York: Simon and Schuster, 1982.
Bhabha, Homi. "Of Mimicry and Man: The Ambivalence of Colonial Discourse." *October* 28 (1984): 125–133.
Blickle, Peter. *Heimat: A Critical Theory of the German Idea of Homeland*. Rochester, NY: Camden House, 2002.
Bounds, Michael, and Alan Morris. "Second Wave Gentrification in Inner-City Sydney." *Cities* 23, no. 2 (2006): 99–108.
Bourdieu, Pierre. *Distinction: A Social Critique of the Judgement of Taste*. Translated by Richard Nice. Cambridge, MA: Harvard University Press, 1984 [1979].
Buck-Morss, Susan. "The City as Dreamworld and Catastrophe." *October* 73 (1995): 3–26.

---. *The Dialectics of Seeing: Walter Benjamin and the Arcades Project*. Cambridge, MA: MIT Press, 1991.
Butler, Tim, and Loretta Lees. "Super-Gentrification in Barnsbury, London: Globalization and Gentrifying Global Elites at the Neighbourhood Level." *Transactions of the Institute of British Geographers* 31, no. 4 (2006): 467–487.
Cameron, Stuart. "Gentrification, Housing Redifferentiation and Urban Regeneration: 'Going for Growth' in Newcastle upon Tyne." *Urban Studies* 40, no. 12 (2003): 2367–2382.
Carson, Rachel. *Silent Spring*. Boston: Houghton Mifflin, 2002 [1962].
Caygill, Howard. "Walter Benjamin's Concept of Cultural History." In *The Cambridge Companion to Walter Benjamin*, edited by David S. Ferris, 73–96. Cambridge: Cambridge University Press, 2006.
Ch'a Pongjun. "Chosehŭi sosŏrŭi saengt'aehakchŏk sangsangnyŏk yŏn'gu" [A study on the ecological imagination of Cho Sehŭi's novels]. *Hyŏndae sosŏl yŏn'gu* 34 (2007): 163–179.
---. "Han'guk hyŏndaesosŏrŭi saengt'aejŏk kanŭngsŏng" [Multilayered ecological possibilities found in Korean modern narratives]. *Munhakkwa hwan'gyŏng* 14, no. 1 (2015): 169–188.
Chang Kyŏngsŏp. "Pokhap wihŏmsahoeŭi anjŏnmunje" [Security problems of a complex risk society]. *Noksaek p'yŏngnon* 33 (1997): 65–85.
Chang, Yu-jeong. "Trot and Ballad: Popular Genres of Korean Pop." In *Made in Korea: Studies in Popular Music*, edited by Hyunjoon Shin and Seung-ah Lee, 63–70. New York: Routledge, 2016.
Chapman, Roger. "Fyodor Dostoyevsky, Eastern Orthodoxy, and the Crystal Palace." In *Historic Engagements with Occidental Cultures, Religions, Powers*, edited by Ann Richards and Iraj Omidbar, 35–55. New York: Palgrave Macmillan, 2014.
Cho, Eun Joo, Jae Hong Lee, and Jong Sung Park. "The Impact of Leverage and Overinvestment on Project Financing: Evidence from South Korea." *Journal of Accounting and Economics* 28, no. 6 (2021): 723–745.
Cho, Haejoang. "National Subjects, Citizens and Refugees: Thoughts on the Politics of Survival, Violence and Mourning Following the Sewol Ferry Disaster in South Korea." In *New Worlds from Below*, edited by Tessa Morris-Suzuki and Eun Jeong Soh, 167–196. Canberra: ANU Press, 2017.
Cho Han. *Sŏul, konggan'ŭi kiŏk kiŏg'ŭi konggan* [Seoul, the memories of space and space of memories: Architect Cho Han explores Seoul]. P'aju: Tolbegae, 2013.
Cho, Mihye. *Entrepreneurial Seoulite: Culture and Subjectivity in Hongdae, Seoul*. Ann Arbor: University of Michigan Press, 2019.
Cho Sehŭi. *Ch'immug'ŭi ppuri* [Roots of silence]. Seoul: Yŏrhwadang, 1985.
---. *The Dwarf*. Translated by Bruce Fulton and Ju-Chan Fulton. Honolulu: University of Hawai'i Press, 2006.
---. *Sigan yŏhaeng* [Time travel]. Seoul: Munhakkwa chisŏng, 1983.
Cho Yunjŏng. "Paekhwajŏm punggoeŭi kiŏkkwa chaenan chabonjuŭi: Samp'ung ch'amsaŭi sŏsahwawa ssŭgi-nodong'ŭi yulli" [The memory of department store collapse and disaster capitalism: The narrative of the Sampung disaster and the ethic of writing labor]. *Hanguk munhak yŏn'gu* 61 (2019): 107–142.

Ch'oe Inho. "Migaein" [Savage]. In *T'ain'ŭi pang* [A stranger's room], 249–290. Seoul: Munhaktonge, 2002 [1971].
Choi, Don Mee. "An Overview of Contemporary Korean Women's Poetry." *Acta Koreana* 9, no. 2 (2006): 97–129.
Choi, Julie. "Right to the City: The Metropolis and Gangnam Style." *Korea Journal* 59, no. 2 (2019): 86–110.
Choi, Seung-ja. *Portrait of a Suburbanite*. Translated by Eunju Kim. Ithaca, NY: Cornell East Asia Program, 2015 [1991].
Chŏng Ihyŏn. *Nangmanjŏk saranggwa sahoe* [Romantic love and society]. Seoul: Munhakkwa chisŏng, 2003.
———. "Sam'pung paekhwajŏm" [Sampoong Department Store]. In *Onŭrŭi kŏjinmal* [Today's lie], 39–67. Seoul: Munhakkwa chisŏng, 2007.
Chŏng Misuk. "Pak wansŏ sosŏlgwa ap'at'ŭ p'yosang'ŭi munhak sahoehak" [The representation of apartments in Pak Wansŏ novel]. *Hyŏndae munhak iron yŏn'gu* 49 (2012): 307–332.
Chŏng T'aesŏk. "Peg'ŭi chaeguijŏk hyŏndaehwa iron'gwa kaeinhwaŭi tillema" [Beck's reflexive modernization theory and the dilemma of individualization]. *Kyŏngjewa sahoe* 55 (2002): 246–271.
Chŏng Yongnim and Yi Nayŏng. "P'ost'ŭ kangnam'yŏk" [Post/Gangnam Station]. *P'eminijŭm yŏng'u* 18, no. 1 (2018): 181–228.
Choo, Eun Joo, Jae Hong Lee, and Jong Sung Park. "The Impact of Leverage and Overinvestment on Project Financing: Evidence from South Korea." *Asia-Pacific Journal of Accounting and Economics* 28, no. 6 (2021): 723–745.
Choo, Hae Yeon. "Selling Fantasies of Rescue: Intimate Labor, Filipina Migrant Hostesses, and US GIs in a Shifting Global Order." *positions: asia critique* 24, no. 1 (2016): 179–203.
Chung, Jae Young, Mi Suk Sun, and Hyun Ju Kim. "What Makes Bullies and Victims in Korean Elementary Schools?" *Children and Youth Services Review* 94 (2018): 132–139.
Cresswell, Tim. *Place: An Introduction*. Chichester: John Wiley & Sons, 2015.
Cumings, Bruce. *Korea's Place in the Sun: A Modern History*. New York: W. W. Norton, 2005.
Davidson, Mark, and Loretta Lees. "New-Build 'Gentrification' and London's Riverside Renaissance." *Environment and Planning A* 37, no. 7 (2005): 1165–1190.
———. "New-Build Gentrification: Its Histories, Trajectories, and Critical Geographies." *Population, Space and Place* 16, no. 5 (2010): 395–411.
Davis, Mike. *City of Quartz: Excavating the Future in Los Angeles*. New York: Verso, 2006 [1990].
Deleuze, Gilles. *The Fold: Leibniz and the Baroque*. Translated by Tom Conley. Minneapolis: University of Minnesota Press, 1993 [1988].
Depoortere, Frederiek. "Reading Giorgio Agamben's *Homo Sacer* with René Girard." *Philosophy Today* 56, no. 2 (2012): 154–163.
Detweiler, Eric. "Hyperurbanity: Idealism, Urbanism, and the Politics of Hyperreality in the Town of Celebration, Florida." In *Disneyland and Culture: Essays on the Parks and Their Influence*, edited by Kathy Merlock Jackson and Mark I. West, 150–170. London: McFarland, 2011.

Dillon, George L. "Montage/Critique: Another Way of Writing Social History." *Postmodern Culture* 14, no. 2 (2004). doi:10.1353/pmc.2004.0005.
Dostoevsky, Fyodor. "Notes from Underground." In *White Nights and Other Stories*, translated by Constance Garnett, 50–155. New York: Macmillan, 1918.
Downey, Anthony. "Zones of Indistinction: Giorgio Agamben's 'Bare Life' and the Politics of Aesthetics." In *Giorgio Agamben: Legal, Political and Philosophical Perspectives*, edited by Tom Frost, 119–142. New York: Routledge, 2009.
Ehrenreich, Barbara. *Fear of Falling: The Inner Life of the Middle Class*. New York: Pantheon Books, 1989.
———. *Nickel and Dimed: On (Not) Getting By in Boom-Time America*. New York: Metropolitan Books, 2001.
Elden, Stuart. *Understanding Henri Lefebvre: Theory and the Possible*. London: Continuum, 2004.
Engels, Friedrich. *Principles of Communism*. Pattern Books, 2020.
Epstein, Stephen J., Mi Young Kim, and Chang Kang-Myung. "Because I Hate Korea." *Asia Pacific Journal* 16, issue 11, no. 4 (2018): 1–12.
Foucault, Michel. *Discipline and Punish: The Birth of the Prison*. Translated by Alan Sheridan. New York: Vintage Books, 1977 [1975].
Gelézeau, Valérie. *Ap'at'u konghwaguk: P'ullansŏ chirihakchaga pon han'gug'ŭi ap'at'ŭ* [The republic of apartments: South Korean apartments seen by a French geographer]. Seoul: Humanit'asŭ, 2007.
———. "Korean Modernism, Modern Korean Cityscapes, and Mass Housing Development: Charting the Rise of Ap'at'utanji since the 1960s." In *Korea Yearbook: Politics, Economy and Society*, edited by Rudiger Frank, James E. Hoare, Patrick Kollner, and Susan Pares, 165–191. Leiden: Brill, 2007.
Girard, René. *Violence and the Sacred*. Translated by Patrick Gregory. Baltimore: Johns Hopkins University Press, 1977 [1972].
Glass, Ruth. "Introduction: Aspects of Change." In *London: Aspects of Change*, edited by Centre for Urban Studies, xiii–xlii. London: MacKibbon and Kee, 1964.
Graeber, David. *Debt: The First 5,000 Years*. Brooklyn, NY: Melville House, 2010.
Gullander-Drolet, Claire. "Bong Joon-Ho's Eternal Engine: Translation, Memory, and Ecological Collapse in *Snowpiercer* (2013)." *Resilience: A Journal of the Environmental Humanities* 7, no. 1 (2019): 6–21.
Gunning, Tom. "Phantasmagoria and the Manufacturing of Illusions and Wonder: Towards a Cultural Optics of the Cinematic Apparatus." In *Cinema, a New Technology for the 20th Century*, edited by André Gaudreault, Catherine Russell, and Pierre Véronneau, 31–44. Lausanne: Payot Lausanne, 2004.
Ha Ŏyŏng. "Kangnam sŏngmaemae t'ŭkkurŭl kada" [Visiting Gangnam, the special district for sex trade]. *Han'gyŏre 21*, no. 887 (November 28, 2011): 44–55.
Ha, Seong-Kyu. "New Shantytowns and the Urban Marginalized in Seoul Metropolitan Region." *Habitat International* 28, no. 1 (2004): 123–141.
Ha Ŭn'gyŏng. "Kangnam'ŭi kogŭp maech'un yŏsŏngdŭl" [High-class female sex workers in Gangnam]. *Wŏlgan mal*, no. 87 (1993): 226–249.

Hackworth, Jason, and Neil Smith. "The Changing State of Gentrification." *Tijdschrift voor Economische en Sociale Geografie* 92, no. 4 (2001): 464–477.
Han, Ju Hui Judy. "High-Altitude Protests and Necropolitical Digits." In *Digital Lives in the Global City: Contesting Infrastructures*, edited by Deborah E. Cowen, Alexis Mitchell, Emily Paradis, and Brett Story, 175–178. Vancouver: University of British Columbia Press, 2020.
Han Sangjin. "Wae wihŏmsahoein'ga" [Why risk society?]. *Kyegan sasang* 38 (1998): 3–25.
Han Yŏnju. *Nanŭn ch'wihaji annŭnda* [I don't get drunk]. Seoul: Tasi, 2006.
Harvey, David. *A Brief History of Neoliberalism*. New York: Oxford University Press, 2005.
———. "Cities or Urbanization?" *City* 1, no. 1–2 (1996): 38–61.
———. *The Condition of Postmodernity: An Enquiry into the Origins of Cultural Change*. Oxford: B. Blackwell, 1989.
He, Shenjing. "New-Build Gentrification in Central Shanghai: Demographic Changes and Socioeconomic Implications." *Population, Space and Place* 16, no. 5 (2010): 345–361.
Hemmings, Clare. "Affective Solidarity: Feminist Reflexivity and Political Transformation." *Feminist Theory* 13, no. 2 (2012): 147–161.
Hong, Jun Sung, Dorothy L. Espelage, Simon C. Hunter, and Paula Allen-Meares. "Integrating Multi-Disciplinary Social Science Theories and Perspectives to Understand School Bullying and Victimisation." In *The Routledge International Handbook of Human Aggression: Current Issues and Perspectives*, edited by Jane L. Ireland, Philip Birch, and Carol Ireland, 109–120. New York: Routledge, 2018.
Hong Poyŏng and Kim Kyŏngmin. "Ŭm'aksan'ŏb'ŭi kongganjŏk punp'o: Sŏulsi ŭm'aksan'ŏp kach'isasŭrŭl chungsim'ŭro" [Analysis on the spatial distribution of the music industry value chain in Seoul]. *Han'guk kyŏngjejirihakhoeji* 18, no. 3 (2015): 335–347.
Hong Sŏngt'ae. *Taehanmin'guk wihŏmsahoe: Saengt'aejŏk pokchisahoerŭl hyanghayŏ* [Risk society, the Republic of Korea: Toward an ecological welfare society]. Seoul: Tangdae, 2007.
Hong Sŏngt'ae, An Hongsŏp, and Pak Hongsin. *Anjŏnsahoero toyakhanŭn kil: Samp'ung paekhwajŏm punggoe isimnyŏn'ŭi yŏn'gu* [A path toward a secure society: A study on the two decades since the Sampoong Department Store collapse]. Kwach'ŏn: Chin'injin, 2018.
Hong Sŏng'yong. "Yŏnghwasok kŏnch'uk iyagi—tongsŏn'ŭi yŏnghwa 'koemul' kwa 'eilliŏn sam'" [Films about the line of flow: *The Host* and *Alien 3*]. *Kŏnch'uksa* 612 (2004): 140–143.
Hong Yŏng'ae, Cho Ŭnju, and Yu Sujŏng. *Kangnam'ŭi pujadŭl* [The rich in Gangnam]. Seoul: Pungnain, 2004.
Horton, Paul. "School Bullying and Social and Moral Orders." *Children and Society* 25, no. 4 (2011): 268–277.
Hwang Chiu. *Kubanp'o sanggarŭl kŏrŏganŭn nakt'a* [A camel walking by the Old Panp'o arcade]. Seoul: Miraesa, 1991.
———. *Saedŭldo sesang'ŭl ttŭnŭn'guna* [Birds, too, leave the world]. Seoul: Munhakkwa chisŏng, 1983.

Hwang Sŏg'yŏng. *Kangnammong* [Dreams of Gangnam]. P'aju: Ch'angbi, 2010.
Johnson, Candace. "Responsibility, Affective Solidarity and Transnational Maternal Feminism." *Feminist Theory* 21, no. 2 (2020): 175–198.
Johnson, Chalmers. *Japan, Who Governs? The Rise of the Developmental State*. New York: W. W. Norton, 1995.
Jung, Eun-Young. "Articulating Korean Youth Culture through Global Popular Music Styles: Seo Taeiji's Use of Rap and Metal." In *Korean Pop Music: Riding the Wave*, edited by Keith Howard, 109–122. Folkestone: Global Oriental, 2006.
Jung, Mi-kyung. *My Son's Girlfriend*. Translated by Young-nan Yu. Funks Grove, IL: Dalkey Archive Press, 2013.
Kang Chunman. *Kangnam, natsŏn taehanmin'gugŭi chahwasang* [Gangnam, a strange self-portrait of the Republic of Korea]. Seoul: Inmulgwa sasang, 2006.
———. *Rumssarong konghwaguk* [The room salon republic]. Seoul: Inmulgwa sasang, 2011.
Kang Chŏnggu and Kim Chonghoe. "Hwang chiuŭi ch'ŏn'gubaekp'alsimnyŏndae ch'ojungban sie nat'anan sinjungsanch'ŭng chaehyŏn yangsang" [A study on the representation of the new-middle strata in Hwang Chiu's poems from the early to mid-1980s]. *Kukche ŏmun* 71 (2016): 67–88.
Kang, Taesoo, and Guonan Ma. "Credit Card Lending Distress in Korea in 2003." In *Household Debt: Implications for Monetary Policy and Financial Stability*, 95–106. Bank for International Settlements, 2009.
Kang-Yu Karam. "Ŏttŏn sagyoyuk k'idŭŭi saeng'ae" [A life of some kid with private education]. In *Hwangnyul kajok* [Probability family], edited by Chaehyŏn Pak and Hyŏngjae Kim, 145–158. Seoul: Mat'i, 2015.
Kee, Dohyung, Gyuchan Thomas Jun, Patrick Waterson, and Roger Haslam. "A Systemic Analysis of South Korea Sewol Ferry Accident—Striking a Balance between Learning and Accountability." *Applied Ergonomics* 59 (2017): 504–516.
Keller, Donald R. "Deep Ecology." In *Encyclopedia of Environmental Ethics and Philosophy*, edited by J. Baird Callicott and Robert Frodeman, 206–211. New York: Macmillan Reference USA.
Kerstein, Robert. "Stage Models of Gentrification: An Examination." *Urban Affairs Quarterly* 25, no. 4 (1990): 620–639.
Kim, Charles R. *Youth for Nation: Culture and Protest in Cold War South Korea*. Honolulu: University of Hawai'i Press, 2017.
Kim Chunsu. "Han'gang'ŭi saengsan: Han'guk palchŏnjuŭi tosihwawa in'gan nŏmŏŭi mul konggan" [The production of the Han River: South Korea's developmental urbanization and more-than-human waterscape]. *Konggan'gwa sahoe* 29, no. 1 (2019): 93–155.
Kim, Han Sang. "*My Car* Modernity: What the U.S. Army Brought to South Korean Cinematic Imagination about Modern Mobility." *Journal of Asian Studies* 75, no. 1 (2016): 63–85.
———. "'My' Sweet Home in the Next Decade: The Popular Imagination of Private Homeownership during the Yusin Period." In *Cultures of Yusin: South Korea in the 1970s*, edited by Youngju Ryu. Ann Arbor: University of Michigan Press, 2018.

Kim, Jae Yop, Sehun Oh, and Seok In Nam. "Prevalence and Trends in Domestic Violence in South Korea: Findings from National Surveys." *Journal of Interpersonal Violence* 31, no. 8 (2016): 1554–1576.

Kim, Ji Youn. "Cultural Entrepreneurs and Urban Regeneration in Itaewon, Seoul." *Cities* 56 (2016): 132–140.

Kim, Jinsook. "Sticky Activism: The Gangnam Station Murder Case and New Feminist Practices Against Misogyny and Femicide." *JCMS: Journal of Cinema and Media Studies* 60, no. 4 (2021): 37–60.

Kim Joohee. "Han'guk sŏngmaemae san'ŏp nae puch'aegwangyeŭi chŏngch'igyŏngjehak" [Political economy of "debt nexus" in Korea's sex industry]. *Han'guk yŏsŏnghak* 31, no. 4 (2015): 217–252.

———. "Instant Mobility, Stratified Prostitution Market: The Politics of Belonging of Korean Women Selling Sex in the U.S." *Asian Journal of Women's Studies* 22, no. 1 (2016): 48–64.

———. "Yŏsŏng momjŭngkwŏnhwarŭl t'onghan han'guk sŏngsan'ŏb'ŭi chŏngch'igyŏngjejŏk chŏnhwan'e taehan yŏn'gu" [The study on Korean sex industry's political economic transformation through "body-securitization" of women]. *Kyŏngjewa sahoe* 111 (2016): 142–173.

Kim, Jung In. "The Birth of Urban Modernity in Gangnam, Seoul." *Arq: Architectural Research Quarterly* 19, no. 4 (2015): 369–379.

Kim, Jung In, and Matjaž Uršič. "Besieged Citizenship—the Social Construction of Inequality in Gangnam District, Seoul." *Teorija in Praksa* 56, no. 1 (2019): 74–310.

Kim Miyŏng. "Hot'erŭi tosi inp'ŭra kinŭng yŏn'gu" [The hotel as an urban infrastructure in Seoul since the 1960s]. PhD diss., Seoul National University, 2016.

Kim Miyŏng. "Welk'ŏm t'u kangnam" [Welcome to Gangnam]. In Yi Hong, *Sŏngt'an p'ik'ŭnik* [Christmas picnic], 213–226. Seoul: Min'ŭmsa, 2009.

Kim Paeg'yŏng. "Olimp'ig'ŭn kangnam kaebare ŏttŏn yŏnghyang'ŭl mich'yŏnnun'ga?" [What kind of impact did the Olympics have on Gangnam development?]. In *Kangnam mandŭlgi, kangnam ttarahagi* [Making Gangnam, imitating Gangnam], edited by Hwang Chint'ae and Pak Paegyun, 231–264. P'aju: Tongnyŏk, 2017.

Kim, Pil Ho. "Branding the Sense of Place: Gangnam as the Epicenter of the Korean Wave." In *Introducing Korean Popular Culture*, edited by Youna Kim, 267–277. New York: Routledge, 2023.

———. "In Liberation Village: The Production of Cinematic Space for Early North Korean Refugees." *Journal of Japanese and Korean Cinema* 11, no. 2 (2019): 137–153.

———. "Korean Rock's Journey from Group Sound to Indie Punk." In *Made in Korea: Studies in Popular Music*, edited by Hyunjoon Shin and Seung-Ah Lee, 71–82. New York: Routledge, 2016.

———. "Songs of the Multitude: The April Revolution, the 6.3 Uprising, and South Korea's Protest Music of the 1960s." *Korean Studies* 46, no. 1 (2022): 107–134.

Kim, Pil Ho, and Hyunjoon Shin. "The Birth of 'Rok': Cultural Imperialism, Nationalism, and the Glocalization of Rock Music in South Korea, 1964–1975." *positions: east asia cultures critique* 18, no. 1 (2010): 199–230.

Kim Ryumi. *Ŭn'gŭn riŏl pŏraiŏt'i kangnam sonyŏ* [Just a little real variety Gangnam girl]. Seoul: T'eksŭt'ŭ, 2011.

Kim Sagwa. *Ch'ŏn'gug'esŏ* [In heaven]. P'aju: Ch'angbi, 2013.

———. "SF." Translated by Bruce Fulton and Ju-Chan Fulton. *Azalea* 7 (2014): 263.

Kim Sanghŏn. *Taehanmin'guk kangnam t'ŭkpyŏlsi* [Special city of Gangnam, Republic of Korea]. Seoul: Wijŭdŏmhausŭ, 2004.

Kim, Seung-Kyung, and Kyounghee Kim. *The Korean Women's Movement and the State: Bargaining for Change.* New York: Routledge, 2014.

Kim Sŏngmin. "Sŏurŭi chaegujohwawa ilbon'in kwan'gwang: Kangnam kaebarŭl chungsim'ŭro" [Japanese tourists and the restructuring of Seoul: Focusing on the developments in the Gangnam area]. *Asia ribyu* 6, no. 2 (2017): 249–268.

Kim Such'ŏl and Kang Chŏngsu. "K'eip'ab'esŏŭi t'ŭraensŭmidiŏ chŏllyag'e taehan koch'al" [Digging Gangnam style: Transmedia storytelling in K-pop]. *Ŏllon chŏngbo yŏn'gu* 50, no. 1 (2013): 84–120.

Kim Yun'yŏng. "Ch'ŏlgabang ch'ujŏk chakchŏn" [Operation Tracking Metalcase]. In *Ruibwittong* [Louis Vuitton], 113–149. P'aju: Ch'angbi, 2002.

Klein, Naomi. *The Shock Doctrine: The Rise of Disaster Capitalism.* New York: Metropolitan Books, 2007.

Koo, Hagen. *Korean Workers: The Culture and Politics of Class Formation.* Ithaca, NY: Cornell University Press, 2001.

———. *Privilege and Anxiety: The Korean Middle Class in the Global Era.* Ithaca, NY: Cornell University Press, 2022.

Koo, Hyojin, Keumjoo Kwak, and Peter K. Smith. "Victimization in Korean Schools: The Nature, Incidence, and Distinctive Features of Korean Bullying or Wang-Ta." *Journal of School Violence* 7, no. 4 (2008): 119–139.

Kwak Chaegu. *Chŏnjangp'o arirang.* Seoul: Min'ŭmsa, 1985.

Kwon Hyŏnsŏk. "Insig'ŭi mobilit'iŭi iron'gwa silche: Kangnam sŭt'airŭi p'aerŏdi hawimunhwaŭi punsŏg'ŭl kŭn'gŏro" [The theory and practice of "mobility" of perception: A reexamination of the parody subculture of Psy's "Gangnam Style"]. *Ŭm'akkwa munhwa* 34 (2016): 5–33.

Kyŏnghyang sinmun. *Kangnam'yŏk sippŏn ch'ulgu, ch'ŏnsegaeŭi p'ost'ŭit: Ŏttŏn aedowa ssaum'ŭi kiŏk* [Gangnam Station Exit Number 10, 1,004 sticky notes: A record of condolences and struggles]. Seoul: Namu yŏnp'il, 2016.

Kyoung, Shinwon, and Kwang-Joong Kim. "State-Facilitated Gentrification in Seoul, South Korea for Whom, by Whom and with What Result." *International RC21 Conference,* Amsterdam, 2011.

Lambert, Christine, and Martin Boddy. "Transforming the City: Post-Recession Gentrification and Re-urbanisation." *Research Paper 6,* ESRC Centre for Neighbourhood Research, 2002.

Lee, Chang-Moo, Jong-Hyun Lee, and Chang-Ho Yim. "A Revenue-Sharing Model of Residential Redevelopment Projects: The Case of the Hapdong Redevelopment Scheme in Seoul, Korea." *Urban Studies* 40, no. 11 (2003): 2223–2237.

Lee, Claire Seungeun, and Yasue Kuwahara. "'Gangnam Style' as a Format: When a Localized Korean Song Meets a Global Audience." In *The Korean Wave: Korean Popular Culture in Global Context,* edited by Yasue Kuwahara, 101–116. New York: Palgrave Macmillan, 2014.

Lee, Fred, and Steven Manicastri. "Not All Are Aboard: Decolonizing Exodus in Joon-Ho Bong's *Snowpiercer*." *New Political Science* 40, no. 2 (2018): 211–226.
Lee, Jin-kyung. *Service Economies: Militarism, Sex Work, and Migrant Labor in South Korea*. Minneapolis: University of Minnesota Press, 2010.
Lee, Jung-min Mina. "Minjung Kayo: Imagining Democracy through Song in South Korea." *Twentieth-Century Music* 20 (2023): 49–69.
Lee, Mun Woo. "'Gangnam Style' English Ideologies: Neoliberalism, Class and the Parents of Early Study-Abroad Students." *International Journal of Bilingual Education and Bilingualism* 19, no. 1 (2016): 35–50.
Lee, Nam. *The Films of Bong Joon-Ho*. New Brunswick, NJ: Rutgers University Press.
Lee, Namhee. *The Making of Minjung: Democracy and the Politics of Representation in South Korea*. Ithaca, NY: Cornell University Press, 2007.
Lee, Seon Young. "Urban Redevelopment, Displacement and Anti-Gentrification Movements." *Journal of the Korean Geographical Society* 49, no. 2 (2014): 299–309.
Lee, Yewon Andrea. "Reframing Gentrification: How Tenant Shopkeepers' Activism in Seoul Radically Reframed Gentrification." *Critical Sociology* 46, no. 6 (2020): 819–834.
Lees, Loretta. "Gentrification and Social Mixing: Towards an Inclusive Urban Renaissance?" *Urban Studies* 45, no. 12 (2008): 2449–2470.
———. "The Geography of Gentrification: Thinking through Comparative Urbanism." *Progress in Human Geography* 36, no. 2 (2012): 155–171.
Lees, Loretta, Hyun Bang Shin, and Ernesto López-Morales. *Planetary Gentrification*. Malden, MA: Polity Press, 2016.
Lefebvre, Henri. *The Production of Space*. Translated by Donald Nicholson-Smith. Oxford: Blackwell, 1991 [1974].
Lerner, Gerda. *The Creation of Patriarchy*. Oxford: Oxford University Press, 1986.
Lett, Denise Potrzeba. *In Pursuit of Status: The Making of South Korea's "New" Urban Middle Class*. Cambridge, MA: Harvard University Asia Center, 1998.
Ley, David, and Sin Yih Teo. "Gentrification in Hong Kong? Epistemology vs. Ontology." *International Journal of Urban and Regional Research* 38, no. 4 (2014): 1286–1303.
Lie, John. "Why Didn't 'Gangnam Style' Go Viral in Japan? Gender Divide and Subcultural Heterogeneity in Contemporary Japan." *Cross-Currents* 9 (2013): 44–67.
Madsen, Richard. *China and the American Dream: A Moral Inquiry*. Berkeley: University of California Press, 1995.
Maliangkay, Roald. "The Popularity of Individualism: The Seo Taiji Phenomenon in the 1990s." In *The Korean Popular Culture Reader*, edited by Kyung Hyun Kim and Youngmin Choe. Durham: Duke University Press, 2014.
Margry, Peter Jan, and Cristina Sánchez-Carretero. *Grassroots Memorials the Politics of Memorializing Traumatic Death*. New York: Berghahn Books, 2011.
Marx, Karl, and Friedrich Engels. *Capital: The Process of Capitalist Production*. Translated by Edward B. Aveling, Samuel Moore, and Ernest Untermann. Chicago: C. H. Kerr and Company, 1912 [1867].
Massey, Doreen. "A Global Sense of Place." *Marxism Today* 38 (1991): 24–29.
McCormack, Gavan. *The Emptiness of Japanese Affluence*. Armonk, NY: M. E. Sharpe, 1996.

Mendes, Luís. "Gentrification and the New Urban Social Movements in Times of Post-Capitalist Crisis and Austerity Urbanism in Portugal." *Arizona Journal of Hispanic Cultural Studies* 22 (2018): 199–215.

Merrifield, Andy. *Henri Lefebvre: A Critical Introduction.* New York: Routledge, 2006.

Mimesisŭ. *Sinsedae: Ne mŏttaro haera* [New generation: Do whatever you want]. Seoul: Hyŏnsilmunhwayŏn'gu, 1993.

Min, Hye Young, Jung Min Lee, and Yoonjung Kim. "An Integrative Literature Review on Intimate Partner Violence against Women in South Korea." *Korean Journal of Women Health Nursing* 26, no. 4 (2020): 260–273.

Moon, Katharine H. S. *Sex among Allies: Military Prostitution in U.S.-Korea Relations.* New York: Columbia University Press, 1997.

Mun Chŏnghŭi. *Nanŭn mun'ida* [I am Mun]. Seoul: Min'ŭmsa, 2016 [2007].

Mun Hongju. *Samp'ung, ch'ukcheŭi pam* [Sampoong: A night of festivities]. Seoul: Sŏn'aenmun, 2013.

Murakami, Haruki. "Barn Burning." Translated by Philip Gabriel. *New Yorker,* October 25, 1982, 86–87.

Naess, Arne, and George Sessions. "The Basic Principles of Deep Ecology." *The Trumpeter* 3, no. 4 (1986): 14.

Namgung Yŏng. "Ssaiŭi 'kangnam sŭt'ail' myujikpidio kiho punsŏk" [A reception pattern analysis of Psy's "Gangnam Style" music video]. *Han'guk pangsonghakhoe haksuldaehoe nonmunjip,* November 17 (2012): 171–174.

Nelson, Laura C. *Measured Excess: Status, Gender and Consumer Nationalism in South Korea.* New York: University of Columbia Press, 2000.

Nietzsche, Friedrich. *Beyond Good and Evil: Prelude to a Philosophy of the Future,* translated by Walter Kaufmann. New York: Vintage Books, 1989 [1886].

———. *On the Genealogy of Morals.* Translated by Walter Kaufmann. New York: Vintage Books, 1989 [1887].

No Chisŭng. "Ch'ŏn'gubaekch'ilsimnyŏndae sŏngnodongja sugiŭi changnŭjŏk sŏngkyŏkkwa kŭlssŭgiŭi haeng'wijasŏng" [The generic nature of sex workers' autobiographical writings in the 1970s and the agency of the writings]. *Sŏgang inmun nonch'ong* 52 (2018): 5–41.

Noriega, Chon. "Godzilla and the Japanese Nightmare: When 'Them!' Is U.S." *Cinema Journal* 27, no. 1 (1987): 63–77.

Norma, Caroline. "Demand from Abroad: Japanese Involvement in the 1970s' Development of South Korea's Sex Industry." *Journal of Korean Studies* 19, no. 2 (2014): 399–428.

O Sejŏng. "Ssaiŭi kangnamsŭt'aire taehan chigak yŏngu" [A study of perceptual factors on Psy's "Gangnam style"]. *Chugwansŏng yŏn'gu* 26 (2013): 163–184.

O Yŏng'uk. *Kŭraedo nanŭn sŏuri chotta: Hŭnjŏkkwa sangsang, kŏnch'ukka ogisaŭi soul iyagi* [Still I like Seoul: Traces and imagination, architect Ogisa's Seoul story]. Seoul: P'eip'ŏ sŭt'ori, 2012.

Oh, Yujeong. *Pop City: Korean Popular Culture and the Selling of Place.* Ithaca, NY: Cornell University Press, 2018.

Pak Ch'ŏlsu. *Ap'at'ŭ: Kongchŏk naengsowa sachŏk chŏngnyŏri chibaehanŭn sahoe* [Apartment: A society dominated by public cynicism and private passions]. Seoul: Ma'ti. 2013.

Pak, Gloria Lee. "On the Mimetic Faculty: A Critical Study of the *Ppongtchak* Debate and Post-Colonial Mimesis." In *Korean Pop Music: Riding the Wave*, edited by Keith Howard, 62–71. Folkestone: Global Oriental, 2006.

Pak Haech'ŏn. *Ap'at'ŭ keim: Kŭdŭri chungsanch'ŭng'i toel su issŏttŏn iyu* [Apartment game: How they were able to become the middle strata]. Seoul: Hyumŏnist'ŭ. 2013.

Pak Paegyun and Chang Chinbŏm. "Kangnam mandŭlgi, kangnam ttarahagiwa han'gug'ŭi tosi ideollogi" ["Making Gangnam, imitating Gangnam" and Korea's urban ideology]. In *Kangnam mandŭlgi, kangnam ttarahagi* [Making Gangnam, imitating Gangnam], edited by Hwang Chint'ae and Pak Paegyun, 13–58. Seoul: Tongnyŏk. 2017.

Pak Sojin and Hong Sŏn'yŏng. "Chugŏrŭl t'onghan sahoejŏk kwasiŭi han'gukchŏk t'ŭksusŏng" [Social conspicuousness and housing culture in Korea: In comparison to the case of Japan]. *Tamnon 201* 25, no. 3 (2009): 35–61.

Pak Soyŏng. "Ch'ŏn'gubaekch'ilsimnyŏndae host'isŭ sugiŭi yŏnghwahwa yŏn'gu" [A study on filmization of hostess memoirs in the 1970s]. *Hanminjok ŏmunhak* 81 (2018): 241–274.

Pak Wansŏ. "Nakt'oŭi aidŭl" [Kids in paradise]. In *Paeban'ŭi yŏrŭm* [The summer of betrayal], 304–329. P'aju: Munhaktongne, 2006 [1978].

Park, Aekyung. "Modern Folksong and People's Song (*Minjung Kayo*)." In *Made in Korea: Studies in Popular Music*, edited by Hyunjoon Shin and Seung-ah Lee, 83–94. New York: Routledge, 2016.

Park, Jeong-Mi. "Paradoxes of Gendering Strategy in Prostitution Policies: South Korea's 'Toleration-Regulation Regime,' 1961–1979." *Women's Studies International Forum* 37 (2013): 73–84.

Park, Kyeyoung, and Jessica Kim. "The Contested Nexus of Los Angeles Koreatown: Capital Restructuring, Gentrification, and Displacement." *Amerasia Journal* 34, no. 3 (2008): 127–150.

Park, Sunyoung, ed. *Revisiting Minjung New Perspectives on the Cultural History of 1980s South Korea*. Ann Arbor: University of Michigan Press, 2019.

Pattison, Timothy James. "The Process of Neighborhood Upgrading and Gentrification: An Examination of Two Neighborhoods in the Boston Metropolitan Area." Master's thesis, Massachusetts Institute of Technology, 1977.

Pihl, Marshall R. "The Nation, the People, and a Small Ball: Nationalism and Literary Populism in Contemporary Korea." In *South Korea's Minjung Movement*, edited by Kenneth M. Wells, 209–220. Honolulu: University of Hawai'i Press, 1995.

Polanyi, Karl. *The Great Transformation: The Political and Economic Origins of Our Time*. Boston: Beacon Press, 2001 [1944].

Porteux, Jonson N. "Police, Paramilitaries, Nationalists and Gangsters: The Processes of State Building in Korea." PhD diss., University of Michigan, 2013.

Porteux, Jonson N., and Sunil Kim. "Public Ordering of Private Coercion: Urban Redevelopment and Democratization in South Korea." *Journal of East Asian Studies* 16, no. 3 (2016): 371–390.

Relph, Edward. *Place and Placelessness*. London: Pion, 1976.

Riordan, D. Vincent. "Suicide and Human Sacrifice; Sacrificial Victim Hypothesis on the Evolutionary Origins of Suicide." *Suicidology Online* 10, no. 2 (2019).

Ryu Sin. *Sŏul akeidŭ p'rojekt'ŭ: Munhakkwa yesullo ingnŭn sŏurŭi ilsang* [Seoul arcades project: Everyday life in Seoul through literature and art]. Seoul: Min'ŭmsa, 2013.

Ryu, Youngju. *Writers of the Winter Republic: Literature and Resistance in Park Chung Hee's Korea*. Honolulu: University of Hawai'i Press, 2016.

Samuel, Lawrence R. *The American Dream: A Cultural History*. Syracuse, NY: Syracuse University Press, 2012.

SCF (Seoul Culture Foundation). *Ch'ŏn'gubaekkusib'onyŏn sŏul, samp'ung* [Sampoong, Seoul, in 1995]. Seoul: Tong'asia, 2016.

Scott, James C. *Seeing like a State: How Certain Schemes to Improve the Human Condition Have Failed*. New Haven, CT: Yale University Press, 1998.

Seol, Dong-Hoon. "International Sex Trafficking in Women in Korea: Its Causes, Consequences and Countermeasures." *Asian Journal of Women's Studies* 10, no. 2 (2004): 7–47.

Seol, Dong-Hoon, and Geon-Soo Han. "Foreign Women's Life and Work in the Entertainment Sector of Korea from the Human Trafficking Perspective." In *Human Security, Transnational Crime and Human Trafficking*, edited by Shiro Okubo and Louise Kelly, 152–179. London: Routledge, 2011.

Shin, Haeran, and Yerin Jin. "The Politics of Forgetting: Unmaking Memories and Reacting to Memory-Place-Making." *Geographical Research* 59, no. 3 (2021): 439–451.

Shin, Heisoo. "Industrial Prostitution and South Korean Dependent Development." In *Women's Lives and Public Policy: The International Experience*, edited by Meredeth Turshen and Briavel Holcomb, 115–132. Westport, CT: Greenwood Press, 1993.

Shin, Hyun Bang. "Property-Based Redevelopment and Gentrification: The Case of Seoul, South Korea." *Geoforum* 40, no. 5 (2009): 906–917.

Shin, Kyoung-Ho. "A Theoretical View of the Globalizing Sex Industry: World System Position, Local Patriarchy, and State Policy in South Korea." In *Analyzing Gender, Intersectionality, and Multiple Inequalities: Global, Transnational and Local Contexts*, vol. 15, edited by Esther Ngan-Ling Chow and Marcia Texler Segal, 75–94. Leeds: Emerald Publishing, 2011.

Sin Hyŏnjun, Yi Yong'u, and Ch'oe Chisŏn. *Han'guk p'ab'ŭi kogohak ilguch'ilgong* [Archeology of Korean pop, the 1970s]. P'aju: Han'gil at'ŭ, 2005.

Sin Kwang'yŏng. *Han'gug'ŭi kyegŭpkwa pulp'yŏngdŭng* [Class and inequality in South Korea]. Seoul: Ŭryumunhwasa, 2004.

Slater, Tom. "Gentrification of the City." In *The New Blackwell Companion to the City*, edited by Gary Bridge and Sophie Watson, 571–585. Malden, MA: Wiley, 2011.

SMH (Seoul Museum of History). *Kangnam sasimnyŏn: Yŏngdong'esŏ kangnam'ŭro* [Four decades of Gangnam: From Yŏngdong to Gangnam]. Seoul: SMH, 2011.

Smith, Neil. "Gentrification and Uneven Development." *Economic Geography* 58, no. 2 (1982): 139–155.

———. "New Globalism, New Urbanism: Gentrification as Global Urban Strategy." *Antipode* 34, no. 3 (2002): 427–450.

———. *The New Urban Frontier: Gentrification and the Revanchist City*. New York: Routledge, 2005.

Sŏ Usŏk and Pyŏn Miri. "Kangnam munhwagyŏngjeŭi sahoehak: Munhwasan'ŏpkwa pyut'isan'ob'ŭi kyŏrhap" [Sociology of Gangnam's cultural economy: A combination of culture and beauty industries]. In *Sŏul sahoehak: Sŏurŭi konggan, ilsang kŭrigo saramdŭl* [Sociology of Seoul: Space, everyday life, and people], edited by Sŏ Usŏk, Pyŏn Miri, Kim Paeg'yŏng, and Kim Chiyŏng, 241–258. P'aju: Nanam, 2017.

Son Chŏngmok. *Sŏul tosi kyehoek iyagi* [Stories of urban planning in Seoul]. Vol. 1. P'aju: Han'ul, 2003.

———. *Sŏul tosi kyehoek iyagi* [Stories of urban planning in Seoul]. Vol. 3. P'aju: Han'ul, 2007.

Son, Min Jung. "The Politics of the Traditional Korean Popular Song Style T'ŭrot'ŭ." PhD diss., University of Texas at Austin, 2004.

Song, Jesook. "Family Breakdown and Invisible Homeless Women: Neoliberal Governance during the Asian Debt Crisis in South Korea, 1997–2001." *positions: east asia cultures critique* 14, no. 1 (2006): 37–65.

———. *South Koreans in the Debt Crisis: The Creation of a Neoliberal Welfare Society*. Durham, NC: Duke University Press, 2009.

Song, Juyoung. "English Just Is Not Enough!: Neoliberalism, Class, and Children's Study Abroad among Korean Families." *System* 73 (2018): 80–88.

Song Ŭn'yŏng. *Sŏul t'ansaenggi: Ch'ŏn'gubaeg'yukch'ilsimnyŏndae muhag'ŭro pon hyŏndae tosi sŏurŭi sahoesa* [The birth of Seoul: A social history of Seoul through the 1960–70s literature]. Seoul: P'urŭn'yŏksa, 2018.

Suh, Jae-Jung. "The Failure of the South Korean National Security State: The Sewol Tragedy in the Age of Neoliberalism." *Asia Pacific Journal* 12, no. 40 (2014).

Suh, Jae-Jung, and Mikyoung Kim. *Challenges of Modernization and Governance in South Korea: The Sinking of Sewol and Its Causes*. London: Palgrave MacMillan, 2017.

Sunwoo, Jacquelyne D. "Aging Population and Slum Resettlement in Guryong Village, Seoul, South Korea." Master's thesis, Columbia University, 2017.

Tan, Marcus. "K-Contagion: Sound, Speed, and Space in 'Gangnam Style.'" *TDR: Drama Review* 59, no. 1 (2015): 83–96.

TBWA Korea. *Karosukiri mwŏnde naliya* [What's all the fuss about Karosukil?]. Seoul: Alma, 2007.

Thornberg, Robert. "School Bullying as a Collective Action: Stigma Processes and Identity Struggling." *Children and Society* 29, no. 4 (2015): 310–320.

Thrift, Nigel J. *Non-Representational Theory: Space, Politics, Affect*. New York: Routledge, 2007.

Tuan, Yi-fu. *Space and Place: The Perspective of Experience*. Minneapolis: University of Minnesota Press, 1977.

UN DESA (United Nations Department of Economic and Social Affairs). *The World's Women 2010: Trends and Statistics*. New York: United Nations, 2010.

Viggiani, Elisabetta. *Talking Stones: The Politics of Memorialization in Post-Conflict Northern Ireland*. New York: Berghahn Books, 2014.

Wagnleitner, Reinhold. "Propagating the American Dream: Cultural Policies as Means of Integration." *American Studies International* 24, no. 1 (1986): 60–84.

Wells, Kenneth M., ed. *South Korea's Minjung Movement: The Culture and Politics of Dissidence*. Honolulu: University of Hawai'i Press, 1995.
Wenner, Jann. *Lennon Remembers*. New York: Verso, 2000.
WHO (World Health Organization). *Violence against Women Prevalence Estimates, 2018*. Geneva: WHO, 2021.
Williams, Ruth. "'Female Poet' as Revolutionary Grotesque: Feminist Transgression in the Poetry of Ch'oe Sŭng-Ja, Kim Hyesoon, and Yi Yŏn-Ju." *Tulsa Studies in Women's Literature* 29, no. 2 (2010): 395–415.
Wright, Erik Olin. *Classes*. London: Verso, 1985.
Yang, Myungji. *From Miracle to Mirage: The Making and Unmaking of the Korean Middle Class, 1960–2015*. Ithaca, NY: Cornell University Press, 2018.
Yi Chaeyul. "T'ugiwa kŏp'um, kŭrigo pudongsan kakyŏg'ŭi pyŏndong" [Speculation, bubble, and fluctuations in real estate prices]. *Kyŏng'yŏng kyŏngje* 37, no. 1 (2004): 315–334.
Yi Hong. *Sŏngt'an p'ik'ŭnik* [Christmas picnic]. Seoul: Min'ŭmsa, 2009.
Yi Hyŏnsŏk. "Ssaiŭi yŏngsang myujikpidio kangnam sŭt'aire tŭrŏnan k'ich'iwa mim'e taehan yŏn'gu" [Analysis of the "Gangnam Style" music video through the concepts of kitsch and meme]. *Han'guk kont'ench'ŭhakhoe nonmunji* 13, no. 11 (2013): 148–158.
Yi Sŏnmin. *Chŏnŭn samp'ung saengjonjaimnida* [I am a Sampoong survivor]. P'aju: P'urŭnsup, 2021.
Yi Soyŏn. "Kongsaeng'ŭi pŏp, sarang'ŭi saengt'aehak" [The law of symbiosis, ecology of love]. *Munhakkwa hwan'gyŏng* 7, no. 2 (2008): 53–82.
Yi Tong'yŏn. "Naega anŭn ssaie kwanhan modŭn kŏt" [Everything I know about Psy]. *Munhwa kwahak* 72 (2012), 307–330.
Yi Yŏngjun. *Chojohan tosi: Sajin'ŭro ingnŭn tosiŭi inmunhak* [Fretful city: Urban humanities through photography]. Seoul: An'grap'iksŭ, 2010.
Yu Ha. *Parambunŭn narimyŏn apkujŏngdong'e kayahanda* [On a windy day we must go to Apkujŏngdong]. Seoul: Munhakkwa chisŏng, 1991.
Yu, Hyun-Seok. "Economic Threat to Human Security: Household Debt Problem in Korea." *Global Economic Review* 32, no. 3 (2003): 67–83.
Yu Kyŏng'wŏn. "Urinara kakyeŭi kŭm'yung kyŏlchŏng'yoin punsŏk" [An analysis of the household financial asset choice decisions in Korea]. *Kŭm'yung kyŏngje yŏn'gu*, no. 185, 1–35. Seoul: Bank of Korea, 2004.
Yun Ch'ungno. "Pet'ŭnam chŏnjaeng ch'amj'ŏn'ŭi an'gwa pak" [The ins and outs of South Korea's engagement in the Vietnam War]. In *Han'guk hyŏndae saenghwalmunhwasa ch'ŏn'gubaek'yuksimnyŏndae* [The modern history of daily life and culture in Korea, the 1960s], edited by Kim Sŏngbo, Kim Chong'yŏp, Hŏ Ŭn, and Hong Sŏgnyul, 165–190. P'aju: Ch'angbi, 2016.
Yun Ilsu. "Homonaraensŭ, kyŏnggyerŭl nŏm'ŏsŏ t'onghapkwa hwahab'ŭro" [Homonarrans toward integration and harmony beyond the border]. *Han'guksasanggwa munhwa* 78 (2015): 405–435.
Yun, Jieheerah. "A Copy Is (Not a Simple) Copy: Role of Urban Landmarks in Branding Seoul as a Global City." *Frontiers of Architectural Research* 8, no. 1 (2019): 44–54.

———. *Globalizing Seoul: The City's Cultural and Urban Change.* New York: Routledge, 2017.

Zhang, Su, and Jingui Wang. "Analysis of South Korea Sewol Sunken Ferry Accident Based on Behavioral Safety." *Journal of Coastal Research* 73 (2015): 611–613.

Zhang, Xiaoling, Jie Hu, Martin Skitmore, and Barbara YP Leung. "Inner-City Urban Redevelopment in China Metropolises and the Emergence of Gentrification: Case of Yuexiu, Guangzhou." *Journal of Urban Planning and Development* 140, no. 4 (2014): 05014004.

Index

Agamben, Giorgio, 122, 124, 192
allegory, 50, 52, 78, 119–121, 123
Amin, Samir, 7, 172
An Ch'ihaeng, 27, 30, 32, 34, 181n27
Ant'a Production, 27, 30, 32, 34
apartment: complex, 11, 18, 29, 31, 32, 36, 46, 47, 53, 55–57, 63, 64, 84–89, 108, 136, 171, 196n16; game, 86, 187; genre, 47, 92, 182n9; high-rise, 11, 12, 34, 65, 79, 91, 112, 148–150, 154, 168, 171; prices, 61, 62, 197n6; republic, 2, 12, 179n3. *See also* Apkujŏngdong: Hyundai Apartments; Tower Palace; Ŭnma Apartment Complex
Apkujŏngdong, 10, 32, 52, 61–63, 121, 133, 139, 157–159, 161; Hyundai Apartments, 11, 16, 45, 48, 49, 67; Rodeo Street, 59, 167. *See also* Yu Ha: *On a Windy Day We Must Go to Apkujŏngdong*
Asian Financial Crisis, 3, 7. *See also* IMF Crisis

Bakhtin, Mikhail Mikhailovich, 20
Benjamin, Walter, 2, 3, 13, 14, 21, 50, 52
Bloom and Goûte, 18, 154, 155, 158, 159, 166
Bong Joon-ho, 16, 23, 186n15, 188n41; *Parasite*, 10, 78–83, 88, 172, 173
Bourdieu, Pierre, 14–16, 63
Buck-Morss, Susan, 3, 52, 179
Bukchon, 150, 168, 197n28
bullying, 121, 123–126, 141, 143, 191n16
Burning Sun, 118, 133, 134, 143, 173

carnival, 15, 16, 19, 20–22, 24, 25, 44
chaebŏl, 86, 102, 172; construction, 86, 172

Chamsil, 16, 49, 68–70; stadium, 7, 35, 171. *See also* Cho Sehŭi
Cho Sehŭi, 16, 48, 66, 183n31, 186n8; *The Dwarf*, 49–53, 56, 67, 75, 76, 171, 185n3; *Time Travel*, 13, 56, 72–79, 85, 88, 91, 93, 171
Cho Tŏkpae, 36, 37
Ch'oe Inho, 16, 46, 47, 66, 127, 128, 171, 175, 184n44
Ch'oe Hosŏp, 36, 37
Ch'oe Sŭngja, 16, 53–55, 77, 171, 184n32
Chŏn Minjo, 16, 48
Chŏng Ihyŏn, 10, 16, 17, 61–63, 112, 172, 188n41; "Sampoong Department Store," 107–110, 175
Chŏng Migyŏng, 16, 61–64, 66, 67, 70, 109, 110, 172
Chŏng T'aech'un, 40, 41
Chŏng Ŭn'i, 26, 28
Ch'ŏngdamdong, 32, 33, 69, 133, 134, 153–157, 159, 161, 194n53
Chu Hyŏnmi, 26–30, 36, 44, 152
Chun Doo Hwan, 6, 51, 128
class: conflict, 73, 82, 88, 90, 126; middle-, 6–12, 15, 23, 28, 32, 38, 43, 51–54, 62, 87, 144–149, 168, 185n52, 187n26; working-, 12, 16–18, 23, 30, 31, 49, 51, 55, 62, 66, 78, 82, 89, 90, 107–110, 142, 144–146, 149, 171, 176, 185n52, 189n12. *See also* hierarchy: class; middle strata
Coca-Cola, 16, 45, 46, 52, 67, 171, 182n3, 183n24
COEX, 21–23, 25, 35, 133
Cold War, 3, 5, 7, 18, 42, 54, 132, 172

Index

collusion (*yuch'ak*), 17, 86, 102, 110, 127, 140, 187
consumerism, 2, 43, 171

Daelim, 65, 102, 103, 104, 112
Daewoo, 102, 160
Davis, Mike, 11, 179n7
debt, 86–88, 127, 129–142, 170, 173, 194nn59–60, 195n70, 196n18
Deleuze, Gilles, 50, 52
disaster capitalism, 17, 93, 98–105, 109, 110, 112, 115, 172
discrimination, 12, 44, 55, 67, 82, 177, 182n7; gender, 44, 90, 117, 176
displacement, 10–12, 23, 85, 100, 147–149, 151, 159, 161, 163, 164, 167, 176
Dostoevsky, Fyodor, 19, 21, 22
dream, 10–14, 19, 43, 44, 52–54, 60–62, 65–68, 170, 171, 175–177; American, 12, 18, 52, 79, 82, 179n2, 183n26, 184n44; polarizing, 10, 170–177; -world, 3, 4, 13, 14. *See also* Buck-Morss, Susan; Hwang Sŏg'yŏng: *Dreams of Gangnam*; Kim Kwangsŏk; middle strata

ecology, 73–76, 78, 79, 81, 83, 186n4, 186n8
economic "miracle," 2, 51, 53, 60, 76, 86
education, 28, 38, 39, 136, 138, 162, 163, 183n23; college-preparatory, 2, 18, 90, 116; English, 66, 169, 197n2; private, 8, 9, 17, 85, 116. *See also hag'wŏn*
Eighth School District, 26, 27, 38, 39, 90, 91, 107, 108
entertainment, 12, 35, 127, 139, 140, 143, 173, 176; adult-, 26, 28, 39, 44, 132, 133, 135, 152, 153, 185n68; company, 33, 39, 118, 173, 194nn52–53; district, 17, 29; establishment, 6, 23, 193n44, 195n67; industry, 16, 21, 25, 32, 33, 116, 139, 143, 173, 176, 195n64; media, 37, 133, 134

Gangbuk, 28–31, 33–35, 84, 93, 96, 107, 108, 129, 133, 134, 148, 150, 171, 197n6; migration, 6, 31, 33, 38, 44, 121
Gangnam: Boulevard, 25–27, 29, 35, 46, 129, 132, 152, 166; development, 16, 17, 43, 58–60, 72, 101, 172–175, 185n68; District, 133, 161; literature, 46–53, 56, 57, 61, 64, 107, 109, 171, 172; noir, 11, 12, 17, 120; Station, 25, 29, 39, 44, 62, 176; Station murder, 44, 116–118, 120, 143. *See also* Hwang Sŏg'yŏng: *Dreams of Gangnam*; Psy
gentrification: classic, 18, 37, 150, 151, 165, 175; commercial, 151, 166, 167; corporate, 157–159; new-build, 145, 147–149, 167, 168; planetary, 8, 68; rip-current, 166–168; super-, 11, 12, 145, 147, 150, 167; wave theory (first, second, third wave), 147–151, 156, 166, 168, 196n11. *See also* displacement
Girard, René, 124–126, 192
globalization, 39, 43, 58, 60, 62, 132, 147, 172
global-polarization, 7–10, 14–16, 18, 67–70, 79, 83, 172, 173, 175, 187n27
Graeber, David, 134, 138, 139, 195

hag'wŏn, 85, 89, 131, 191n1
hallyu (Korean Wave), 10, 133, 173
Hanbo, 86, 91, 102
Hannam Bridge, 5, 31, 133, 152
Han River, 23–25, 29, 31, 35, 49, 55, 56, 72, 76–78, 93, 107–108, 148, 187n22, 188n43; Comprehensive Development Project, 6, 7, 16, 77, 79, 186n13; parks, 78–81, 186n19; water quality, 78–84, 93, 186n11, 187n23
hierarchy: business, 131, 135; class, 14, 88, 89, 120–125, 141; gender, 91; school, 121, 122
homo sacer, 122, 124, 126, 141, 192n25
Hongdae, 150, 157, 196n22
Hotel Riverside, 26, 29, 32, 34, 110, 129
Hwang Chiu, 16, 55, 56, 59, 60, 63, 171
Hwang Sŏg'yŏng, 17, 110; *Dreams of Gangnam*, 15, 29, 67, 100, 101, 104, 110, 170, 195n67
Hyundai, 65, 86, 102, 183n16; Motors, 162, 183n29. *See also* Apkujŏngdong: Hyundai Apartments

IMF Crisis, 42, 43, 69, 83, 86–91, 102, 127, 133, 136, 138, 150, 153, 156, 172, 174, 187n26
Insadong, 41, 150, 152
Iran, 102–104, 189n15; Iran-Iraq War, 102, 112

Japan, 16, 26, 39, 78, 131, 153, 180n2, 186n15, 187n33; colonialism, 4, 21, 26, 65, 100, 128. See also sex industry

Kangyu Garam, 85–88, 91
Karosukil, 68, 146, 151–159, 161, 163, 166, 167, 175, 196n24
Kim Bora, 17, 187n37; *House of Hummingbird*, 88, 90–93, 176
Kim Kwangsŏk, 40, 94–98, 107, 112, 176
Kim Sagwa, 16, 67–70, 169, 172
Kim Yun'yŏng, 16, 66, 67, 172
kisaeng, 126, 127, 135; tourism, 129, 132, 173, 192n37, 193n39
Korean War, 5, 56, 101, 112
K-pop, 16, 21, 24, 33, 39, 41, 116, 118, 133, 173, 194n52. See also Burning Sun; *hallyu*; Psy
Kwak Chaegu, 16, 45, 46, 49, 52, 170, 171

Lee Chang-dong, 18, 120, 169, 170, 173, 197n1, 197n3
Lee, Young June, 84, 85, 91, plate 3
Lefebvre, Henri, 12–15, 17, 119, 120, 139, 141, 191n9

maekin (advance pay), 131, 132, 137–141
Malchukkŏri, 26, 27, 120
Marx, Karl, 52, 54, 99, 119, 142, 183n25, 184n33, 191n7, 197n6
memorial, 12, 55, 93, 95, 111–115, 117, 143, 175, 190n43
middle strata, 11, 54–56, 58, 61, 66–69, 77–79, 82, 83, 110, 128, 149, 171, 184n33
minjung, 3, 45, 51, 52, 183n23
misogyny, 44, 116, 138
modernity, 3, 42, 102, 183n31; modernism, 2, 179n3

Mun Chŏnghŭi, 10, 16, 61, 65
Mun Hongju, 17, 67, 110–112
Mun Hŭiok, 26–28, 30, 152
Murŭng, 47, 48, 57, 59, 71, 82, 83, 85; American, 60, 82, 171

Nam Kug'in, 26, 28, 32, 34
National Assembly, 99, 171, 183n16, 187n22
Nochatsa, 40, 94, 176, 182n3
Nonhyŏndong, 29, 30, 32, 33, 96, 152

O Yun, 52, 183n24, plate 2
Olympics, 41, 72, 77, 99, 103, 132, 171, 194n51

Pak Wansŏ, 16, 47, 53, 57, 93, 171, 182n11, 188n41; "Kids in Paradise," 47, 71, 77, 83–85, 93
Pangbaedong, 35–37, 44, 151, 159–161, 167, 173; ballad, 32, 38; Café Street, 36, 37, 164. See also Saikil; Sŏrae Village
Park Chung Hee, 26, 51, 55, 56, 101, 128, 129, 149, 172, 185n3, 193n39
parody, 19–21, 24, 60
People's Song Movement (PSM), 39, 40, 94, 98, 182n3, 187n38. See also Kim Kwangsŏk; Nochatsa
phantasmagoria, 10, 13, 15, 24, 25, 52, 61, 69, 70, 170, 171
place, 15, 22, 55–57, 76, 82, 139, 161, 165, 191n5; sense of, 14, 17, 18, 118–120, 139–143, 173, 176. See also displacement; space
polarization, 15, 18, 25, 51, 53, 63, 85, 90, 113, 125, 141; dreams, 4, 7, 10, 18, 170, 173, 177. See also global-polarization
Psy, 28, 39, 154, 197n2; "Gangnam Style," 10, 11, 15, 19–31, 35, 39, 44, 67, 77, 171, 173, plate 1
public amnesia, 17, 112, 114, 115

real estate, 44, 62, 148, 150, 154, 156, 164, 166, 180n24, 185n52, 188n40; prime, 101, 111; speculation, 8–11, 23–26, 28, 37, 47–49, 85, 87, 91, 116, 120, 145, 146, 168, 179n11, 185n68. See also apartment: game

reconstruction (*chaegŏnch'uk*), 62, 84, 85, 87, 144, 150, 188n40
room salon, 29, 127–136, 140, 142, 170, 193n44

Saikil, 146, 151, 152, 160–165, 167, 175, 176, 197n25
Sampoong Department Store, 12, 17, 43, 60, 86, 96, 102, 104–107, 112, 114, 150, 170, 172. *See also* Chŏng Ihyŏn; Mun Hongju; Yi Chun
Samsung, 11, 44, 65, 102, 150, 158, 176, 198n11
Seo Taiji, 41–43
Seoul: Metropolitan Government, 75, 79, 106, 111, 161, 186n19, 192n29; National University, 39, 69, 182n3; Seoul-Busan Expressway, 27, 29, 31, 33, 35, 46, 148, 172
Sewŏl, 99, 112–115, 175, 190n39
sex industry, 12, 17, 18, 29, 127–140, 173, 193n46, 193n49; prostitution, 118, 132, 136, 142, 192n30, 193n45, 195n72. See also *kisaeng*; room salon
shantytown, 32, 149, 175
Sinch'on, 72, 94, 96, 150
Sinsadong, 26–29, 35, 36, 44, 46, 48, 151–154, 159, 166; Circuit, 32–34, 38, 96, 129, 139, 173, 181n29, 194n52. *See also* Karosukil
Sŏch'o, 7, 29, 34, 38, 111; District Office, 44, 111, 161–163
social evil, 18, 116, 120, 139, 142, 143, 191n16
social mobility, 10, 18, 38, 60, 118, 148, 149, 167, 171, 175
solidarity, 12, 17, 18, 51, 88, 105, 114, 115, 143, 177; affective, 109, 112, 114, 172, 190n30, 190n38, 190n41; cross-class, 109, 110, 175; feminine, 63, 64
Sŏngsu Bridge, 17, 43, 60, 84–86, 91, 93, 98, 99, 102, 112, 150, 172, 188n43
Sŏrae Village, 159–161, 164, 165
space: abstract, 119, 139, 140, 142, 143; geometric, 15, 118, 119; production of, 17, 57, 144, 171; representational, 12–15, 141, 143; representation of, 14, 18, 142, 176; social, 12, 15, 16, 18, 119; spatial practice, 12, 14, 18, 141–144, 176. *See also* Lefebvre, Henri
suburbanization, 5, 12, 145, 148, 149, 168, 174; American suburbia, 78, 79, 83, 179n2, 196n16
subway, 24, 32, 105, 162, 186n19; Line Number 2, 6, 25, 35, 36, 46, 133, 194n51; Taegu Subway fire, 98, 110–112

Teheran Road, 25, 35, 44, 133, 137, 140, 194n51, plate 4; Valley, 42, 133, 139, 142, 173
Tower Palace, 11, 65, 67, 116, 150, 175
trot, 16, 26–30, 34, 36, 38, 173, 180n6, 181n19

Ŭnma Apartment Complex, 85–93, 150, 188n42. *See also* Kim Bora: *House of Hummingbird*
utopia, 7, 10, 47, 53, 62, 141, 171, 175; and dystopia, 4, 14, 18, 179n7. *See also* Murŭng

Vietnam War, 5, 101, 102, 172
violence, 47, 51, 83, 99, 120, 122–126, 139–142; domestic, 90, 137, 138, 177, 194n61; gender, 44, 116, 117, 127, 138, 176, 177, 194n60; school, 125, 143, 173

Yeon Sang-ho, 173; *The King of Pigs*, 18, 120–126, 141, 143
Yi Chun, 100–102, 104, 105, 170, 189n21
Yi Hong, 11, 16, 62, 70, 172
Yŏngdong, 27–29, 32, 33, 46, 49, 84, 85, 181n20
Yoon Jong-bin, 120; *Beastie Boys*, 18, 134–143, 173
Yoon Soo Il, 30–32, 34
Yu Ha, 11, 16, 120, 171, 185n68; *On a Windy Day We Must Go to Apkujŏngdong*, 10, 53, 59–63, 120, 171
Yusin, 1, 128

About the Author

Pil Ho Kim is associate professor of Korean studies in the Department of East Asian Languages and Literatures, The Ohio State University. As a researcher and educator, he is interested in the intersection of political economy, class analysis, and cultural studies.